Quilts in a material world

Linda Eaton

Quilts in a material world

Selections from the Winterthur Collection

Abrams, New York, in association with

The Henry Francis du Pont Winterthur Museum, Inc.

contents

acknowledgments

I have had such fun researching and writing about Winterthur's quilt collection. I thank Leslie Greene Bowman, Winterthur's director, and Patricia Halfpenny, director of collections, for their support and encouragement of the project. I also thank my talented curatorial colleagues and friends Wendy Cooper, Donald Fennimore, Anne Verplanck, Leslie Grigsby, Ron Fuchs, Ann Wagner, Cheryl Payne, Margaretta Frederick, and Tom Savage for their kindness. Maggie Lidz has been generous in sharing her research with me, and I have enjoyed our many discussions about du Pont and his collecting. I have also benefited from the work of my predecessor, Deborah Kraak, and her organization of the quilt collection. Significant contributions have been made by fellows in the Winterthur Program in Early American Culture and the McNeil interns, including Amanda Isaac, Katherine Hunt, Katherine Haas, and Justina Barrett. Without the help of Lois Stoehr this book would never have been completed.

I am eternally grateful to Joy Gardiner, Kathleen Kiefer, and Lynne Hoyt in the textile conservation laboratory at Winterthur. Their care and handling of both collection and curator have been outstanding. I also thank the graduate students in the Winterthur/University of Delaware Program in Art Conservation, particularly Anne Peranteau, Yadin Larochette, Allison McCloskey, Christina Ritschel, and Kate Sahmel, and intern Heather Hansen. Seminal discoveries have been made by Winterthur's Scientific Research and Analytical Laboratory, and thanks go to Jennifer Maas, Catherine Matsen, Chris Peterson, Joe Webber, and particularly the late Janice Carlson, senior scientist emerita. I am also grateful to Richard Wolbers for adapting his technique of fluorescent microscopy to printed textiles.

The most outstanding resources in the Winterthur library are the staff, and I am grateful to Cate Cooney, Emily Guthrie, Kathy Coyle, Rich McKinstry, Jeanne Solensky, Laura Parrish, and archivist Heather Clewell, all of whom patiently dealt with my numerous queries and directed me to material I would never have discovered on my own. Thanks as well to Neville Thompson for her help and advice in the early stages of this project.

I am indebted to Onie Rollins in the Publications Office for her continued enthusiasm as well as support at crucial stages. It has been a pleasure to work with Jim Schneck, who photographed many of these quilts so beautifully, and Susan Newton, who accomplished the amazing task of tracking all the images. My thanks as well to Harriet Whelchel and Darilyn Carnes at Abrams. Friends and colleagues working to make this dream into an exhibition include Felice Jo Lamden, Doug McDonald, Nat Caccamo, Amy Marks Delaney, and Mary Jane Taylor. Major support for the exhibition is provided by The Coby Foundation, Ltd., New York, and the Estate of Sally Behr Pettit and Samuel L. Pettit.

I am grateful to many people outside Winterthur. Perhaps first and foremost are the librarians at the Rhode Island Historical Society Library and Museum, in particular Karen Eberhart, Dana Signe, Jennifer Betts, and ex–staff member Rick Stattler, who were all kind enough to share my excitement about Mary Remington's letters. Museum curator Kirsten Hammerstrom kindly searched their collection for Remington family material. Jack Braulein, Eric Roth, and Leslie Lefevre-Stratton at the Huguenot Historical Society helped enormously in my quest for Walkill Sheeting and Jane Ten Eyck Hardenbergh. Local historian Barbara Barker found the Watermans, while Barbara Parshley and

Nancy Tatnall Fuller provided information about quiltmakers Eliza Bennis and Abigail van Nostrand. Donna Thomas, Robert Emlen, Jean Whitall, Reed and Virginia Clayton, and other donors shared information about their family quilts. Thanks to Doris Bowman at the National Museum of American History, Ellen Endslow at the Chester County Historical Society, and other colleagues who have helped in various ways: Patricia Keller, Janneken Smucker, Dawn Heefner, Diane Fagan Affleck, Kathryn Berenson, Karen Herbaugh, Dilys Blum, Celia Oliver, Amelia Peck, Linda Welters, Jacqui Atkins, Cynthia Fowler, An Moonen, Arlette Klaric, Marilyn Zoidis, Titi Halle, Michelle Majer, Leigh Wishner, Shelly Zegert, Merikay Waldvogel, Patricia Crews, Carolyn Ducey, Jonathan Holstein, Joan Quinn, Jan Whitlock, Grace Snyder, Laura Stutman, Laura Fisher, Stella Rubin, Trish Herr, Linda Baumgarten, Kim Ivey, Aimee Newell, Mary Schoeser, Lynn Felsher, Jane Nylander, Sandi Fox, Margi Hofer, Kary Bresenham, Henry Joyce, Stacy Hollander, Lee Kogan, Rita Barber, and Virginia Whalen.

Lynne Bassett kindly commented on my manuscript and has been unfailing in her help and support. She has always been quick to respond to numerous enquiries, both vague and specific, and I have benefited tremendously from her scholarship.

And, finally, I would like to thank my family, Herb, Emmalou, Craig, and Stef Eaton, who were surprised to discover that I was writing a book but never doubted that I could do it.

foreword

Winterthur Museum & Country Estate, nestled in the Brandywine Valley of Delaware, is the ancestral home of Henry Francis du Pont, one of most acclaimed collectors and horticulturists of the twentieth century. The one-thousand-acre estate offers a world-class museum of fine and decorative arts, a sixty-acre naturalistic garden, and a superlative research library that supports the museum's joint graduate programs with the University of Delaware in early American culture and art conservation.

Born at Winterthur in 1880, H. F. du Pont not only continued the development of his family property into a grand country estate but also played a national role in his advocacy of American decorative arts. Over the course of his lifetime, he amassed one of the nation's greatest and most comprehensive collections of decorative objects, comprising every medium from furniture, ceramics, and metalwork to glass, paintings, and textiles. In this catalogue and its accompanying exhibition, we celebrate his superlative collection of quilts, many made by young ladies like Mary Remington of Rhode Island.

Mary Remington was just twenty-three years old in 1815 when she created a beautiful and intricate whitework quilt. The fact that she was quilting was not at all unusual, for such needlework activities were the norm for young women in the early 1800s. Equally as expected is the fact that Mary enjoyed letter writing, corresponding with a gentleman named Peleg Congdon, who would eventually become her husband.

What is unusual is the survival of Mary's whitework quilt and, with it, the letters that she penned over the years to Peleg. What a record of those years they provide, allowing us a glimpse into Mary's life and the lives of her contemporaries.

The topics of her letters—everyday life, politics, social history, design, and trade—provide the perfect framework within which to interpret the outstanding quilt collection at Winterthur. The themes that resonated with Mary can be found in abundance among the textiles so eagerly acquired by Henry Francis du Pont. With the strength of the collection falling into the period of the late 1700s and early 1800s, these rare survivals are themselves a grouping of unusual depth and beauty.

Henry Francis du Pont collected textiles because he loved the fabrics, he loved the colors, and he loved the history. He also loved to decorate. At Winterthur and at Chestertown, his summer residence in Southampton, textiles were used on beds, on walls, on dressing tables, and were even cut up to help reupholster the furniture. Du Pont was among the vanguard of early twentieth-century decorators.

This catalogue is much more than the exquisite presentation of a significant quilt collection or the record of a superlative museum exhibition. It is also an extraordinary opportunity to peer into the life of Mary Remington and discover, through her quilt, that the passing of time does little to alter human nature.

Leslie Greene Bowman
Director
Winterthur Museum & Country Estate

introduction

Quilts are not made in isolation. With few exceptions, they are created from fabrics that were woven, bleached, dyed or printed, transported, advertised, and sold within either a national or an international context of industry and commerce. The selection of a particular design or technique by a quilt maker in America—or on the southeast coast of India—is influenced by the fashions of the time and the materials that are available. While individual choices may be conditioned by local preferences and experiences, the general techniques and designs are part of a wider design vocabulary that is international in nature.

One aspect of recent quilt scholarship is the identification of the individual maker, almost always a woman, and the social context in which she made her quilt. Now treasured by private owners and museums alike, historic quilts are often the only evidence that survives of the maker's skill, artistry, or existence. It is unusual for a quilt to survive with enough primary documentation to inform us of the significance of the object within the life of the maker or the context of her community. Winterthur's collection includes a beautiful whitework quilt made in 1815 by Mary Remington of Warwick, Rhode Island. The survival of a group of letters, written between 1811 and 1817, by Mary to her friend, fiancé, and future husband, Peleg Congdon, provides a rare opportunity to understand her quilt within the wider world in which she lived.

This is not the story of a young woman in a rural backwater. Through her needlework, her reading, and her travels, the activities of business and pleasure undertaken by her friends and family, and the effects of politics, international trade embargoes, and war on her happiness and well-being, we can see that Mary's life was an integral part of a wider history. Such a life can only be understood in the context of local, national, and international events.

Women's history, a booming specialty within the wider academic discipline, has by necessity forced historians to glean information from a variety of primary sources. Commonplace books, diaries, membership lists of benevolent societies, and personal letters written by women with no thought of future publication have all been mined for the information they contain. The academic field of material culture, whose development has been more or less contemporary with that of women's history, has devised its own methodology for using objects, rather than written words, as evidence of cultural history. It is one that informs aspects of the daily lives of people from previous generations so difficult to recover from printed sources. Many scholars have looked at these fields in their research about quilts. The history of quilt scholarship has been well described by Virginia Gunn, and Patricia Keller has proposed methodologies that can be used in the quest for cultural meaning in the creation of quilts.[1]

The survival of Mary Remington's quilt, and a significant number of personal letters, provides a rare opportunity to combine these disciplines. Various aspects of Mary's life form the major themes of this book. Placing other, often more anonymous, quilts within the context of what is known about one quilter's life provides a basis for their interpretation.

Winterthur's collection of quilts has never before been published as a whole, although individual examples have been illustrated from time to time. The collection was started by Winterthur's founder, Henry Francis du Pont.

Intended to furnish his homes on Long Island and in Delaware, the early purchases were acquired not as individual objects of folk art but as part of the stylish interiors he created, ones that were widely admired by his contemporaries. Ranging in date from the seventeenth to the late nineteenth century, Winterthur's collection includes approximately 285 quilts. It is an unusual grouping. Because of du Pont's particular interests, described in chapter 7, almost half are wholecloth quilts, which were often bought for the fabrics from which they were made. Others were acquired for their patriotic imagery or for their beautiful design. It was only in the 1940s, as du Pont worked to focus toward the more academic interests of a museum, that he began to search for the personal histories behind the objects. The content of this publication necessarily reflects this bias in Winterthur's collection of quilts.

Once Winterthur Museum opened in 1951, many visitors offered donations of quilts that were family heirlooms. The curators carefully gathered information about their histories and ensured that this information was recorded in the Registration Office. Through judicious purchases, the collection was augmented with examples of types not previously represented. Winterthur's collecting policy, articulated only after du Pont's death, stated that the museum should acquire examples of decorative arts made or used in America between 1640 and 1820. Although the latter date was subsequently extended to 1860, the majority of Winterthur's quilts date from between 1760 and 1840.

Correspondence between du Pont and the many dealers with whom he worked document the fact that he would often pass up new acquisitions of furniture, silver, or paintings because he did not have a place for them. This, however, was not true for the quilts and textiles that he amassed in considerable quantity. He built special storage areas for them and brought Dr. Harold Plenderleith, head of the research lab of the British Museum in London, to measure the environmental conditions in these areas and advise on preventive conservation, which resulted in the installation of an air conditioning system. In 1962 du Pont told an interviewer that Winterthur "is really a textile museum." This book presents, for the first time, the quilts that form but one part of the textile collection founded by Henry Francis du Pont—a collection that continues to grow through the care of subsequent curators and the generosity of many benefactors.

Page 1 A stuffed-work pinwheel shows the influence of fashionable classical designs on Mary Remington's quilt. Although it is not known if Mary designed the quilt herself, there is no evidence that anyone helped her to make it. Mary spent a year quilting between ten and thirteen stitches per inch to create her extraordinary masterpiece.

Page 2 **Rebecca Scattergood Savery Quilt**
Rebecca Scattergood Savery pieced a sunburst quilt from a variety of small-patterned printed cottons purchased for a quilt intended to celebrate the marriage of her daughter Elizabeth. This Quaker quilt attests to the love of bright colors and busy patterns among a religious community often thought to value only muted colors and plain designs.

Pages 4–5 Representing a cross-section of Winterthur's collection, these quilts document different quilting styles and techniques, as well as changing fashions in fabrics.

Page 9 **Cotton Quilt Scraps**
This bundle of scraps, the remains of an 1840s wholecloth quilt, has been carefully preserved at Winterthur for more than sixty years. Henry Francis du Pont was acutely aware of the damage caused by the prolonged display of quilts and other textiles in his period rooms. He instructed his upholsterers to save every scrap for future repairs.

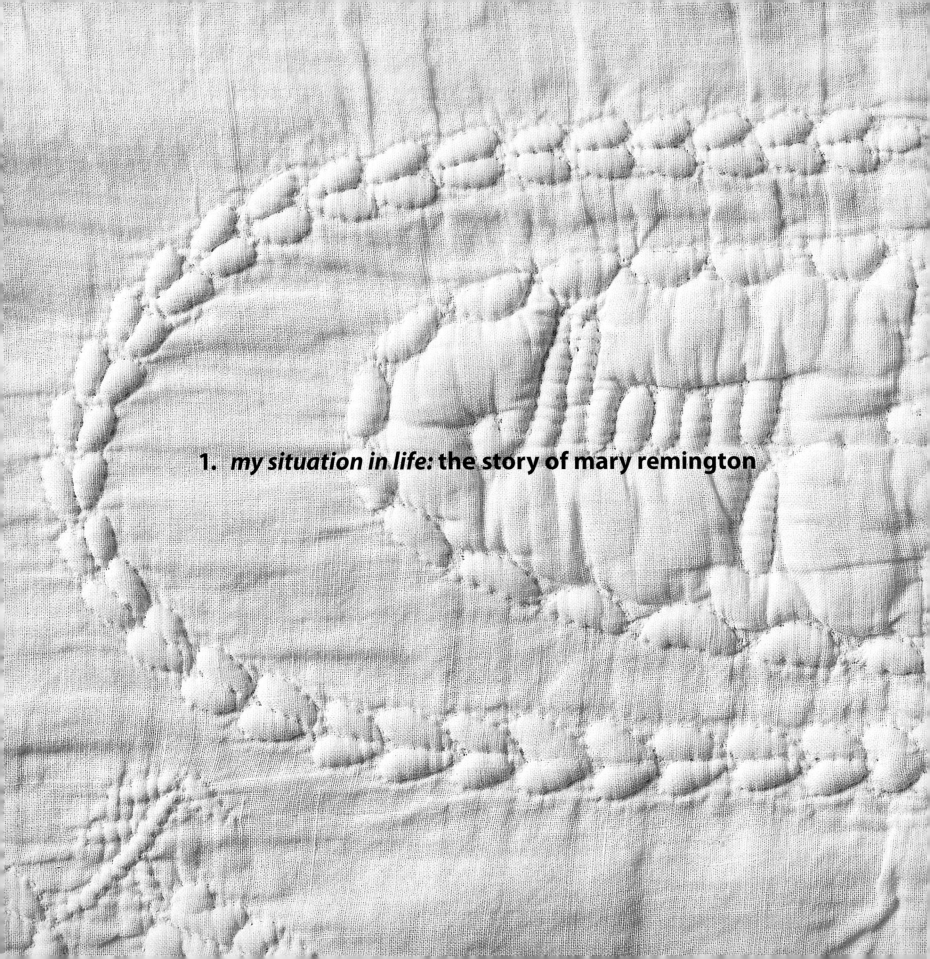

1. *my situation in life:* **the story of mary remington**

"My situation in life is easy, and as long as my Parents are spared to remain with me is every way pleasant; my advantages are much greater than I deserve, or by making good use of them merit." This assessment was written by Mary Remington, a young woman of twenty-three who was being pressed by her suitor, Peleg Congdon, to marry. Mary was suffering agonies of indecision. On one hand, she had been corresponding with Peleg for more than three years. Many of her family and friends had been expecting an announcement for some time. On the other hand, Mary suspected that Peleg's motive for marrying her might be pecuniary, rather than romantic, in nature. The story, which reads like a soap opera, is told in a series of twenty-nine letters written by Mary to Peleg between November 1811 and January 1817. The story is somewhat lopsided. Peleg requested that Mary burn his letters to her, which she did. The draft of one letter from Peleg did survive, as did three from Mary's cousin Sarah Holden to Peleg. Interspersed among these is the tale of a white stuffed-work quilt that Mary was making. This chapter is the story of that quilt, in the context of her life.[1]

Mary's letters read like an epistolary novel. Such novels of sensibility were read voraciously by young women on both sides of the Atlantic. Mary's early correspondence, however, also closely resembles the prescribed format found in letter-writing manuals of the period. Even her later letters conform in some ways to the published models, as they more closely resemble written conversations. "As letters are the copies of conversation, just consider what you would say to your friend if he was present, and write down the very words you would speak, which will render your epistle unaffected and intelligible."[2]

Letter writing was a burgeoning activity in the early nineteenth century. The format in which the prescriptive literature was sold underlines its availability to people in various economic circumstances and all walks of life. For example, *The New and Complete Letter Writer* by Rev. Thomas Cook, which was printed in Wilmington and sold by Robert Porter in 1820, is made from poor-quality paper bound in a pressboard cover.[3] By contrast, *The New Complete Letter Writer: Or, the Art of Correspondence Composed by Writers Eminent for Perspicuity and Elegance of Expression*, printed by Charles R. and George Webster at their bookstore in Albany, New York, in 1802 has higher-quality paper and a more elegant tooled-leather binding. It includes a model letter "From a young Woman, just gone to Service in Boston, to her Mother in the Country."

An examination of this prescriptive literature shows close similarities of content, consistent with the blatant plagiarizing that went on in the publishing world at the time. These similarities also show that there was certainly an accepted model for correspondence, one to which Mary's early letters conform quite closely. The tables of contents in these guides put Mary's situation (her concern that Peleg is only interested in her money, or that he is romantically involved with the young ladies of New York) into context among her contemporaries. Reverend Cook provides examples in the section "Love, Courtship and Marriage" that include a standard love letter "From a young Gentleman to a Lady with whom he is in love," but also "From a young Gentleman in expectation of an estate from his penurious Uncle, to a young Lady of small fortune, desiring her to elope with him to New England. And The Lady's prudent Answer." We also find "From a rich young Gentleman to a beautiful young Lady with no fortune," as well as "From a Lady to a Gentleman, complaining of Indifference," which accuses him of loving a Miss Benson; his reply tells her that she should not entertain "groundless jealousies." As well as dealing with infidelity and elopement, the booksellers from Albany include such "useful" examples as "The Earl of Strafford to his Son, just before his Lordship's Execution." Other useful models include "Of

Warwick March 12th

Respected Friend P.C.

I have repaired to my chamber with an intention of writing you and perhaps for the last time for several months. And have vainly endeavoured to collect my scattered ideas that I might arrange them in some form, but I am perfectly at a loss how to begin. When I wrote my last letter I scarcely thought of the distance that it must travel to reach you and of the uncertainty of its arrival. Should this fall into the hands of any one except yourself I hope it will be one possessed of a generous heart, and who will not take pleasure in exposing it.

When I have ever written to you I have considered it as writing to a friend and have therefore not made use of those compliments, professions of friendship and kindness that we frequently meet with and which in my opinion are not natural where the heart is well inclined, they are rather a prostitution of Speech seldom intended to mean what they express and never all. I think it a very just observation that among the many errors we commit the want of sincerity is none of the least. Many people are so full of dissimulation that their words are hardly any signification of their thoughts. I think sincerity a necessary and glorious virtue so it is also an obvious and easy one; it is so obvious that wherever there is life there is a place for it, and so easy that there is but little labour required in preserving it. ___

The Rev. Mr Wilkes in his advice to his niece says that the duties that are owing to friends are integrity, love, counsel and assistance. That it is not intimacy or frequency of conversation that makes a friend but a disinterested observation of these duties; I never expect to find one without imperfections and those who do will never find what they seek.

Few examples survive of bed quilts, bed valances, and dressing-table covers quilted en suite. Mary Remington never mentions her quilted accessories in her letters, but they survived together and were made from the same fabrics and by the same hand. Today they are displayed in one of Winterthur's period rooms.

Consolation to a Friend in Prison for Debt" and "From a sensible Lady, with a never failing Receipt for a Beauty Wash." Many of the volumes include quotes from classical literature, and sometimes even complete letters, and fifty pages of maxims, listed under convenient headings so the appropriate quotation for every occasion can easily be found.

Reading Mary's letters, one could be forgiven for coming to the conclusion that she was a scatterbrained, hysterical, indecisive young woman. Put into the context of the literature of her time and the conventions of sensibility within which she operated, the language of her letters seems less so. The popular American novel *Charlotte Temple* was about the difficulties that a young woman has in making choices in her life. Charlotte's situation is much worse than poor Mary's, as it involves seduction and pregnancy out of wedlock, but Mary's letters sometimes contain the same tone. This elevated, emotional language is common to the whole concept of sensibility, a concept that pervaded the spheres of men and women, and of public and domestic life.[4] It is a style that can be found in sermons and political orations of the time, as well as in letters and diaries, but it is so different from the linguistic conventions that are used today that it is easily misunderstood.

Mary's Life
Mary Remington was born on April 13, 1792, the only child of doting parents, Henry Remington and Margaret Le Valley, who were both descended from early settlers of the town of Warwick in Kent County, Rhode Island. Her father was a lawyer and a judge who served on Rhode Island's Supreme Court, between 1801 and 1808, and was known as "a fluent, energetic debater."[5] Less is known about her mother, but from evidence scattered throughout Mary's letters, she seems to have been a nervous woman who was often not well. Mary, herself, was a small, fragile child whose health was also of some concern to her family.

Mary's father was quite well off, although his wealth did not rival that of the great Rhode Island merchants. In addition to his legal career, Henry Remington owned land in the eastern side of Warwick, on the peninsula known as the Neck or Old Warwick. His will indicates that he raised sheep and a few cattle on this property, leasing some of his sheep to neighbors. In 1813, Henry purchased a farm in Plainfield, Connecticut, which Mary visited on a number of occasions.[6] Plainfield is just over the border and had much closer social and commercial ties to Rhode Island than to the western part of Connecticut. There is also some evidence that Henry Remington was in a mercantile partnership with his neighbors, Henry and Thomas Arnold, and he seems to have invested in a business operated by his brother Thomas.[7]

When Mary was about nine years old, her father built a new house on the Post Road in Apponaug, one of the villages that make up the larger town of Warwick. The neighborhood later came to be known as Judges Row.[8] Mary lived next door to her good friend Catherine T. Warner, whom she describes as her "only intimate acquaintance."[9] Both houses, almost identical, are still standing. The Remington house backs onto Apponaug Cove, which was a center for shipbuilding and trade. It is said that large sloops would off-load at the store of Jacob Greene & Co., which was next door to the Remingtons. Although now a sleepy little town behind the T. F. Green airport, in the early nineteenth century Apponaug was a thriving center of commerce and manufacturing. It was once thought that Apponaug would grow to rival London in size.[10] It was here that Mary made her quilt.

Peleg Congdon's situation in life was considerably different from Mary's, which was a source of some concern both before and after their marriage. He was the youngest of the fourteen children of John Congdon and his third wife, Abigail Carr. Peleg's father had been a yeoman farmer in Exeter, Rhode Island, who died in

1785, the year after Peleg was born. John Congdon's personal estate was sold at his death and the proceeds were divided among his wife and children, according to his will.[11] Peleg is not listed in his father's will because he was not yet born when it was written. It is unclear whether Peleg received a share of his father's estate. Noah Webster defined a yeoman as "a gentleman farmer, freeholder, officer," in his first *Compendious Dictionary* of 1806.[12] No land is listed in John Congdon's will or probate inventory and, judging from his household furnishings, he was not a wealthy man.

Peleg had gone to sea as a young boy and worked his way up to become a ship's captain for the merchant house of Minturn & Champlin, an old and prestigious firm based originally in Newport, Rhode Island, and later in New York City. He may have met Mary when visiting his brother Gideon, who operated a blacksmith shop in the Four Corners section of Apponaug, just across the bridge from Mary's home, although another brother, Joseph, seems to have known the family since Mary was a child. Joseph was a frequent visitor who was very kind and took a particular interest in Mary's happiness and welfare. He seems to have had business with Mary's father, as she and her father spent the day of June 11, 1815, with him on "the neck."[13] The Congdon family was very close, and Mary mentions many of them with affection in her letters to Peleg.

Mary Remington and Peleg Congdon were just recent acquaintances when both Mary and her cousin Sarah Holden began to correspond with him in November of 1811. By the end of 1812, Peleg had mentioned the possibility of matrimony. Although Mary was clearly attracted to him, she hesitated to commit herself, and with some reason. Peleg had a reputation for liking the young ladies of New York. Cousin Sarah, who clearly did not think highly of Captain Congdon, mentioned these ladies in her very first letter. Mary also worried that Peleg was only interested in her money and was not shy to say so. She recounts a conversation she had with

her mother in which she noted, "I wish'd if I ever gave my hand to any one it might be to a person of good character one who was respect'd by his acquaintance a man of business if not of fortune and one who would make a kind and affectionate husband to such a one so that could I feel assured I was preferred from laudible motives." Later in the same letter to Peleg she is even more blunt: "Soon after your first arrival in R Island I was told you had courted a young lady in N York, and acknowledged your love for her was sufficient to have been married, but from the persuasions of your brother and her want of fortune, you was not, and further that you should say in company you could fancy any lady was she possessed of a handsome fortune."[14]

By March of 1815, Peleg seems to have won her over, and she encouraged him to write to her father, although not with any particular enthusiasm: "You mentioned writing to Papa. I have no objection but should be pleas'd with it if it is your wish."[15] Mary's parents only wished for her happiness. She writes that her mother told her, "Mary In your getting a husband property is not my object neither is it your Papa's if you have a prudent one we have a sufficiency to render us both happy with very little exertion. All they wanted was a worthy Man that would make me a kind tender and affectionate husband."[16] In the early nineteenth century, the choice of a marriage partner was increasingly the decision of the couple themselves, and Mary certainly felt the strain.

Sadly for them both, the firm of Minturn & Champlin failed in 1815, and Peleg experienced great difficulty finding other employment, a situation that he found understandably depressing. Peleg remained in New York City for some time, evidently searching for work. In July of that year she writes, "For me to know that you preferred N.Y. to R.I. without the prospects of business being better there than here, or if I really thought you was waiting wholly for me to write you my wishes for an immediate union it would for a while be

a source of grief." She had also been upset by Peleg's earlier demand that, "Unless I [Mary] write you my arms are open to receive you as a Husband I must not look for you and that my withholding my hand caused you to leave R.I. and is now the only reason for your not returning immediately."[17]

Mary finally made up her mind and married Peleg Congdon in January of 1816. The marriage was not one made in heaven. Considering the evidence that survives, it would seem that Peleg did marry Mary for her money rather than for love. It is unclear whether Henry Remington refused to support them or whether Peleg was too proud to become dependent on him, but Peleg left Rhode Island to look for work soon after the wedding, while Mary remained at home for at least a year.

During that time, her letters, which began with a gush of newly wedded bliss, become increasingly frantic. Peleg must have come to visit Mary in the early spring, when he quarreled with his mother-in-law. In April, Mary writes, "Of what is past pray let us think as little as possible. I know my dear your feelings have been too often hurt; and in that mine have been tried also. But let us forbear reproach."[18] In Peleg's defense, Mary's mother seems to have been a difficult and unstable woman; she may have suffered some form of mental breakdown. Mary is compelled to explain to Peleg that "from Mama we can expect but little she is but a child to what she once was . . . She knows what is past and my being separated from you renders me unhappy that with other ideas has wore upon her mind till it may truly be said to be a disorder at times she is very nervous and I think some hypocondriacal, we have persuaded her to have medical advice but as yet to no purpose."[19]

Mental instability seems to have run in the family. Sarah C. Cook, who was related to Mary's mother, lived for a while with the Remingtons. Sarah's mother, Abigail Allen Cook, lived in various asylums while her daughter lived with relatives or boarded at Mary Balch's school in Providence. One of the asylums, run by a Dr. Willard,

The Remington house still survives in Warwick, Rhode Island, as does the Warner-Harrison house next door. Mary's letters mention Captain Harrison, who boarded with her cousin's family in Providence but often came to Warwick to court Catherine T. Warner, Mary's best friend. When Catherine's father, Thomas, died in 1847, Catherine and her husband, William Harrison, inherited the house. Mary's father's second wife, Lucy Ann Arnold Remington, and her daughters inherited the Remington house when Henry Remington died.

The Apponaug Cove behind the Remington home was a center of shipbuilding and trade. A commercial building, just across the stream from the Remington property (at the right in this photograph), occupies the former Jacob Greene & Co. warehouse property. Later, the Oriental Print Works, one of the largest printers in the country, was located just down the road.

Mary worked a marking sampler in 1799, when she was seven years old. The sampler included her nickname, Polly, as well as a middle initial "L." There is no other reference to her middle name, although it may well stand for LeValley, her mother's maiden name. Like the Remingtons, members of the LeValley family were early settlers in Warwick and owned a significant amount of farming land in the town. The Queen-stitch pocketbook, with a silver clasp engraved with the initials "M.R.," was probably made as a gift by Mary's second cousin Sarah Cook, who lived for a time with the Remingtons.

was among the best available at the time, where other patients included John Hancock's nephew and Paul Revere's son-in-law.[20] It is likely that the Queen-stitch pocketbook attributed to Mary was in fact made as a gift for her by Sarah, who is known to have made another in similar circumstances.

Soon Mary begs Peleg to write to her more often, "in evidence to Papa and Mama that I am not forgotten."[21] By July, she is really worried that he doesn't love her, and writes, "If you have business and on that account cannot leave I will not complain only assure me that it is not your unwillingness that prevents."[22]

That summer, Peleg gets work building a ship in New York and, while he refuses to come live with her in Warwick, or perhaps more particularly her mother, he also has not requested for Mary to come to New York. She writes about her concern that Peleg has injured himself from heavy lifting, so he may have been little more than a common laborer. (This experience stood

him in good stead, however, as later in his life he built ships for the U. S. government.)[23] Peleg's shame over his living conditions may be one reason why he did not bring Mary to New York, although he evidently would not admit this to her. While Mary hesitates "to leave my father and mother and more than all to leave them unhappy on my account," and claims that she would have no particular objections to living in New York, she worries that for her to leave her father would be "more than he could bear." She writes to Peleg, "I feel anxious to do every thing for our future happiness and good that in my power lies but what will be for the best I know not. I can't write as I wish now, my ideas are confused."[24] By the next month, however, she writes, "I must say that I have at times felt that you was not as willing to make sacrifices as I or as condescending. You have never been sensible of my situation to that I think it is owing."[25] Their separation is the talk of both towns. "By your mentioning that many observations are made respecting our situation it appears N. York or its inhabitants are not altogether, in that respect, unlike those in Warwick. We cannot wonder my dear that people are anxious to know why we are separated and remain at so little distance from each other."[26]

At this unhappy juncture, with his illness and depression probably exacerbated by his young wife's continuous complaints, Peleg writes a letter that contains "expressions" that were "truly distressing to the feelings of a fond wife or a tender Father," whereupon her father counseled Mary not to respond. When she did, two months later, she noted, "You reminded me in one of your letters of my past conduct with other young men as well as yourself and wish'd me to take a retrospective view of it and see if I was guilty of no faults. I am willing to aknowledge to you all my errours and can say with sincerity that I never knew of my character being calld in question before and little my dear did I once think that my husband would be the first to remind me of it." In later letters, however, Peleg had given her "much satisfaction" by his "willingness to acknowledge [his] fault."[27]

By the end of the year, Peleg is asking for a reconciliation, having heard rumors that Mary's father was about to obtain a divorce for his daughter. Divorce was not common at that time, but there had been an increase in petitions after the American Revolution, when some scholars speculate that "women enjoyed new feelings of individualism, self-confidence, and self-assertion."[28] These were certainly not Mary's feelings; from her letters she seems self-effacing, indecisive, and willing to do whatever her husband wished. One can only assume that the sole reason Mary's father could have cited would have been desertion. This would seem to be a bit unlikely within one year of the marriage, especially since so many women in Rhode Island were married to merchants or seamen who could be away for months or even years at a time. There were a few precedents set in the 1790s of divorce petitions by women who were deserted immediately after their wedding. The rumor about a possible divorce, however, proved to be false, as Mary asserted: "Papa never insinuated a thing of that kind to me nor will he ever without my requesting it."[29]

At the end of 1816, Peleg finally obtains a ship and feels more confident about the future. Mary wrote to him: "You have often said in your letters that the want of property you believ'd had been the cause of our troubles; I am loath to believe it, yet I am sorry to say that I think your future, or our happiness will depend some on your success in business; this voyage should you be successful will determine much." He had written to Mary from Savannah as well as New York, and maybe on his way to New Orleans and possibly to Europe.[30]

And there the story comes to an abrupt end. We do know that Peleg eventually came back to live in Warwick and kept a hotel in Apponaug from 1819 (the year their first son was born) until 1832. Mary died on November 14, 1820, a few months after the birth of her second son. Mary's mother died shortly thereafter, and

Henry Remington so shocked the town by his choice of a second wife (she was younger than his daughter) that the fact was mentioned in a town history written nearly fifty years later.[31] They went on to have two sons and three daughters, who inherited all of Remington's real estate; in his will, he left Mary's sons each five hundred dollars. John Remington Congdon became a sea captain like his father and took his wife with him on many voyages. Henry Remington Congdon founded a successful business in Providence. Peleg Congdon died in 1862 at the age of seventy-seven.

The Congdon family were Quakers, but the Remingtons were Baptists. Rhode Island was founded on the principle of freedom of religion, and both Baptists and Quakers were among the earliest settlers. There were many different interpretations of faith within the Baptists. The church in Warwick was part of the group know as Six-Principle Baptists, from Hebrews 6:1–2, which lists those principles as repentance, faith, baptism, laying on of hands, resurrection of the dead, and eternal judgment.[32] The Remingtons attended the church organized in either 1785 or 1792 by Pastor David Corpe. It occupied an old house on a hill east of the village of Apponaug. Corpe was succeeded by Elder Spooner (mentioned in Mary's letters) who was appointed by the yearly meeting to preach once a month. The history of the Baptists at this time is unclear, but it is believed that the church in Apponaug "became extinct" in 1805. Many of Mary's friends were later associated with the Central Free Will Baptist Church, founded in Warwick in the 1830s, including Thomas W. Harrison, Catherine Westcott, William D. Brayton, Elizabeth Wickes, and Mary E. Wilbur.[33]

Mary lived at the start of the Second Great Awakening—a time when there were numerous preachers traveling the country. She describes the social aspects of attending meetings but never discusses her own beliefs. The correspondence between her Quaker cousin Sarah and Peleg Congdon feature more of the self-

conscious introspection that was a feature of religious practice in the Society of Friends.

Mary's letters are limited to what she would say to a young man, a suitor about whom she has some qualms, and describes to some extent the course of their romance. The general tenor is consistent with other, more revealing diaries of young women of the period, in particular concerning her hesitation to set a wedding date.[34] Once betrothed, it was not uncommon for young women to delay the actual marriage. What is less clear is whether other young men felt the same level of exasperation as Peleg did.

The extent of Mary's reading, which included both classical and contemporary literature, history, and modern travelogues is revealed in her letters. The only novel she mentions is *Self Controul* by Mary Brunton, lent to her by cousin Sarah. This is a moral tale that concerns thwarted love, honor, seduction, and marriage, incorporating distinct levels of what we would consider to be melodrama. Mrs. Brunton's work was lampooned by Jane Austen in her own novel *Sense and Sensibility*. "Although by the late eighteenth century the British deplored sensibility as foolish sentimentalism, the literature of sensibility still sold well in the former colonies."[35] The heroine of *Self Controul* rushes off to America to get away from her persistent suitor, whose conduct made her feel she couldn't marry him. Again, the novel features a woman making choices about her future. At a time when a woman's personal wealth would be controlled by her husband, the decision about whom to marry becomes a crucial one.

Mary read the classics, specifically mentioning Petrarch. Such reading was not unusual for the daughters of the American elite. Although Mary could not be considered among the intellectuals of her time, she was certainly reading many of the same texts.

In January of 1815, Mary began writing to a mysterious Alfred and signing herself Laura. This, too, was a common ploy. Young couples often adopted pet names for each other that referred to classical literature—John and Abigail Adams renamed themselves Lysander and Diana (it was only later that she started calling herself Portia). It is perhaps indicative of Mary's uncertainty about marrying Peleg that the name she selects is Petrarch's unrequited love, Laura, for whom he wrote many poems in the courtly or troubadour convention, a style beloved and revived by the sentimental poets and novelists of the eighteenth and early nineteenth centuries. On the other hand, Peleg, as Alfred, is portrayed as the King of England, who has been credited with establishing the British navy. Mary had been reading *A History of England*, perhaps David Hume's 1810 edition that describes Alfred as, "the model of the perfect character. . . . He knew how to reconcile the most enterprising spirit with the coolest moderation; the most obstinate perseverance with the easiest flexibility; the most severe justice with the gentlest lenity [*sic*]; the greatest vigour in commanding with the most perfect affability of deportment; the highest capacity and inclination for science, with the most shining talents for action." In addition to saving the English nation from the Danes, he also encouraged "the vulgar and mechanical arts" (navigation, commerce, and industry).[36] One wonders whether these names were selected by Mary or Peleg.

The Flowers of Literature, published annually between 1801 and 1809 by Benjamin Crosby & Co. in London, was also on Mary's reading list. It consisted of extracts from what were considered to be the most popular writing published each year, including poetry, travel writing, biography, and prose fiction. Each issue contained commentary by the editors. An important publisher, Crosby & Co. is forever associated with the unfortunate decision not to publish Jane Austen's manuscript, sold to them as "Susan" in 1803 but eventually published in 1818 by John Murray as *Northanger Abbey*.[37]

Mary was also reading *The Seasons* by James Thomson, a compilation of four poems that was a best-seller throughout the eighteenth and early nineteenth centuries. Mary stitched a needlework picture inspired by John Fairburn's 1796 print depicting Autumn. Mary's best friend, Catherine Warner, embroidered a similar picture at the same school, which remains unidentified. If not in Warwick, the school may well have been in Plainfield, Connecticut, which Mary mentions in her letters.[38] She also mentions reading John Milton's *Paradise Lost*.

Mary speaks of *Silliman's Journal*, which has relevance to the local textile industry. In 1810 Benjamin Silliman (1779–1864) published *A Journal of Travels in England, Holland and Scotland and of Two Passages Over the Atlantic, in the Years 1805 and 1806*. Silliman had been commissioned by the trustees of Yale to further his own learning and purchase books and scientific apparatus in Europe, but at least part of his journal was kept for his brother, Gold S. Silliman, who lived in Newport, Rhode Island, and who had an interest in textile manufacturing.[39] Silliman was "purposefully reporting to a growing body of scientific and technical professionals in America," but was also widely read by people like Mary, who were keeping up to date with events and developments in the wider world.

Mary's Quilt

Mary never describes her quilt in any of her letters, and in fact does not even call it a quilt, but instead uses the words "counterpane" and "spread" (an early use of these terms). According to the *Oxford English Dictionary*, the use of the words "spread" and "bedspread" to mean a bedcovering originated in America. The earliest usage is 1845, although the term can be found earlier in probate inventories.[40] The word "quilt" often just meant some form of a bedcover, usually a soft and warm one. Today we define the word more precisely, to mean a bedcovering made with two layers of fabric that have been stitched together, often in a decorative pattern with some form of filling between. In 1864, however, *Godey's Lady's Book* provided directions for knitting "Three Summer Quilts" and describes them as "more easily washed, and kept of a snowy whiteness than heavier counterpanes, pleasant and convenient for summer use."[41]

Mary's quilt combines motifs and stylistic elements that are both traditional and contemporary, at a time when the most up-to-date fashions were based on classical designs. The overall format of a rectangular shape formed by a wide band with arcs or quarter circles cut in at each corner is one found in many design sources from the late eighteenth century, based on earlier, classical prototypes. A plate from George Richardson's *A Book of Ceilings, Composed in the Style of the Antique Grotesque* is just one of many examples.[42] It is not inappropriate to use an architectural model for the design of a bedcover. Robert Adam, one of the greatest British architects of the late eighteenth century, designed a counterpane for a state bed at Osterley Park, just outside London, which was a simplified version of the pattern he used for the ceiling of the room.[43] In fact, floors and ceilings were related to each other in terms of interior design in the same way that the designs for counterpanes are often more elaborate versions of designs found on the testers of state beds. Even the pinwheel motifs in Mary's quilted borders, which are often associated with "fancy" taste, have a prototype in a design for a patera published by N. Wallis in 1771.[44] There was considerable overlap between "classical" and "fancy" taste, and the distinction in the current scholarship would seem to be one of wealth and class, as well as urban versus rural. Mary's quilt seems to fit the higher end of this scale.[45]

One aspect of the design that Mary quilted is certainly unusual and possibly unique. The primary focus within the central medallion is the only example known of a quilted armorial device. The design conforms to the description of the Remington arms in *Bolton's American Armory*, with a "Gryonny of 8" (which means that the shield was divided into eight equal parts radiating

Classically inspired designs for formal bedcovers were closely related to architectural designs for ceilings. Published in London in 1776, George Richardson's book of designs for ceilings includes many examples with layouts similar to those in Mary's quilt.

In the eighteenth and early nineteenth centuries, many books were published for architects and designers with patterns that could be copied or adapted for a variety of purposes. Wallis's *A Book of Ornaments in the Palmyrene Taste* was published in London in 1771, and includes a design for a pinwheel with curving arms similar to those found on Mary Remington's quilt.

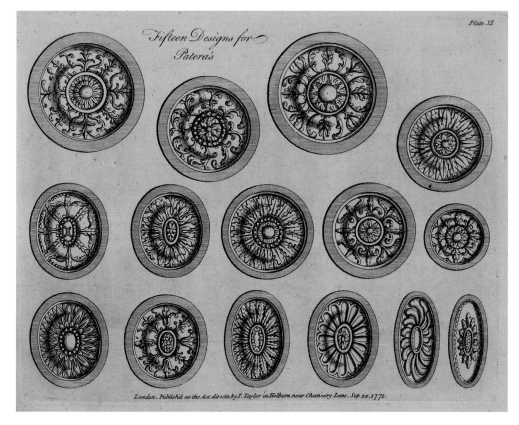

from the center) on which a dolphin was depicted. The helmet is facing left (which, according to the rules of heraldry, indicates a family that is not of the nobility), and the crest is a lion's head.[46] Although the stuffed-work technique is not conducive to finely delineated detail, it is clear that Mary has quilted a very accurate rendition of her family's coat of arms, identified on the motto ribbon with the words "By the Name of Remington."

From Mary's letters we get no hint of whether she drew the design of her quilt herself or had it drawn for her. Although based on classical prototypes, the formal layout and the floral sprigs and pinwheel motifs were part of the standard design vocabulary of the day. The design of the her coat of arms can be compared to contemporary embroidered examples worked at some of the most prestigious schools of the period. Embroidered coats of arms had been stitched by wealthy and well-connected schoolgirls in New England from the 1740s through the early nineteenth century, often drawn on their silk or canvas by professional artists. Mary was probably aware of this practice, if indeed she didn't work one herself. Surviving are a small number of silkwork coats of arms, worked at the school run by Mary Balch in Providence, Rhode Island, and dating to 1806 and 1809, but these examples are characteristically different from Mary's, and there is no evidence that Mary attended this school.[47] Another group of silkwork armorials thought to date to about 1804 has been identified as the product of the Misses Patten School in Hartford, Connecticut, an interesting comparison because of Mary's articulated desire to attend school in that state. But Mary's quilted coat of arms more closely resembles a silkwork one worked in Newburyport, Massachusetts, which author Betty Ring has identified as being stylistically related to arms painted by John Coles, Sr. (1749–1809), of Boston.[48] The feature that has been identified by Harold Bowditch as characteristic of Coles's work is the fact that the composition can clearly be divided into two levels: "the upper containing helm,

crest and mantling, and the lower the shield, palm branches and motto-ribbon." The palm branches on either side of the shield are also similar to those painted by Coles (which Bowditch reports are sometimes called cornstalks or leeks). Charles Knowles Bolton records the existence of an example of the Remington arms painted by Coles, which he dates to about 1800.

What significance can be read into the use of the Remington coat of arms on a quilt made in preparation for a marriage to which Mary would be expected to bring considerable wealth? Certainly the presence of the coat of arms indicates pride in her family heritage. In the United Kingdom, it was a common practice for a man to take another surname, sometimes that of his wife or another relative, either wholesale or hyphenated with his own, when the inheritance of considerable wealth was involved. In the United States, where family names are not so closely associated with wealth and status, there is little evidence of this practice, despite the fact that wealth was often inherited through gen-

Opposite In the early nineteenth century, it was fashionable for a young girl to create embroidered silkwork pictures depicting her family's coat of arms. Mary Remington's quilt is the only example discovered to date of an American quilted armorial device, carefully positioned to fall in the center of the bed.

Above Detail of name and date on Mary's quilt.

erations of a family. But Americans were not oblivious to the fact that women lost their nominal identity upon marriage. Abigail Adams, spending time with the wife of another delegate to the Continental Congress, asked her husband John, "Why should we not assume your titles when we give you up our names?"[49] Clearly Mary felt strongly about the significance of the Remington family name, using it as a middle name for both of her sons, but she did not go as far as Martha Laurens Ramsay, who gave her father's full name to four of her children.[50] In the field of anthropology, cultural naming practices are considered to be highly significant, yet no study has been done on early America, although the choice of names for children was clearly significant. Not only were family names used, but many male children were named after patriotic heroes such as George Washington. Mary's own father named his first son Henry Clay Remington, after the senator from Kentucky who had strong popular support in Rhode Island.

How long did it take Mary to make this quilt? The stitching is beautifully done, with between nine and thirteen stitches per inch, and was almost certainly all worked by Mary herself. She mentions her "bedspread" or "spread" a number of times in her correspondence with Peleg, but never mentions anyone working on it with her. She has started the quilt by the middle of January of 1815, when she tells Peleg that "the bedspread gets along finely."[51] Although by this date Mary and Peleg have been corresponding for just over three years, there is no evidence of a formal understanding between them, but marriage has certainly been on Mary's mind. By March, she has clearly recognized that her quilt project will be a long one. In a letter dated March 11, 1815, she writes that she "staid at home and work'd on my spread. When it will be finished I know not if I am not more industrious than I have been of late. You may circumnavigate the Globe before it is done." Although as far as we can tell, Peleg's travels did not include sailing around the world, the quilt was com-

pleted by the end of the year, and on January 7, 1816, Mary and Peleg were married.

Three quilted valances and a dressing-table cover worked by Mary Remington Congdon also survive. Although she never mentions these in her letters to her husband, the iconography she quilted would seem to indicate that she made these after her marriage. On her valances, Mary quilts pomegranates and cornucopia, alongside bunches of flowers with fashionable swags and bows, while her dressing-table cover features a central sheaf of wheat. This imagery connotes fertility, fecundity, and abundance, all attributes associated with marriage.

Mary occasionally mentions other needlework in the course of her correspondence, but rarely until after her marriage. She is asked to "prepare grave clothes" for a neighbor, and she helped her sister-in-law to make a new carpet, but she states that she would like to do more personal sewing for her husband. She had knit him some stockings and a shawl for herself, but expresses regret that Peleg has not sent her a piece of shirting for her to make up for him.[52]

American Textile Manufacturing

Warwick, Rhode Island, was a vibrant community in the early nineteenth century, at the center of the mechanization of American textile production. The village Mary lived in, known as Apponaug, was also called Fulling-mills, for the fulling mill that had been built in 1696 on the Kickemuit Brook next to her home. Fulling is a finishing process for wool that shrinks the cloth and raises the nap after the fabric has come off the loom. One wonders whether Mary was knitting Peleg's stockings and her shawl with wool from her father's sheep or with locally spun cotton yarn.

Warwick was a center for cotton spinning and weaving, and many of Mary's relatives, friends, and neighbors were involved in this fast-growing business. Approximately seventy-five cotton mills were built in

Opposite, above Mary Remington quilted three valances to hang on a bed with her quilt. Alternating pomegranate and floral bouquets are centered within alternating bows and swags, above a series of cornucopia and bordered with a floral and foliate design. Although none of the motifs match those on her quilt, the materials, including the fringe, are identical.

Opposite, below Mary also quilted a dressing-table cover depicting a basket with flowers and sheaves of wheat. It was fashionable in the early nineteenth century to cover fairly crude, pine demi-lune tables with fabric tops and skirts that would hide the wood. The skirt (which does not survive) would have been pinned or sewn into place to cover the unfinished edges of the quilted cover.

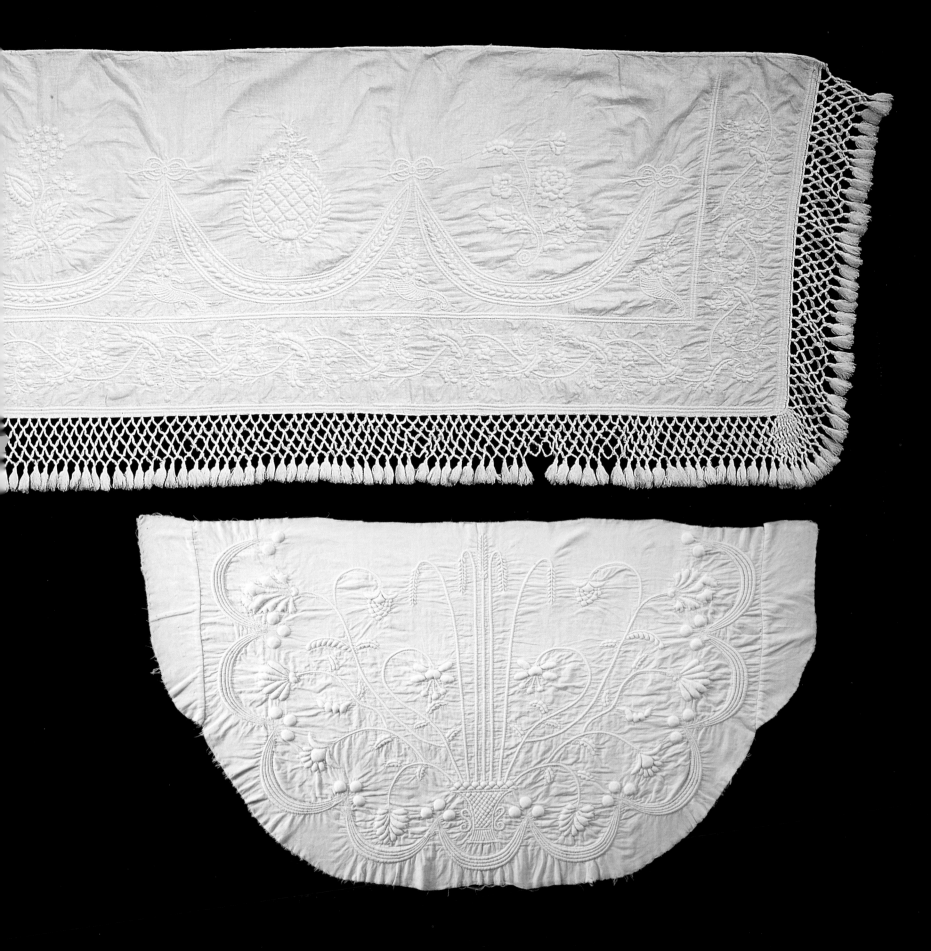

Above Mary used a fine white cotton fabric for the front of her quilt (shown here) but a much coarser, more loosely woven fabric for the back. She carefully inserted the cording used to create the three-dimensional effect without cutting any threads in the backing fabric. The backing may have been woven locally, but the fine fabric on the front was almost certainly imported.

Below Tench Coxe, a great promoter of American industry and Assistant Secretary of the Treasury under Alexander Hamilton, reported that 260 yards of cotton fringe were made in Providence, Rhode Island, in 1791, providing evidence that the fringe Mary Remington used for her quilt and valances may well have been made locally.

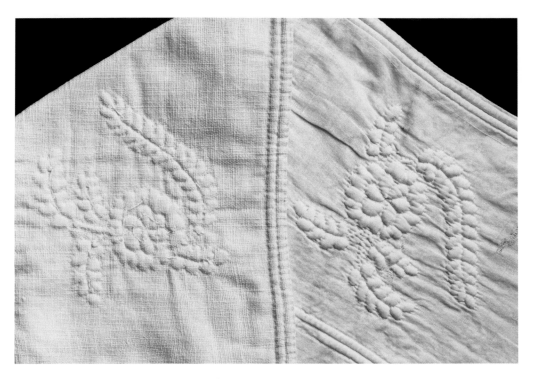

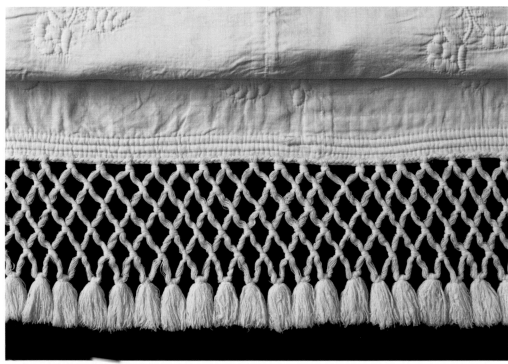

Rhode Island between 1810 and 1815, many of them in Warwick.[53] Tench Coxe described the importance of the local textile manufacturers, listing 25,265 yards of linen, 5,858 yards of cotton, and 260 yards of fringe as having been made in the town and vicinity of Providence, Rhode Island, in 1791.[54] Mary's first mention of this industry is in December of 1812, when she tells Peleg that "Mr. Wilbur has for some time past been doing business for the Washington Mrg. Co. and for several weeks has been at the Mill."[55] Warwick, however, had been involved in mechanized spinning since 1794, when Colonel Job Greene and other investors built the Centreville Mills, the second Arkwright spinning mill in Rhode Island.[56] In the early nineteenth century, a number of other spinning factories were opened, involving many of Mary's friends and relations, including the Lippetts, the Warners, the Arnolds, and the Greenes. Her uncle, Benjamin Remington, was one of the owners of the Crompton Mills in West Warwick. Built in 1807, this is probably the earliest stone textile mill in Rhode Island.[57] In 1813, Mary went riding with Mr. Waterman and was taken to see the cotton factory that Mr. Wilbur was building.[58]

Not all of these manufacturing businesses prospered. After the end of the War of 1812, the British dumped massive stocks of textiles onto the American market, undercutting the cost of domestic products and causing many of these businesses to fail. In June of 1815, Mary writes that "Mr. Smith, Mr. Westcott, Mr. Wilbur, and Capt. Harrison have all done with the Manufacturing business and at present idle." Her uncle's company, Crompton Mills, failed in 1816. But some of the struggling companies were bought by Almy & Brown, who later combined with Samuel Slater, who had founded the first mechanized spinning mill in America in 1792 (in Rhode Island).

So where were the fabrics that Mary used for her quilt manufactured? The front is a cloth with tightly spun yarns that was probably woven on a mechanized loom.[59] The power loom was only introduced to Rhode Island in 1817. The earliest mechanized weaving in Massachusetts was in 1814, but samples of these products do not survive. The likelihood is that this fabric was imported. Given the disruption to international trade during the War of 1812, this fabric would have been more expensive than usual. The backing fabric, however, is much looser in structure, and consists of three panels of cloth.[60] This is the type of fabric extensively woven by outworkers in Rhode Island.[61]

White bedcovers had been fashionable in elite homes for generations. The use of white cloth for clothing or bedcovers had implications that are little thought of today—the extra time, effort, and expense needed to keep them clean. In fact, Quaker schools in the 1820s would routinely ask that their students not bring light-colored clothing because of the extra washing. Bleaching, to obtain a good, bright white cloth, was also part of the finishing process for manufacturing fabrics. The Warwick Manufacturing Company, founded in 1807, bleached the cloth that was handwoven locally using the time-honored system of grass bleaching. Their bleaching green was across the river from the Baptist parsonage where "the cloth was spread and occasionally wet until the desired whiteness was secured."[62] The Clyde Bleachery and Print Works in Warwick, founded by 1828, later became the most important textile printworks in Rhode Island.[63]

One end use for the multitude of cotton yarns being spun in Warwick and other towns near Providence was for fringes. Mary never mentions knotting her fringe, a fashionable activity for elite women of the time, but one not associated with the type of fringe found on her quilt. It is more likely that she purchased hers but it may well have been locally made.[64]

International Trade

The technique that Mary used to make her quilt, now called stuffed-work, was also known as Marseilles quilting. This is a term that can be confusing. Marseilles quilting would have been familiar to many in the United States, as it is often found in lists of imported textiles advertised in newspapers. It originated in the style of white-corded quilting that was made professionally in Marseilles, France, in the seventeenth and eighteenth centuries, and was used to make items of clothing as well as bedcovers.[65] Similar materials and techniques, however, were used by quilters not only in England and other parts of Europe but also in America.[66] In the seventeenth and eighteenth centuries, this technique involved pulling cording through channels formed by parallel lines of stitching, but in the late eighteenth century, the technique of pushing stuffing through the backing fabric into spaces shaped by stitching became fashionable. The same term was also used to describe a woven fabric used for bedcovers, clothing, and men's waistcoats, made in Bolton, England (see also page 126).

In the early nineteenth century, Rhode Island became famous for its manufacturing, but prior to the War of 1812 its fortunes were generally made through international trade. Rhode Island merchants were very active in trade with ports in Britain, Russia, France, and the Baltic, as well as with the East Coast ports of the United States, South America, and the West Indies. Scholarship has traditionally focused on the more exotic China trade, so called despite the fact that a considerable proportion of this trade was with India. Huge fortunes were made, as with the Brown family of Providence. Merchant families from Warwick, such as the Arnolds and the Greenes, also took part in trade along the coast of North America, the West Indies, and South America, which required smaller ships and less capital investment. Sarah Holden mentions her brother's return from Lisbon in one of her letters to Peleg Congdon, while Mary cites seeing the *Trident* off Warwick Neck bringing back a cargo of 22,000 bushels of salt from Lisbon.[67]

The Baltic trade was also important to the merchants of Rhode Island. The only surviving letter from Peleg to Mary was from Copenhagen, a major port in the Baltic Sea. She clearly thought that he was on his way to Russia. Commodities traded with Russia, Silesia, and other ports on the Baltic Sea included hemp, rope, and cordage, which are not nearly as beautiful as the tea, silks, cottons, and porcelains of the China trade. Mary asks Peleg to purchase a muff and tippit for her in Russia: "I shall give you no instructions concerning the kind but leave it to your judgment to get such a one as you think would be becoming for me to wear, such a one Papa will without doubt be willing to satisfy you for. Think not that I wish it as a present but that my motive in sending to you is because they can be procured much cheaper in Russia than in N. England should you send it by cousin C Holden any presents that you think proper for me to accept will be received with pleasure."[68]

Ships entering the Baltic through the Sound had to stop to pay a toll in Helsingør, Denmark (which Peleg spells Elsinore, of Shakespearian fame), where a careful record was kept. Between 1783 and 1807, a total of 171 ships from Rhode Island registered to pay the toll, while during the same period, 104 ships from New York registered.[69] Many of these ships stopped in Hamburg and/or Gothenburg before continuing on to the Baltic ports of Rostock, Danzig, Riga, or St. Petersburg.

Disruptions of international trade through embargoes and blockades of European ports caused by the Napoleonic Wars in Europe severely affected the international merchant trade in Rhode Island. The War of 1812 decimated the Rhode Island shipping industry, while the port of New York continued to grow, although some of the more successful Rhode Island merchants survived. Peleg tells Mary that that "Nay Greene is here doing business on the acct of Ives & Brown" (the largest firm in Providence). Minturn & Champlin, the merchant firm for which Peleg worked for twelve years, was founded in Newport, Rhode Island, in the early eighteenth century, but its main center of operations moved

to New York after the Revolution when that city grew in importance as a port. Providence had overtaken Newport in size by the late 1700s, but the trade embargoes and disruptions drastically reduced its international trade in the early nineteenth century.

Peleg, with his usual bad luck, wrote to Mary from Copenhagen on May 16, 1812, while the Napoleonic Wars were raging in Europe, and only one month before the outbreak of war between Britain and the United States, which was declared at the height of the shipping season. Immediately upon hearing news of the war, Minturn & Champlin "sent the pilot-boat schooner *Champlin*" racing to the Baltic "to warn the captains and supercargoes of their vessels of the danger of British capture." "The existence of an embargo on foreign trade, the chief weapon of Madison in his economic duel with Britain, obliged the *Champlin's* master, Captain Summers, to declare to the harbor officials that her destination was Eastport, Maine. Once outside the harbor, he laid a course for Gothenburg," and was the first to bring the news to the American vessels in various Baltic ports.[70] At this time, John Quincy Adams was the United States minister in Russia, and the young Richard S. Smith was the American consul in Gothenburg, a port whose importance had grown as many of the northern European ports had been closed to Great Britain and neutral countries such as the United States by Napoleon's Continental System.[71] The American ships, to protect themselves, sailed in convoys with the British, their new enemies.

Peleg had traveled to Copenhagen using a circuitous route via Sweden because there were no vessels going there directly from New York. He was hoping to take charge of a ship, but the shipping industry was already in decline. He discovered on arrival that it was impossible, and on the advice of a friend he decided to stay in Copenhagen from six weeks to three or four months "in hope of an alteration favourable to the commerce of the U States, and if disappointed in this I shall

return in the Fall to some port in the U States as most convenient to take a passage. I shall prefer landing at Boston or some port East of R Island and proceed to New York by land as I would then have the pleasure of spending a few Days with my friends in R Island this fall."[72] He had a rough passage from New York to Gothenburg in the schooner *Experiment*, owned by Minturn & Champlin. They were at the mercy of a gale for five days, and after a two-day reprieve, "It came on again with greater Violence," with heavy seas, "which Stove our Boat," obliging them to stuff the holes with "old nets Shaveings and then Nail canvass over the rack to prevent her from going Down." But they survived, and "arriv'd at Gottenburg after a teadious passage of 49 Days from New York."

Peleg describes his journey on land from Gothenburg down the coast to Helsingborg, a distance he says of 150 miles, traveling at first in an open cart (though later in a proper carriage) with post horses that were changed every eight miles or so. He then crosses the sea channel to Elsinore and travels the remaining twenty-five or twenty-six miles to Copenhagen on a paved road, which he says made the journey "rather unpleasant." Peleg does not speak Danish and has to describe the city of Copenhagen from "ocular evidence" alone. After speaking of the streets and buildings, the shops, the churches, and the various inhabitants (who don't impress him), Peleg describes visiting the Royal Museum, which contains many "anticus Curiosities among the rest is an Egyptian mummy which from its appearance is no dout genuine. The Lady is surrounded by a great number of thicknesses of some kind of cloth on which appear to have been put a composition like Pitch, to make the Bandages stick firmly together. But what is more singular is a humane boddy which was found buried in the sand in a state of almost perfect preservation. What prevented it from decaying I will not pretend to say."[73]

Politics

Peleg Congdon noted in his memorandum book, "The Republican virtues of our yeomanry may they never been conkered by avarice, corrupted by ambition or Poisoned by foreign influence."[74] Although Peleg never knew his father, it may have been his father's position as a yeoman farmer that influenced his son's political opinions, which he claims are different from what one would expect of someone making a living as a merchant seaman. The early development of the two main political parties in the U.S. can be confusing, but essentially the Federalists supported a strong central government while the Republicans believed that the individual states should have more power. Many merchants and industrialists were associated with the Federalists, while farmers often supported the Republicans. Political opinion in Rhode Island seemed to fluctuate with the boom-and-bust cycles of foreign trade. "After 1800 a majority of Rhode Islanders had appeared to identify with the principles of the Republican party. . . . Discontent with the economic consequences of the embargo, however, produced a resurgence of Federalism in Rhode Island, and the Federalists remained a viable political force in the state through the end of the war."[75]

Peleg is a Republican, and he tells Mary that, "Nay Greene . . . is to use his own words a staunch Federalist and was rather supprised to hear me express my sentiments on political affairs they being in opposition to his own & several of my Brothers who he knew to be Staunch federal Republicans."[76]

Historians have been revising their opinions about women's involvement in politics, citing the importance of social gatherings and networks to the politics of the day.[77] All this presupposes a knowledge and interest in politics, which is seen not only in Peleg's one surviving letter to Mary, but in numerous letters from more active politicians to their wives. Mary read newspapers, kept up with current events, and discussed martial and political events with others. She had firsthand knowledge of some events during the War of 1812, having viewed Stephen Decator's squadron near the shore in Long Island Sound: "We could plainly see and distinctly hear them on board, the barges were constantly leaving and returning to the ships. The sound of the piper or whistle was to one quite a novelty, indeed the whole scene was. I had formed but an incorrect idea of the size and form of those vessels, they appear'd to me when viewing them so near the shore with such rural prospects around them, to be as it were quite out of their element."[78]

She was particularly delighted when the war ended, having worried about the possibility of Peleg being shipwrecked or captured. "In the morning the news of Peace was ushered in by the firing of guns. Every person almost young and old seemed ambitious to make noise, even the little children that could speak reiterated the sound of Peace."[79] But she was also fully aware of the political consequences, telling Peleg of a conversation she had with his brother. "He appeared very much surprised at the late news and was unwilling to rejoice until he would know on what terms the Treaty was made, he was fearfull he said it was such a one as would reflect little honour to America."[80]

Conclusion

Mary Remington was a young girl whose life centered around sewing, reading, and socializing with friends and family. Her correspondence with Peleg Congdon during their courtship and marriage describes how her life is affected by politics and war, the vicissitudes of international trade, and the growth of the American textile industry. Her letters also describe the literature she read, her decision to marry, the social difficulties she experienced living apart from her husband, and the pride she took in her family heritage, which is reflected in the design of her quilt. The story of Mary's life and the survival of her quilt provide a framework for examining other quilts in the Winterthur collection.

2. *the hurry of work:* **the role of quilts in women's lives**

Previous pages Rachel Goodwin Woodnutt Quilt

Silks in muted colors, such as those in this quilt, were a public demonstration of the Quaker faith in the late eighteenth and early nineteenth centuries. The prescriptive literature of the 1820s also advocated simplicity in dress at a time when mainstream fashions were becoming more colorful and elaborate.

Opposite Detail, Rachel Goodwin Woodnutt Quilt

This subtle and beautifully made quilt has a stuffed-work central basket of fruit. A traditional symbol associated with abundance, baskets of fruit were popular motifs that can be found on samplers from the Mid-Atlantic region in the 1820s and early 1830s.

"I thought every day or evening to write you, but the hurry of work such as knitting and sewing on my counterpane prevented."[1] In 1815, Mary Remington was working on an extraordinary white stuffed-work quilt (her counterpane) while trying to make up her mind about marriage. Many quilts survive with stories connecting them with important events in the life of their maker, or which commemorate networks of family and friends. Other quilts, often more simple in design and construction, are part of their maker's everyday life. But whatever the purpose behind them, each quilt documents choices or changes that can tell us much about the often anonymous lives that they have come to represent.

The quilts presented in this chapter touch on many important elements of women's lives, including marriage, religious beliefs, social networks, and kinship, all aspects of quilts that have been widely recognized.[2] Behind these topics is an overarching sensibility that became widespread as America moved into what became known as the Romantic Age, when memory and emotion, once belonging to private life, became publicly acknowledged and even celebrated.[3] This romantic sensibility influenced both the style of quilts and the materials used to make them. It also encouraged the preservation of quilts, often handed down through generations of one family together with memories about their makers. This influence spread throughout America via novels, poetry, religious tracts, and popular women's magazines. Once only available to the daughters of the wealthy elite, by the early nineteenth century, books were published in both cheap and more expensive editions, and magazines and newspapers were widely disseminated through subsidized postage and advances in transportation. Quilts, repositories of history and memory, reflect these stories.

Mary Remington spent a year making her quilt in anticipation of her marriage. The decision to marry, and whom to marry, was perhaps the most important choice in any woman's life. Bedding has long been associated with a woman's dowry and preparation for marriage.[4] Whether made by the bride-to-be herself, as was the case with Mary, or by the bride's mother or friends, many nineteenth-century quilts are associated with marriages. Winterthur's collection includes several quilts made by members of the Society of Friends from the Mid-Atlantic region, some of which are, by tradition, associated with weddings.

A considerable body of research exists about Quakers, and particularly Quaker women, benefiting from the fact that the Society of Friends had always encouraged personal reflection and individual accountability, and stressed the equality of men and women.[5] Such attitudes fostered the writing of diaries and letters describing personal opinions and beliefs, providing valuable information for later generations.[6]

Rachel Goodwin Woodnutt did not leave a written record, but her quilt has been treasured by her descendants, who lived in Salem County, in southern New Jersey. Salem was settled by Quakers in the seventeenth century; it was the first permanent English settlement on the east side of the Delaware River. Although once the home of Caspar Wistar's early glassworks, and in the later nineteenth century, a center of ketchup production, Salem has remained primarily an agricultural community with a strong Quaker heritage and close ties to Philadelphia.[7] According to family tradition, Rachel made this quilt for her daughter Elizabeth G. Woodnutt, who then gave it to her great-niece and namesake, Elizabeth Newlin Baker, who in turn donated it to Winterthur. The actual date when it was made is uncertain, but if the family history is true, Rachel may well have been making it toward the end of her life in anticipation of her daughter's marriage. Rachel's exact death date has remained elusive. One family member believes that she died in 1828; she is listed as deceased in the record of her daughter Elizabeth's marriage to Ansley Newlin in 1833.[8]

The light cream, green, and dove-colored silks in Rachel Woodnutt's quilt are said to have come from Quaker wedding dresses. Saving scraps of clothing and other personal items was not unusual at this period, and many Quaker quilts have survived, "reportedly made from recycled silk fabrics taken from wedding dresses and shawls."[9] A doll in Winterthur's collection, which can be dated to between 1835 and 1845, was said to have been dressed by the daughters of Mary Ann Warder Bacon, a Quaker woman from Philadelphia, using fabrics from their mother's wedding dress.[10] Scrapbooks of fabrics put together by Sarah Bradway Harris and her two daughters, Catherine Harris and Sarah Marion Harris Johnson, in the 1880s, contain many swatches cut from Quaker wedding dresses as well as aprons, bedhangings, and quilts, among many other types of fabrics. Dating between 1860 and 1881, the scrapbooks have also included fragments of young girls' first silk dresses, clearly a memorable event in their lives.[11] A less personal scrapbook of fabrics survives in the collection of the Friends Historical Collection at Swarthmore, collected by Rachel D. Griscom of Reading, Pennsylvania.[12] Coincidentally, Rachel's family was originally from Salem, New Jersey. Rachel included examples of "linsey" made by the Griscom family in Salem, New Jersey, as well as mummy cloth, fabric from clothing worn by slaves, and cotton raised, spun, woven, and dyed in Liberia.[13] The preservation of scraps of fabric in quilts has long been associated with the rise of paper-based scrap albums and autograph books.[14] What seems to be consistent in examples studied, all made within the Quaker community, is that the majority of the fabrics were cut from silk dresses. It is possible that the fabrics in Rachel Goodwin Woodnutt's quilt represent the wedding dresses of Rachel's six sisters, but there are at least eight different fabrics in the pieced diamonds. It is also possible that the quilt was made by Elizabeth G. Woodnutt herself, incorporating fabric from wedding dresses of her friends and family. The central stuffed-

work basket of fruit is a motif signaling abundance, and is often found on quilts and samplers. Recent research indicates that in the early nineteenth century, there was little or no difference between dresses worn to Quaker meetings and Quaker wedding dresses. It is also noticeable that the clothing kept by Quaker families tends to be the dress worn in the early nineteenth century, a time when Quakers in the Mid-Atlantic region were consciously wearing a distinctive form of plain dress, at least on Sundays.[15]

Contrasting with the subtly hued silks of Rachel's quilt is a colorful sunburst pattern quilt made by Rebecca Scattergood Savery.[16] The story that has come down in the family is that the quilt was made by Rebecca for her fourth child, Elizabeth Savery, in anticipation of her marriage, planned to take place in 1827. In 1827 there was a split within the Society of Friends that was not healed until the middle of the twentieth century. The Society of Friends, also known as Quakers, was founded by George Fox in 1652, in part as a reaction against the perceived Catholicism of the Church of England. Fox did not advocate any specific doctrine, but stressed that the "inward light of Christ" was present in every person. Over time, however, the Friends acquired various rules and disciplines. With the increased evangelicalism associated with the Second Great Awakening in the early nineteenth century, a difference of opinion arose culminating in the division of the Society, known as the Great Separation.

The more evangelical group became known as the Orthodox Quakers, advocating greater concentration on scripture and emphasizing belief rather than behavior.[17] The more conservative faction, known as the Hicksites, continued to believe in the primacy of the inner light—an individual's personal experience of Christ rather than elaborate interpretations of the Bible. "Quakers divided into Hicksite and Orthodox camps based on social, economic, and geographic factors. Orthodox Quakers tended to be urban merchants and

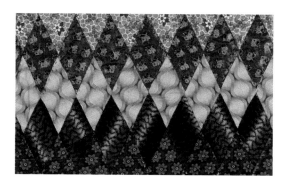

Opposite **Detail, Rebecca Scattergood Savery Quilt**
Rebecca Scattergood Savery pieced a sunburst quilt from a variety of small-patterned printed cottons purchased for a quilt intended to celebrate the marriage of her daughter Elizabeth. This Quaker quilt, like many others, attests to the love of bright colors and busy patterns among a religious community often thought to value only muted colors and plain designs. (See page 2 for an image of the full quilt.)

Left, above **Detail, Rebecca Scattergood Savery Quilt**
Because the fabrics on the Scattergood Savery quilt have not been washed, they retain their original glazed finish. The colors and designs, at the height of fashion in 1827, look modern today.

Left, below **Detail, Paper Label, Rebecca Scattergood Savery Quilt**
The label stitched to the lower edge of this quilt gives details of its maker and the number of its "patches." The label was added later in the nineteenth century, when there seems to have been a competitive spirit among quilt makers vying with one another to make quilts from the greatest number of pieces.

their rural relatives, while the Hicksites were comprised of rural Quakers, rural immigrants to the cities, and Philadelphia's old established families who resented the rising merchant class."[18] The Savery family went into the Orthodox camp while the family of the man Elizabeth was to marry, James Cresson, became Hicksites. Despite the fact that Elizabeth's older brother William was already married to James Cresson's sister, it is said that their families prevented the marriage of Elizabeth and James, and Elizabeth remained single all her life.

The contrast in color and tonality between these two Quaker quilts does not necessarily represent an aesthetic distinction between Orthodox and Hicksite beliefs. All of the brightly colored quilts illustrated in Jessica Nicoll's seminal book *Quilted for Friends* were made by Hicksite women and are as vibrant as the one made by the Orthodox Rebecca Scattergood Savery.[19]

When discussing one particular group of people, be they a religious sect or an ethnic group, it is tempting to consider the individuals as one large homogeneous group. Recent scholarship suggests that members of the Society of Friends have always included a range of opinions, beliefs, and behaviors that emphasized introspection and an individualized interpretation of faith.[20] There was always a tension between the individual and the group. The constant movement of preachers and visitors both within America and across the Atlantic and a constant reinterpretation of the rules and disciplines were two ways that the Society of Friends attempted to keep some form of unity of purpose and belief. Contemporary scholars continue to seek ways to interpret the iconic Quaker phrase "of the best sort but plain," one that has become inextricably linked to Quaker material culture.

Not only did Quakers look inward for their spiritual guidance, but the lives of most young Quaker women were closely circumscribed by a tight circle of faith and family. Nancy Tomes has studied these social net-

works using surviving letters and diaries of prominent Quaker women from the late eighteenth century.[21] A study by Katherine Hunt of one quilt in Winterthur's collection shows how friendship quilts can be used as primary-source material, providing evidence of personal connections that extend beyond standard documentary sources. "The quilt cannot reveal information about how often visits occurred or what form these relationships took, but the quilt does provide a window into the life of at least one unmarried Quaker woman in the mid-nineteenth century."[22]

The silk quilt opposite, pieced in a design sometimes known as the LeMoyne pattern, was made to celebrate the marriage of Sarah Williams to Samuel Emlen, which took place on September 30, 1851, at the Sixth Street Meeting-house in Philadelphia. Ninety-one of the pieced stars contain names of people commemorating this event, but because of the quilt's poor condition, only about seventy are still legible. Distinguished by color, rather than design, the quilt features a central section that contains names of family members, including Sarah's parents, aunts, uncles, and cousins. Both Sarah Williams and Samuel Emlen attended Westtown School in Chester County, Pennsylvania, and the second cluster of names are friends that Sarah made there, about twenty in all. A third group of names relates to friendships formed through Sarah's work with the Female Society of Philadelphia for the Relief and Employment of the Poor. Although Sarah's name only starts to appear on the list of members of this group after her marriage, her mother, Hannah Newlin Williams, had been an annual contributor since 1818. The last group of names on the quilt are people who attended the same Quaker Meeting and lived near her family's home in the Franklin Square area of Philadelphia. The significance of placement of names on this quilt correlates with the practice of specific placement of family and friends in Quaker silhouette albums.[23]

The Orthodox-Hicksite split that occurred in 1827

was painful for individuals and the Society of Friends as a whole. Thomas P. Cope, whose wife signed Sarah Williams's quilt, confirmed this in 1844 when he wrote that even at that date the Society of Friends was "rent from one end of the continent to the other." Cope did not personally avoid contact with Hicksite Quakers. He wrote, "I have not as yet felt it my duty to shun social intercourse with others, merely because of a difference of faith," but his comment implies that others did so, and the extent of interaction between the two groups is not known.[24] The presence of Mary A. Shourds's name on Sarah Williams's quilt is therefore significant. Mary was the daughter of William and Martha Shourds and joined the Hicksite Green Street Monthly Meeting in 1836.[25] "With the records available it is impossible to determine how Sarah Williams and Mary A. Shourds met each other as Mary did not attend the same meeting, the Emlen-Williams wedding, or Westtown Boarding School, nor did she belong to the Female Society for the Relief and Employment of the Poor. Yet, their friendship was strong enough to commemorate on the quilt despite their theological differences."[26] What the presence of Mary A. Shourds's name does tell us is that while the extensive records of Quaker organizations provide much information about the networks that define the lives of Quaker women in the mid-nineteenth century, these documentary sources do not offer a complete picture of their lives.

By an extraordinary coincidence, Winterthur's collection includes a quilt that is remarkably similar to the Sarah Williams piece, yet with only a single name in the central star. Elizabeth Webster, together with her sisters, Mary Ann and Hannah, signed Sarah Williams's quilt, in three of the four outer corners. They were the daughters of Stephen and Mary (Thorpe) Webster of Frankford, just north of Philadelphia. According to family tradition, Elizabeth's quilt was also made in anticipation of her marriage, planned for 1852. Sadly, the young man she hoped to wed changed his mind. Elizabeth never

married, and gave her quilt to her niece and namesake Elizabeth Webster Smedley. Elizabeth became an elder, a position of importance within the Society of Friends, and died in 1892. One wonders how many other of the young women represented on Sarah Williams's quilt also had similar works of their own.

The Mid-Atlantic region is credited with originating the fad for signature quilts that was strongest between 1840 and 1860.[27] The majority that have survived were made from printed cottons, with the distinctive Turkey Red prints being most popular. In addition to the wider social networks exhibited in the Emlen quilt, other examples document family connections. Historians have noted the importance of familial relationships to Quaker business practice.[28] Other studies show that this is not exclusive to Quakers.[29] An overt, yet unspoken practice, kinship was an integral part of the social networks that informed the lives of men and women in the past as well as today. For men, family networks could provide access to financial credit, contacts with overseas merchants, political strategies to control local or even national government offices, paths to successful careers, and access to educational opportunities. No less important for women, family relationships often influenced membership in benevolent societies, and they have even been recognized as a major factor in determining who attended the Seneca Falls Women's Rights Convention in 1848.[30]

In the nineteenth century, as society increasingly perceived the role of women through the rose-colored spectacles of romanticism, women were considered to be the keepers and promoters of family networks through letters and visits, and through family-based signature quilts. Quilt historians have long recognized that names found on signature quilts can be used to identify a network of family and friends. Even when a kinship network is not central to the design or decoration of a quilt, it was the family that preserved most quilts, ensuring their survival and therefore their pres-

ence in the public and private collections in which they are celebrated today.

Despite the fact that the fad for signature quilts started in the Mid-Atlantic region, stretching from northern New Jersey to the Chesapeake Bay, the collection at Winterthur (located in northern Delaware) included few examples until relatively recently.[31] A typical quilt from Delaware identifies the family connections spanning two generations of the Clayton family, descendants of three brothers, Dr. Joshua Clayton, John Clayton, and George Clayton, who somewhat confusingly was renamed James after the early death of an older brother.[32] Descended from another Joshua Clayton, who came to Pennsylvania with William Penn on the ship *Submission* in 1682, the Clayton family were landowners active in local and national politics. Perhaps the most illustrious name on the quilt is John M. Clayton, who served in the United States Senate for three terms, and was the chief justice of Delaware between 1837 and 1839. He served as Secretary of State under President Zachary Taylor, negotiated the Clayton-Bulwer Treaty with Great Britain, and was said to have paved the way for the subsequent building of the Panama Canal. His cousin Thomas Clayton also served in both the United States Senate and in the House of Representatives. Characteristic of signature quilts from southern Delaware, a quilt of the same design and materials is in the collection of the Historical Society of Delaware.

Associations of people through their religious beliefs, be they Quaker meetings, churches, or synagogues, were an important aspect of many women's lives and continue to be so today. Many of Baltimore's elaborate album and presentation quilts are linked to the Methodist movement, one of the fastest growing evangelical sects in the period of heightened religious fervor known as the Second Great Awakening. Where their origins and intentions are known, all the quilts featuring a Bible in one block were made for Methodist ministers or class leaders, although the converse is not true;

Page 39 Sarah Williams Emlen Quilt
Few silk quilts survive from the early and mid-nineteenth century, but many were probably made. Silks of the period were not washable; the dyes were often fugitive and would bleed when damp or wet. Once badly damaged, many quilts were thrown away. This quilt, made to commemorate the marriage of Sarah Williams and Samuel Emlen in 1851, demonstrates that the historic value of a quilt may remain even if its visual beauty has been compromised.

Opposite Detail, Elizabeth Webster Quilt
Godey's Lady's Book recommended the use of silks for patchwork quilts in the 1850s, as printed cottons had become quite cheap due to advances in the mechanization of spinning, weaving, and printing technology. Luminous silks were fashionable for both day and evening wear by the wealthy elite, and a young girl's first silk dress was an event worthy of celebration.

Above Detail, Elizabeth Webster Quilt
The only name on Elizabeth Webster's quilt is her own.

Above **Turkey Red Quilt Blocks**
Intended for a friendship quilt that
was never made, these squares of
Turkey Red fabrics have papers
pinned to them with the names
intended for the blocks for which
they were to have been used. The
names include Eliza Sinquet, Ann L.
Hicks, Hannah S. Pawling, and
Lydia Cox, all from Chester County,
Pennsylvania.

Right **Clayton Family Quilt**
Small-patterned Turkey Red printed
cottons are a notable feature of many
Delaware Valley signature quilts of
the 1840s. Centers of production for
the fabric were Manchester, England,
southwestern Scotland, and Mulhouse, France. This particular style
of friendship quilt was prevalent
in Delaware.

Opposite **Coles Family Quilt**
This friendship quilt was made by
Hannah Woolston Coles of Camden
County, New Jersey, around 1841. A
recent donation to Winterthur, the
quilt was the gift of two sisters in
memory of their mother.

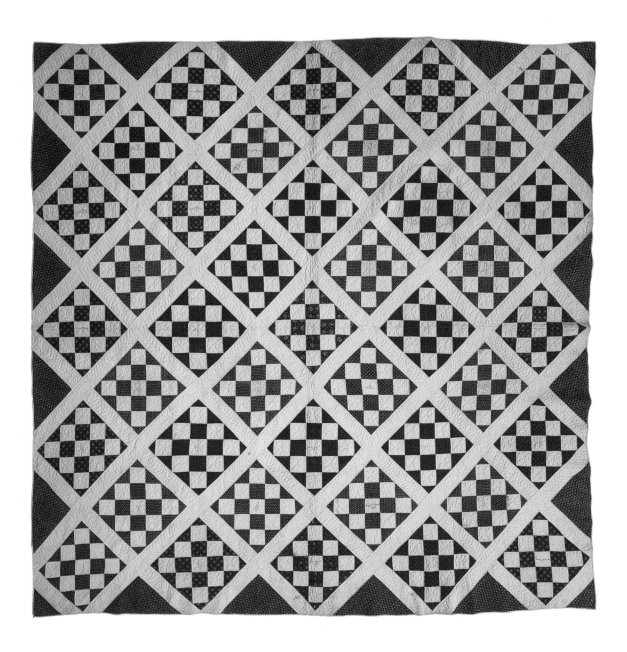

not all quilts made for Methodist ministers depict representations of the Bible.[33] Each Methodist minister was stationed in a church or geographic area serving a group of churches for a period of usually only two years, providing ample opportunities for members of their congregations to make presentation quilts. Identification of individuals represented by name on an 1854 Baltimore album quilt in Winterthur's collection has enabled us to relate it to a separate denomination with interesting connections to Methodism.[34]

Many of the individuals identified on this album quilt were associated with a church known as Old Otterbein, or the Second German Reformed Church on Howard's Hill. The quilt was therefore probably made for presentation to departing minister John Russell, who had served Old Otterbein since 1851, and was replaced in 1854 by Samuel Enterline. The church was named in honor of Philip William Otterbein (1726–1813), who arrived in Pennsylvania in 1752 as a German missionary. It is said to be the oldest church building in continuous use in Baltimore. Known for his radical piety, Otterbein came to serve a church formed by a group that had broken away from the First German Reformed Church of Baltimore in 1771 under the influence of Benedict Swope, a charismatic lay preacher who left Baltimore in that year for Kentucky. Otterbein became closely involved with the Methodists, taking part in the 1784 ordination of Francis Astbury as general superintendent of the Methodist church, centered in Baltimore. The offshoot of the German Reformed movement that Otterbein founded, known primarily as the Evangelical United Brethren, combined with the Methodists in 1968 to become the United Methodist Church, the largest Protestant denomination in the United States.[35]

Old Otterbein was one of the many German-language churches in Baltimore, and only stopped holding services in that language when the United States declared war on Germany and entered the First World War on April 6, 1917.[36] Three German-language

Opposite **Old Otterbein Church Quilt**
Many names on this quilt made by members of the Old Otterbein Church in Baltimore, Maryland, in 1854 are worked in cross or marking stitch. A few of the blocks, notably the basket of flowers, may have been produced in kit form by Mary Simon, a Bavarian immigrant.

Top **Detail, Old Otterbein Church Quilt**
Images of Bibles are often found on quilts made for departing ministers. This central block was signed by Louisa Messersmith, who was twenty-four years old when it was made. She may have been the woman who organized the making of the quilt.

Center **Detail, Old Otterbein Church Quilt**
Ruched and padded flowers are found on many album quilts made in Baltimore, Maryland. Those seen here are characteristic of the style of an anonymous quilter known as "Designer II."

Bottom **Detail, Old Otterbein Church Quilt**
This particular design of a basket of flowers is found on many Baltimore album quilts. It is attributed to Mary Heidenroder Simon, who is known to have designed and basted blocks. A Catholic from Bavaria, Mary emigrated to Baltimore in 1844 and married a carpet weaver, Philip Simon, also from Bavaria.

newspapers were published in the city, in 1850. Germans were by far the largest ethnic group in Baltimore, which was also home to a sizeable Irish community as well as the largest population of free blacks in the country. These ethnic and racial groups did not congregate in separate parts of the city but lived side by side throughout each ward in a pattern described as a "social quilt . . . a patchwork of nationalities and establishments stitched together by a complex thread of economic and demographic change."[37] Appliquéd rather than pieced together, this quilt features names that connect German families who had been in America for at least one generation with recent immigrants. The use of Baltimore album quilts as primary-source material for a study of patterns of immigration, however, is frustrated by the difficulty in identifying and tracing so many of the women whose names are only known by the quilts they made.

We know much about Mary Remington's life just before and after her marriage, but almost nothing about her life after her husband, Peleg Congdon, returned to live with her in the village of Apponaug; however, the reminiscences of Adeline L. Dorr, daughter of quilt maker Abigail Horton Van Nostrand, provide a rare insight into the daily life of a quilt maker roughly contemporary with Mary.[38]

Abigail Horton married John Van Nostrand in 1808. Their daughter Adeline did not record how her parents met, but both families had business interests in the old part of New York City, at the tip of Manhattan Island. Abigail's whitework quilt was probably started in anticipation of her marriage in March 1808, but an inscription added sometime later records that it was completed in 1809, perhaps just before the birth of her first daughter, Almira, in February of that year. Abigail's father, Thomas Horton, was a merchant with offices on Canal Street in New York and was lost at sea in 1803.[39] Her mother, Lavinia Purdy Horton, was descended from early settlers of Connecticut. Her husband's family, the Van

Nostrands, were early settlers and influential landholders in Brooklyn, New York. According to his daughter, John Van Nostrand had a shop in the city. He is listed in the city directories as a grocer, but there is no relationship between his business interests and fruit Abigail depicted on her quilt.[40] The word "grocer" originally referred to a wholesale merchant and only later became associated with purveyors of foodstuffs. In 1807, John's firm, Thompson and Van Nostrand, imported seventeen casks of nails, and a J. Van Nostrand imported 105 pots and kettles in the same year.[41] John and his brother Abraham bought out their partner, Abraham G. Thompson, in 1809.[42]

John and Abigail Van Nostrand made their first home on Harrison Street, but just before the birth of their daughter Adeline, in May 1821, they moved to a large brick house in Washington Street, where pinks and sweet Williams grew in the small yard and morning glories twined around the porch. At that time commercial properties were intermingled among private residences, and their house was next to a marble-cutting yard, creating noise and dust by the continuous sawing of marble slabs. Adeline remembered their parlor and its "large patterned ingrain carpet, its red curtains with many draperies culminating in a graceful fall over the pier glass, the slender legs of the German pianoforte, and the very hard but handsome mahogany sofa covered with black haircloth, studded with black nails [and] the tilting mantle glass reflected a pair of candelabra and smaller candlesticks of beautiful bronze and gilt."[43] The family took the Chambers Street Ferry to Hoboken, where they would picnic in the woods and drink lemonade of mead, "an effervescent drink which seemed to be peculiar to Hoboken."[44] Adeline also recorded the cholera epidemic of 1832 and the first great fire of 1835.

At that time, the family was living on Morris Street (previously known as Beaver Alley, but said to have been renamed because Abigail Van Nostrand refused to live in an alley). Adeline remembered that, "Though the

Above **Inscription, Abigail Van Nostrand Quilt**
The label attached to the back of Abigail Horton Van Nostrand's quilt was added later by a descendant. The detail seen here shows not only the coarser backing fabric of the quilt but also the white cotton tape that binds the edges.

Opposite **Detail, Abigail Van Nostrand Quilt**
In the early nineteenth century, all-white quilts made from fine fabrics were a hallmark of the wealthy who had the resources to keep them clean. This task must have been a particularly difficult one in urban centers such as New York City, the home of Abigail Horton Van Nostrand, who completed her quilt in 1809.

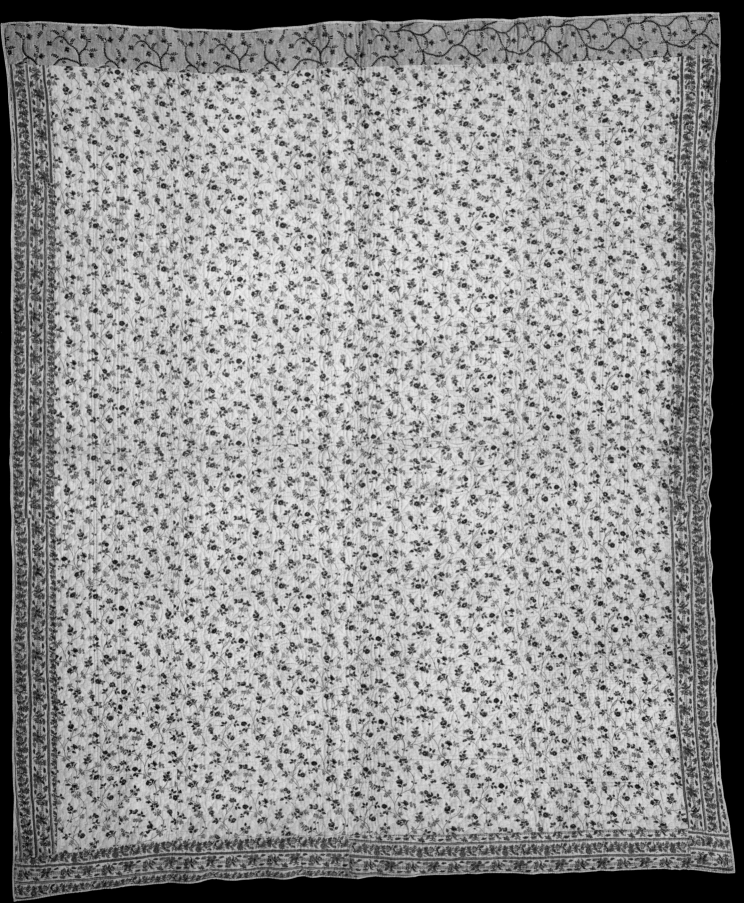

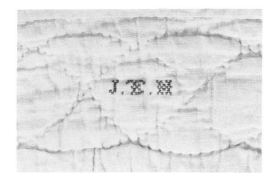

Opposite **Hardenbergh Quilt**
Fewer wholecloth quilts made with printed cottons survive than pieced or appliquéd examples, although they were made in great numbers in the late eighteenth and early nineteenth centuries. Jane Ten Eyck Hardenbergh's quilt was given to Winterthur by a descendant of her brother, James B. Hardenbergh. Two period rooms at Winterthur feature architectural elements from a stone house built in 1762 by Jane's grandfather, Johannes G. Hardenbergh.

Above **Detail, Hardenbergh Quilt**
Marked in cross stitch on the back of this otherwise anonymous quilt are the initials of its maker, Jane Ten Eyck Hardenbergh. It was common practice to mark household linens in this way until the 1820s, when ink marks become more prevalent.

fire was over on the east side of the city, the streets on the west side were as light as day."

By 1845, the year of the second great fire in New York, John Van Nostrand was the president of an insurance company with a very keen professional interest in the damage. "The fire was so fierce that many thought it was the end of the world. People moved out their furniture and the Battery was full of furniture with great resultant squabbles. At our house the window lintels were covered with wet blankets on account of the sparks."[45] Adeline also remembered attending the theater, visiting art exhibitions, and seeing the windows of the City Hotel that were illuminated with the name of George Washington to celebrate the centenary of his birth.[46]

In 1846, the extended family moved to Brooklyn, where John, his brother James, his son John, and son-in-law Harman Westervelt bought about fourteen lots to form a family compound on Strong Place and Henry Street. Everyone lived with John and Abigail until their own houses were built.

John and Abigail Van Nostrand hosted enormous family celebrations at Christmas. Adeline remembered the last Christmas before her mother's death, when twenty adults and eleven children ate "soup served from a tureen on the table, a handsomely glazed boiled ham standing opposite at the other end of the table. Later, the tureen being removed, the ham was placed before Ma and a very large boiled turkey stuffed with oysters and oyster sauce and all the vegetables suitable to boiled turkey with it. Then came duck and a juicy sirloin of beef, carved by Pa after the removal of the turkey, celery in two tall glasses and cranberry sauce and every sort of vegetable and chicken salad. Dishes filled with fruit and nuts graced the corner of the table and later came mince pie and a pleasing plum pudding. The feast ended with nuts and raisins and wine."[47] Abigail Van Nostrand died of pneumonia in 1856, and her husband died two years later.

Both Mary Remington and Abigail Horton Van Nostrand made elaborate whitework quilts that were extremely fine and stylish, and expressive of their skill, taste, and the time they had available to make such works of art. A quilt of a similar date but made to be used, rather than as a showpiece, was similarly treasured by family members, but less is known about its maker or owner. Marked on the back with the initials "J TE H," the quilt was probably made by or for Jane Ten Eyck Hardenbergh. Also descended from illustrious early settlers in New York, Jane was the oldest child of Johannes I. Hardenbergh and Blandina Bruyn, christened with the Dutch form of her name, Jenneke Tennijk, at Wawarsing, Ulster County, New York, on August 22, 1795.[48] Jane never married, and little is known about her life, although census records show that during her long life she lived with a number of different family members. As an unmarried daughter, she may have cared for her elderly parents. In the 1840 census for the town of Hurley in Ulster County, a Jane Hardenbergh is listed as the head of a household consisting of two teenage boys and an older man, probably her father. In 1850, she was living with her brother John Gerardus Hardenbergh in Rochester, Monroe County, New York. In 1870, she is recorded living with her nephew Daniel and his family in Shawangunk, Ulster County, but she was in New York when she died in 1888, perhaps with her niece Margaret Hardenbergh Van Kleeck from whose family this quilt descended. Margaret was the daughter of Jane's younger brother, James Bruyn Hardenbergh, a well-known and respected minister of the Dutch Reformed Church. Jane's extended family was successful and well-connected, consisting of farmers, landowners, wealthy merchants, bankers, lawyers, and politicians. Jane is buried in Green-Wood Cemetery in Brooklyn among many more famous people, such as DeWitt Clinton, governor of New York; F. A. O. Schwarz, founder of the famous toy store; and Samuel Morse, inventor of the telegraph. This beautiful cemetery with its Gothic-style entrance, was founded in the 1830s and became not only the most fashionable place to be buried in New York City, but also a place for family picnics and outings for people from the area.[49]

Despite her wealth and family connections, Jane's quilt was made by reusing dress fabric that had been fashionable in the 1780s, before she was born. The fabric that forms the border on three sides, however, is from the 1810s or early 1820s, when the quilt was made. The frugal reuse of older fabrics is not uncommon among quilters, but its use as the primary fabric of a wholecloth quilt is most often found in quilts intended for use rather than for show. How much can we read into the survival of a utilitarian quilt rather than an ornamental one owned by a woman who chose never to marry? Given her wealth and connections, we must assume that Jane would have been attractive to potential husbands whether or not physical beauty was added to her financial and dynastic attractions. At a time when the choice of a marriage partner, or indeed the choice of marriage over remaining single, was increasingly becoming the responsibility of the woman and not her parents, it is interesting that Jane did not marry.

Mary Remington worried that her attractiveness to Peleg Congdon was financial rather than personal, and perhaps Jane Ten Eyck Hardenbergh had the same concerns about less-successful suitors. But she may also have purposely decided not to marry. The number of unmarried women was very low during the colonial period but began to grow during the last decades of the eighteenth century, when Jane was born. By the middle of the nineteenth century, about eleven percent of the women born at that time never married.[50] In a climate of heightened sensibility in the early nineteenth century, together with the increasing importance of companionate marriage, it has been argued that women electing to remain single were doing so because of their idealization of marriage. They were

living up to the high principles of their religious beliefs, which had become all-pervasive during the course of the Second Awakening, a time of increasing religious fervor.[51] Jane Hardenbergh was a respected member of the Dutch Reformed Church. She was related to Jacob Rutsen Hardenbergh, one of the denomination's most famous ministers and the first president of Queens College, which later became Rutgers University.[52] Her brother, James Bruyn Hardenbergh, in whose family this quilt has descended, was also a highly respected minister, preaching in churches in both New York and New Jersey. No record has been found of any philanthropic activities that Jane may have engaged in, nor of any interest in teaching or the arts, common activities for unmarried women of her wealth and time. While assumptions can be made from extensive research through women's diaries in New England and, to a certain extent, Pennsylvania, it would be dangerous to extrapolate the same ideas and opinions to women of different social, economic, religious, or geographic origin. Much research remains to be done.

Mary Remington carefully documents the books she read in her letters to Peleg Congdon. An important part of many women's lives was reading for the purpose of furthering their education as well as for pleasure. Ranging from *A Patch-Work Screen for the Ladies* by Jane Barker, published in 1723, to the 1991 novel *Alias Grace* by Margaret Atwood; and from Eliza Calvert Hall's *Aunt Jane of Kentucky*, published in 1907, to the contemporary mysteries of Barbara Michaels, Earlene Fowler, and Jean Hager, quilts have often been used as a literary metaphor for many different aspects of women's lives, many of them specifically American. Reading played an important part in women's education, at first only for the wealthy elite. By the late eighteenth century, reading classics in translation as well as contemporary novels had come to be accepted as part and parcel of genteel behavior. Someone would often read to the young women learning fancy needlework at school, and

the subjects of their silkwork pictures often reflected the literature they read. A great favorite at many schools was James Thomson's poems *The Seasons*. Mary Remington is known to have embroidered an illustration of "Autumn."[53] Reading for pleasure was also important to women in the late eighteenth and early nineteenth centuries. Many novels were targeted specifically at this large and growing audience, often overlaying moral endings with swashbuckling tales of intrigue and adventure.

Quilt maker Mary Remington read *Self-Controul* by Mary Brunton at the behest of her cousin Sarah Holden. In this somewhat improbable tale, the heroine escapes from an ardent lover of libertine propensities who she has agreed to marry if he would reform his life. Her father dies, the heroine sells her own artwork to survive, is abducted and taken to Canada by her unreformed lover's minions, and escapes by going through rapids and over a waterfall in a canoe. Meanwhile, she has met a more worthy man whom she eventually marries, and her original lover commits suicide.[54] In addition to the obvious morality tale about virtue rewarded, *Self-Controul* is about a young woman being independent and making her own choices in a life determined by her own personal values. The influence of literature was widespread throughout contemporary culture. Illustrations of subjects from both classical and contemporary literature could be found as prints, framed and hung on walls, and literary subjects could be found on wallpaper and furnishing fabrics, which were sometimes made into quilts.[55]

The most widely read book in early America was the Bible. Two quilt centers made by Sarah Furman Warner Williams around 1810 feature stories from the New Testament: the Annunciation, the Nativity, and the Flight into Egypt.[56] Examples of figurative designs in appliqué have been found in both England and America. The technique of cutting figures from one fabric and stitching them to others is an ancient one. It can be found on heraldic banners as early as the fourteenth century, and can be related to the technique of embroidering "slips."[57] An example more closely related stylistically is thought to depict the marriage procession of George III.[58] It is interesting that many of the American examples similar to Sarah Furman Warner Williams's work are associated with quilt makers in New York and Charleston, the two cities with which William Williams, the artist who drew Sarah's portrait, was associated.[59]

Both of Sarah's appliqué panels at Winterthur depict biblical scenes from the New Testament. The first depicts the Annunciation and the Birth of Christ, complete with shepherds, the three kings, an inn, and a stable with livestock. The narrative is presented on two levels, much like plate-printed furnishing cottons that were fashionable in the late eighteenth and early nineteenth centuries. The narrative on the second panel is less overt: the Holy Family is seen going into Egypt and then coming out again after what is believed to have been about four years. Both pictures contain printed cottons manufactured in Europe in imitation of the palampores imported from India, many of which featured flowering trees. This motif is a multicultural phenomenon with representations in the arts of China, India, the Middle East, as well as in Europe.[60] Often mentioned in the Bible, the tree of life is contrasted with the tree of knowledge—the cause of many of the troubles of humankind. The tree of life, on the other hand, represents hope and trust in salvation and eternal life.

In addition, two full-size appliquéd bedcovers attributed to Sarah Furman Warner Williams are known; one is in the collection of the Metropolitan Museum of Art in New York and the other at the Henry Ford Museum in Michigan. Both bedcovers were made for relatives—a niece and a younger cousin—and were probably given as gifts in celebration of their marriages. Although similar in design and materials, neither depicts a biblical scene, which begs the question of why Winterthur's panels were made. A second version of

the Nativity panel survives in a private collection, which only compounds the mystery. All three examples have cut edges, indicating their probable use as the central panels of unquilted bedcovers or counterpanes, but they are all smaller in size than the central panels of the complete bedcovers.

Sarah Furman Warner and Azarius Williams were married in Trinity Church in New York City on December 30, 1788.[61] He was a merchant with a business, listed at 23 Liberty Street in the New York Directory for 1797. She was the step-daughter of a sail-maker. The baptismal records of Trinity Church indicate that both the Warner and Williams family attended there. Founded in 1698, Trinity was "old-line Episcopalian, conservative, and Anglican in its traditions."[62] Located at the corner of Wall Street and Broadway, Trinity is where George Washington worshipped after his inauguration ceremony, and where Aaron Burr was buried. Reliable records containing information about Sarah and Azarius are sparse; he may have died sometime before 1805, when a widowed Sarah Williams was listed as living at 12 Chambers Street in New York. In 1814, the probable year of her death, there were two widowed Sarah Williamses in town. What we do know is that Sarah Furman Warner Williams was a woman of faith, with strong ties to an extended family for whom she delighted in making gifts that were highly personal.

Although not as widely read as the Bible, *The Adventures of Telemachus* was nevertheless a best-seller in America in the eighteenth and early nineteenth centuries. It was written by François de Salignac de la Mothe Fénelon and first published in 1699. The story was ostensibly about Telemachus, son of Ulysses and Penelope, who, together with the goddess Athena disguised as his guardian, Mentor, went in search of his father who was taking a long time to return home at the end of the Trojan War. Fénelon was writing for Louis XIV's grandson, the Duke of Burgundy, and his tale has been interpreted as both a criticism of the lavish display and

despotism of the French monarchy and as an advice manual for youth, emphasizing self-control and financial economy. An earlier work by Fénelon, translated in 1707 by George Hickes as *Instructions for the Education of a Daughter*, was also widely read in America. Despite deploring the "weaker" minds of women (a common refrain of male authors) Fénelon believed that women should learn to write, keep accounts, understand the law, read classical literature in Latin (to provide examples of virtuous conduct), and read for pleasure.[63]

The Adventures of Telemachus was translated, adapted into poetry, reinterpreted, and illustrated by many artists in the form of paintings and engravings. Various editions were published throughout the eighteenth and early nineteenth centuries. Sarah Logan, the daughter of James Logan, William Penn's agent in Philadelphia, and the only one of his children intellectual enough to take part in his literary and scientific pursuits, owned an edition published in Amsterdam in 1719 in French.[64] Wallpaper depicting scenes from this tale, produced by the French firm of Joseph Dufour et Cie, was one of the most popular of the scenic wallpapers fashionable in the early nineteenth century. Andrew Jackson hung Telemachus in the hallway of his home in Nashville, Tennessee, and many examples have been found in homes in New England.[65]

Winterthur's collection includes two examples of *The Adventures of Telemachus* on plate-printed fabrics that date from 1785 to 1795, one of which is in the form of a quilt. The front has been pieced in places indicating that it had a previous use, possibly as a set of bedhangings. Like many printed-cotton wholecloth quilts where the design of the fabric is the key decorative element, the actual quilting is a fairly standard grid formed from diagonal rows of running stitches approximately five to six stitches per inch, and one and a half inches apart.

Oliver Goldsmith's poem "The Deserted Village," published in London in 1770, was also a best-seller in America.

Above **Portrait of Sarah Furman Warner**

In the late eighteenth century, it was fashionable for family portraits to be rendered in pastel. Artist William Williams signed the back of Sarah Furman Warner's portrait and dated it "Novr. 30th 1781," seven years before Sarah's marriage to Azarius Williams. A label attached to the back of the frame by a descendant indicates that Sarah was ten years old at the time. Winterthur's collection also includes pastel portraits of her two half-brothers, Effingham and Garrett Brass Warner.

Right **Appliqué Quilt Center**

Quilts and counterpanes were often made as gifts to commemorate important events in the recipients' lives. Sarah Furman Warner Williams is known to have made two pictorial bedcovers for members of her extended family, so perhaps these two appliqué panels (this page and opposite) were made for the same purpose.

Left **Appliqué Quilt Center**
Creativity, a sophisticated sense of design, and considerable skill were needed to make these appliqué pictures that may once have formed part of larger quilts or unquilted counterpanes. Sarah Furman Warner Williams clearly had a considerable amount of printed cottons to use in her work.

Overleaf, above **Telemachus Quilt**
The visual appeal of wholecloth quilts made from printed cottons was in the design of the fabric, not the design or skill of the quilting. Although this quilt could have been professionally made as part of a complete set of bed furniture (the bedcover and associated hangings), the piecing at the upper right is evidence that the quilt was probably made with fabric that was once a set of bed curtains.

Overleaf, below **Design Repeat, Telemachus Quilt**
The English plate-printed cotton used to make this quilt depicts scenes from *The Adventures of Telemachus*, by François Fénelon. The designs were copied from two illustrations published in London in 1785. One image shows Telemachus and Mentor arriving on the island of Calypso after having been shipwrecked. The other represents the nymph Echo. A best-seller in America during the seventeenth and eighteenth centuries, the story would have been a familiar one.

Opposite, above **Design Repeat, "Deserted Village" Quilt**
Goldsmith's epic poem was a best-seller, so the meaning of these two scenes would have been well-known to the owner of this quilt. Although based on original prints by John Keyse Sherwin, the scenes were adapted, showing the people wearing clothing of the early 1800s, when the fabric was printed.

Opposite, below left **"Deserted Village" Quilt**
This roller-printed cotton depicting scenes from Goldsmith's poem has been attributed to the Manchester printworks of John Marshall. A similar quilt in the collection of Shelburne Museum in Vermont was once owned by the Dutton family of Wilmington, Connecticut.

Opposite, below right **Plate Print**
This earlier version of "The Deserted Village" shows the same scenes but with the individuals wearing clothing from the late 1700s. Printed with a flat copper plate, the design has a vertical repeat of 34 inches. The later roller-printed version has a repeat of only 21 inches and lacks many of the secondary details seen here.

Steeped in the pedantry of pastoral poetry, it tells the story of the land clearances and enclosures of the eighteenth century, when many rural tenants were displaced as the face of British agriculture changed dramatically. Some of these people moved to the new industrial cities, while others crossed the Atlantic to start anew in America. Two scenes from this poem are depicted in textiles at Winterthur, a design repeat of the late eighteenth-century plate-print in red, and also on a printed cotton wholecloth quilt, with a roller-printed version of the same scenes in blue.

The literary conventions of the pastoral featured the wickedness of the city, with its wealth, luxury, and folly of fashion, against the carefree bliss of rural life, full of frugal, honest, and deserving peasants. This contrast is illustrated in the two scenes depicted on both of these fabrics. The first, known as "The Dance," shows innocent youth dancing after their daily work is done, and contrasts with "The Departure," which portrays a family leaving their village before embarking on a ship for the new world:

> Good Heaven! What sorrows gloom'd that
>   parting day,
> That call'd them from their native walks away;
> When the poor exiles, every pleasure past,
> Hung round their bowers, and fondly look'd
>   their last,
> And took a long farewell, and wish'd in vain
> For seats like these beyond the western main,
> And shudd'ring still to face the distant deep,
> Return'd and wept, and still return'd to weep!

Goldsmith does not describe our country in flattering terms:

> Far different there from all that charm'd before,
> The various terrors of that horrid shore,

Yet "The Deserted Village" struck a chord with Americans who saw themselves as having brought the rural virtues to a new world. A number of authors wrote sequels, and Philip Freneau, in *The American Village*, went so far as to suggest that Britain's loss was America's gain. Many American towns were named Auburn, in reference to Goldsmith's British village, and Timothy Dwight used "The Deserted Village" as a model for his amazingly long poem "Greenfield Hill," about a utopian village now part of Fairfield, Connecticut.[66]

The roller-printed fabric has been dated to between 1815 and 1825 and attributed to the print works of John Marshall of Manchester, England. This was a period when many British fabrics were dumped on the American market, but it was also a time of increased immigration, when depictions of people leaving their homes would resonate with a large proportion of the population, despite the fact that many of them were coming from urban rather than rural settings.[67] Another quilt, made from the same fabric, is in the collection of the Shelburne Museum in Vermont. That quilt had once been owned by the Dutton family of Wilmington, Connecticut; but the one at Winterthur has no provenance.[68]

Memory, emotion, family pride, and history all come together in a quilt made in 1860 for a beloved grandchild. In the eighteenth century, silk dresses were expensive luxuries only available to the wealthy, although the less-well-off could purchase them on the second-hand market. Not only did such fabrics have high monetary value, but they were passed on as personal treasures. Soon after the death of his wife, Thomas Willing, a wealthy merchant, a member of the Continental Congress, and the first president of the Bank of North America wrote to his unmarried sister, Abby, "I send you a piece of Brocade Silk which my dearest Nancy intended to make up for herself, as soon as she was well—please to accept it in remembrance of her, who had for you a sincere affection, the highest opinion, & the greatest good will."[69]

This silk from which Winterthur's quilt was made was designed and woven a little earlier, between 1753 and 1755, in Spitalfields, the major silk weaving area in east London.[70] Evidence of fold and sewing lines indicate that this was once the petticoat of a gown. An inscription on the back identifies it as a cherished family heirloom, made into a quilt for a grandchild. The maker was Ann G. Boker, who made it for her granddaughter Amanda Boker Bunn, who was only three years old. Ann was the wife of a Philadelphia merchant, and may have met her husband when he was in New York on business. The silk probably came down through the family of her mother, Martha Hitchcock, who was living with the Boker family in Marcus Hook, just south of Philadelphia at the time the quilt was made. No further information has yet been found about the family or original owner of the dress, but its presence in a quilt made more than one hundred years later speaks to the depth of personal sentiment, handed down through generations of one family, and still highly valued today.

Quilts are often admired for their aesthetic beauty, their richness of pattern and color, and the skill with which they were made. They are often treasured as memorials to friends and relatives, providing an emotional connection between generations. This appreciation can only be enhanced by a greater understanding of the lives of their makers, and the cultural context within which they were made.

Left **Detail, Ann G. Boker Quilt**

In the eighteenth century, the design of fashionable dress silks changed every season. This quilt is made from a Spitalfields silk that can be dated to between 1753 and 1755. The silk was used for a dress worn by an ancestor of the maker, Ann G. Boker. Wider than it is long, the quilt was made for one of the high beds popular in the mid-nineteenth century.

Above **Inscription, Ann G. Boker Quilt**

At least part of the family history about the origin of this dress is inaccurate. The fabric was only about 105 years old when it was made into this quilt. Although the fashion for white weddings did not begin until the nineteenth century, many earlier dresses made from white fabrics have been mistakenly identified as wedding dresses. As the original owner has not been identified, it is impossible to know if the fabric used was once worn for a wedding.

3. *the bedspread gets along finely:* **making quilts in early america**

In January of 1815, Mary reported her mother's comment, "You have sewed steadily all day and must be tired," but then went on to assure Peleg that, "the stockings . . . are nearly finished and the bedspread gets along finely."[1] The techniques used to make stockings and quilts are considered to be plain sewing. Knitting and stitching are very different processes, but both use basic skills that were central to every woman's life. The distinction between Mary's stockings and her bedspread, however, lies in the difference in their end uses. Stockings are objects of everyday apparel, and while homemade stockings provide evidence of the close personal relationship between the maker and the receiver, they are fairly standard products. Mary's quilted bedspread, by contrast, was a tour de force of decorative needlework.

Some scholars who study samplers and needlework pictures would have us believe that needlework skills declined during the first half of the nineteenth century. This attitude can be understood by comparing the quality of needlework in a series of samplers that range in date from 1790 to the early 1850s, worked by successive generations of one family. Hannah McIntire's sampler, worked when she was eleven, is what is often termed a "fancy" sampler, one with decorative embellishments that were indicative not only of her skill with a needle but also the investment made in her education. Her daughter, Ann Jane Couper, worked a plainer sampler at school in New Castle, Delaware, in 1824. Her teacher, Mrs. Deborah H. Mundall, later moved to Philadelphia, where she operated a seminary for women until 1842.[2] Annie C. Smith, Ann Jane's much younger cousin, worked her sampler around 1850, using the soft zephyr wool that came into fashion for canvaswork embroidery in the second quarter of the nineteenth century. The deterioration in both the aesthetic and technical quality of the embroidery is not so much due to a decrease in skill as a change in the nature of women's education.

Education in general, and the education of women in particular, was a contested topic in the early years of the American republic. The debate centered on the perceived need to educate children to become good citizens and to provide them with the practical skills that they would need throughout life—a debate that continues today. Emphasis was put on educating the underprivileged, providing them with the means to improve their prospects. At a minimum, this type of education consisted of the ability to read, write, and cast accounts. The concept of education was not limited to schools, but was actively sought by many people through access to books and magazines that were increasingly made available by enterprising publishers, a phenomenon that has been termed "the village enlightenment."[3]

The value of knowledge was a fundamental precept of the philosophical movement known as the Enlightenment, which promoted a rational understanding of arts and sciences. Eighteenth-century prescriptive literature, widely read on both sides of the Atlantic, encouraged women to improve their education through reading and a comprehensive study of subjects such as astronomy, mathematics, history, and the natural sciences. In the early eighteenth century, such advanced studies for women in America was reserved for the wealthy and was also limited by aptitude and personal interest. Then, as now, some women were more interested in academics than others, but many acquired a high level of learning. Sarah Logan (1715–1744) was the only child of James Logan intelligent enough to take part in his studious pursuits. Sarah Wistar (1738–1815) became the first woman to be voted a share in the Library Company of Philadelphia, in 1769. Evidence that such a sophisticated level of education was not limited to Philadelphia is evidenced by women such as Mercy Otis Warren and Abigail Adams in New England, and Martha Laurens Ramsey in the South.[4]

Previous pages **Detail, Mary Keller Quilt**
Mary Keller made this quilt in 1851. It is a superb example of her skill in plain sewing.

Opposite **Samplers**
Making a sampler was part of almost every young girl's schooling, but its significance changed over time. By the mid-nineteenth century, greater importance was placed on a wide variety of academic subjects. The poor quality of samplers from that time does not reflect a change in skill or ability but rather in the nature of women's education. These samplers are dated 1790, 1824, and c.1850 (viewed clockwise).

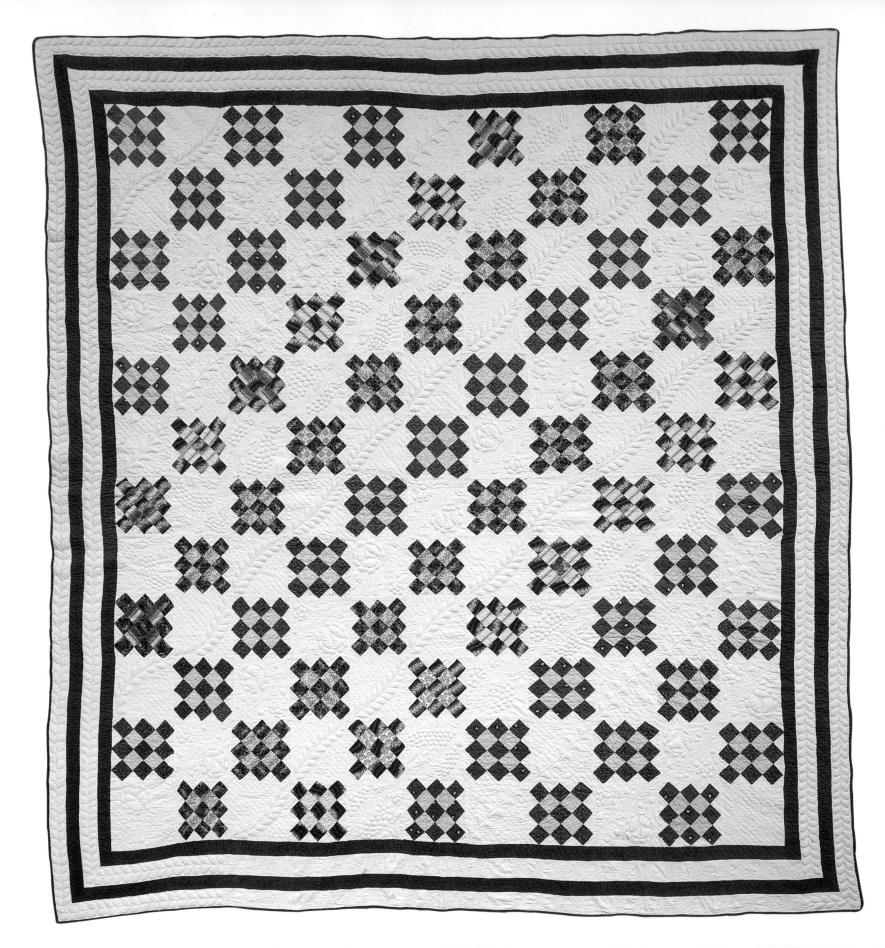

Opposite **Mary Keller Quilt**
Mary Keller's quilt is made in a design sometimes known as "Album Patch." The pieced blocks alternate with white stuffed work. Although made from common and inexpensive fabrics, the exquisite stitching ensured that this quilt would be treasured by subsequent generations.

Above right **Detail, Mary Keller Quilt**
Initials and the surname of ten family members are quilted along the lower borders of this quilt. The quilt descended in the family from mother to daughter until it was donated to Winterthur in 1994.

Below left **Detail, Mary Keller Quilt**
Mary Keller of Hagerstown, Maryland, was nineteen years old when she dated her quilt March 1, 1851. She married Jeremiah B. Cromer in 1856, and they raised ten children.

Below right **Specimens of Needlework, British and Foreign School Society Manual**
The British and Foreign School Society was founded in 1808 as The Society for Promoting the Lancasterian System for the Education of the Poor. Their manual for teaching needlework provides detailed instructions for hemming, including how to turn raw edges, which fingers to use when holding the work, which direction to point the needle, and the number of threads in the fabric to leave between each stitch. No leeway was granted to students who were left-handed or who felt more comfortable holding their needle differently.

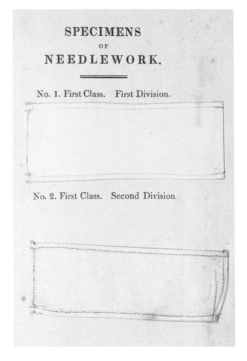

Detail, Martha Agry Vaughn Quilt
Martha Agry Vaughn employed an unusual technique to make her 1805 pieced-silk quilt. Instead of using newspaper to stabilize her pieces, she merely put it as a backing for various-sized blocks, sewing them together through the paper. The full quilt is illustrated in chapter 5.

After the American Revolution, educational opportunities for women expanded, and the early years of the nineteenth century saw the founding of literally hundreds of private female academies and the growing accessibility of public schools.[5] And if a young woman wished to extend her education, she could engage in a program of reading, either by herself or with friends.

Mary Remington read classical authors, in translation, in addition to history, travelogues, literary compendiums, and novels. Her contemporary, Rachel Van Dyke of New Brunswick, New Jersey, continued to study botany, chemistry, biology, history, and Latin after her formal schooling had finished, reading many of the same works as Mary Remington, such as Petrarch, Thomson, and Zimmerman.[6] Although a college education was not open to young women at this time, one should not underestimate the level of education they could achieve.

As formal educational opportunities for women became more widespread, and the subjects they studied became more academic, the emphasis on making elaborate samplers diminished. This did not mean that learning needlework was less important, but that the focus changed from fancy to plain sewing skills. These were the useful techniques that every woman needed to know in order to stitch bedding and table linens, personal underclothing, and men's shirts. These are also the sewing skills needed to make quilts.

There is a remarkable continuity in the technique of plain sewing from the seventeenth through the early twentieth centuries. Early examples include hems and seams on bedding and personal linens. Written evidence of how young girls were taught to sew, together with examples, is found in manuals published by the British and Foreign School Society in the early nineteenth century.[7] Based on the Lancasterian system of education, widely adopted in America in the early nineteenth century, each child developed skill in a particular technique before moving on to the next, usually under

the supervision of an older child. Little fingers practiced folding tiny hems on paper before graduating to fabric and learning to stitch hems, seams, and gathers, as well as different techniques for darning, patching, and repairing holes and tears. Even after the use of sewing machines became widespread, young girls continued to learn fine hand-sewing skills.[8]

Who could doubt the sewing skills of Mary Keller, whose quilt is dated 1851. Made about the same time that Annie C. Smith was working her sampler, Mary's quilt is a good example of the exquisite workmanship found throughout the nineteenth century. It is all hand-stitched with alternating blocks of piecing and stuffed work, quilted with between eleven and fifteen stitches per inch. Along the lower border, Mary has carefully quilted the names of many members of her family while the date, March 1, 1851, is quilted into the block in the lower right corner.

By contrast, Martha Agry Vaughn's pieced silk quilt, made in the early years of the nineteenth century, is very coarsely sewn. Although this might be due to her lesser skill with a needle, it is also likely to relate to the type of materials she chose to make her quilt, primarily fine silks for the pieces and a glazed worsted, sometimes known as tammy, for the backing. Martha's quilt was sewn using newspaper templates, but not in the traditional manner. Templates are usually cut to shape, and the fabric folded and basted around them to provide the shape of each piece, which are then whip-stitched together. Instead, Martha pieced each block by seaming her patches together without using a paper template. She then backed each block with a paper "template." These templates did not provide the overall shape for the block but were instead stitched and folded right into the somewhat lumpy seams that join each block. The reason for this odd construction technique is not known. It is almost as if someone had described the technique to Martha but she had never actually seen a demonstration or the final product.

Fine sewing skills have always been associated with clothing that requires constant washing. Fabrics made from silk and wool were not laundered and, in the late eighteenth century, the sewing on even a good quality silk dress is often quite coarse when compared to that found on a fine linen shirt. The looser stitching allowed the expensive fabric to be unpicked and remade easily.

Some quilts that are embellished with embroidery combine both plain and fancy needlework skills. More than just the buttonhole stitching that secures many appliqué motifs, embroidered designs used as part of the primary decoration can be found on a group of quilts that date to the 1820s and 1830s, just as teaching fancy needlework was falling out of favor in many schools and academies.

Embroidered wool quilts are relatively rare, but Winterthur's collection includes two glorious examples from New England. Their forms show the incorporation of crewelwork techniques, grounded stylistically in the rococo style of the mid-eighteenth century, with the block-and-strip style quilts so heavily influenced by later classical taste. No provenance for these quilts is known, but they closely resemble other examples from New England, originating possibly in western Massachusetts or in southern Maine.

Curvilinear designs and the large, exotic floral motifs relate the embroidered decoration in a wool-strip quilt back to the crewelwork designs of the previous century, but the selection of colors, materials, and technique of embroidery set the work within the context of the early nineteenth century. The frugality of New England quilt makers at this time is evidenced by the reuse of heavy fulled-wool breeches used to make the darker strips.[9] The embroidered motifs within a square block set on point on a second quilt can be related to the diagonal trellis patterns filled with individual motifs that have been identified in northern New England, and in turn related to embroidered motifs embellishing checkered woven blankets.[10]

Opposite **Embroidered Strip Quilt**
The dark brown wool stripes seen
here have been embellished with
an embroidered design of curving
stems and exotic flowers. A few of
the motifs include coarsely woven
wool appliqués. Quilting surrounds
the embroidered designs while the
rest of the piece is quilted in interlac-
ing circles.

Right **Pieced and Embroidered Quilt**
Pieced with alternating blocks of
embroidered designs, this quilt has
been altered and repaired over time.
It is missing side panels on three
sides, and the embroidered motifs
on the triangular blocks around the
edges are later additions. The original
embroidery is worked with crewels
made from worsted wool. Commercial crewel wools were a standard
two-ply construction, but some of
the threads found on this quilt are
singles and therefore are certainly
homespun. The later embroidery
includes soft zephyr woolen thread.

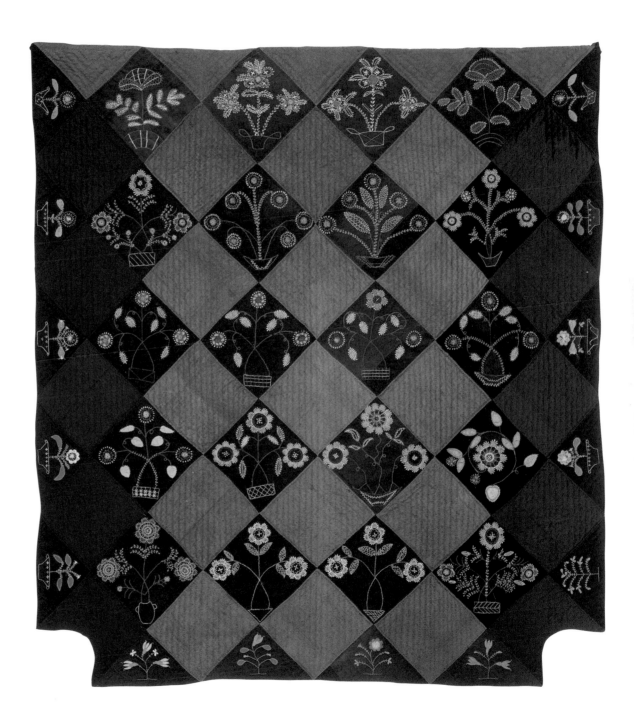

Above Detail, Pieced and Embroidered Quilt

The initials "E. S." embroidered at the center of the quilt are probably those of a member of the Schliefer family. A related quilt dated 1832 has the name "Euphemia Kichlein" embroidered in the center. Born in 1818, Euphemia was the daughter of Christiana Schleifer and Jacob Kichlein of Bucks County, Pennsylvania. Two other related quilts associated with the Kichlein and Schliefer families survive, one at the Moravian Museum in Bethlehem, Pennsylvania, and the second in a private collection.

Opposite Pieced and Embroidered Quilt

This 1830 quilt is one of the earliest dated examples of a reel design. The red fabrics used to piece the quilt are a lightweight worsted wool. The reel or orange-peel design resembles the jacquard coverlet designs made by Pennsylvania German weavers. Most of the fringe is original.

Textile scholar Lynne Bassett has shown a stylistic relationship between designs of wool wholecloth quilts made in New England and a group of related embroidered bed rugs.[11] Janneken Smucker has extended Bassett's work to include a group of embroidered bedcovers made by those with family connections to the Connecticut River Valley and that have strong similarities to wholecloth quilts and bed rugs from that area.[12] Smucker was unable to directly connect the two embroidered quilts illustrated here to any identified group of decorated bedcovers, but the work of these two scholars shows clearly that research on the design and techniques of quilting should not be done in isolation from other types of bedcovers.

The unknown maker of an embroidered quilt marked "E.S." in the center block was probably a member of the Schleifer family of Bucks County, Pennsylvania. One of two related quilts, this represents some of the earliest known examples of quilting within the Pennsylvania German community, better known for its exquisitely decorated hand towels and float-weave bed coverlets. The embroidered designs reflect those found on fraktur, decorative birth certificates and other family documents whose characteristic lettering has also been linked to quilts from the ethnic German communities.[13] Similar in technique but different in design, examples of crewel-work embroidery can be found on medallion-style quilts associated with Chester County, Pennsylvania.[14] As further examples come to light, these quilts may provide visual evidence of cross-cultural influences between the strong German and English communities who settled these areas.

Painting and drawing, once important elements in women's education, also fell out of favor as school curricula became more academic in the 1830s and 1840s. This was the time when young women started to create theorum paintings with stencils rather than their drawings. Stenciled designs were also used to create bedcovers and quilts, some of which were decorated with designs resembling quilt patterns. Mary Ann Hoyt, of Reading, New York, alternated blocks of stenciled designs with blocks of nine patch on a quilt she dated May 15, 1834.[15] Easier to do than embroidery, stenciled designs are achieved with methods and materials that are very different from the stamped designs produced by printing pigments in oil with wooden blocks. The same pigments could be used for either process, but the medium used to bind the pigments with the stencils was a water-based gum (usually gum arabic or gum tragacanth), while linseed oil was used to bind the pigments for the stamped designs. Stencils could be cut from pasteboard or varnished paper to shape the design and prevent paint being applied outside the area of the motif. Carved wooden blocks, used for the process called stamping, are more difficult to make but are sturdier and enable the commercial production of greater quantities of yardage.

The period spanning the late eighteenth and early nineteenth centuries saw great changes in the location of beds in the household, as new concepts of privacy took them out of public parlors and into separate bedrooms.[16] The role of the bed as a symbol of status was changing as well; they were no longer the vehicle for the display of costly textiles, as the processes of mechanized production brought the cost of such bedding lower and lower. These changes can be related to evidence of quilt design that shows tension between the value of tradition and delight in the new.

Information on the origin of quilt designs is difficult to document as is evidence of their actual designers. Connections have been made between the design of quilts and other objects, such as furniture and ceramics, showing that these designs were heavily influenced by the global world of fashion.[17] Designs could be drawn on wholecloth quilts by the maker herself, a friend or relative (either male and female), or by a professional artist. Because so many of Winterthur's quilts are without provenance, their designs can only be interpreted through evidence provided by their style.[18]

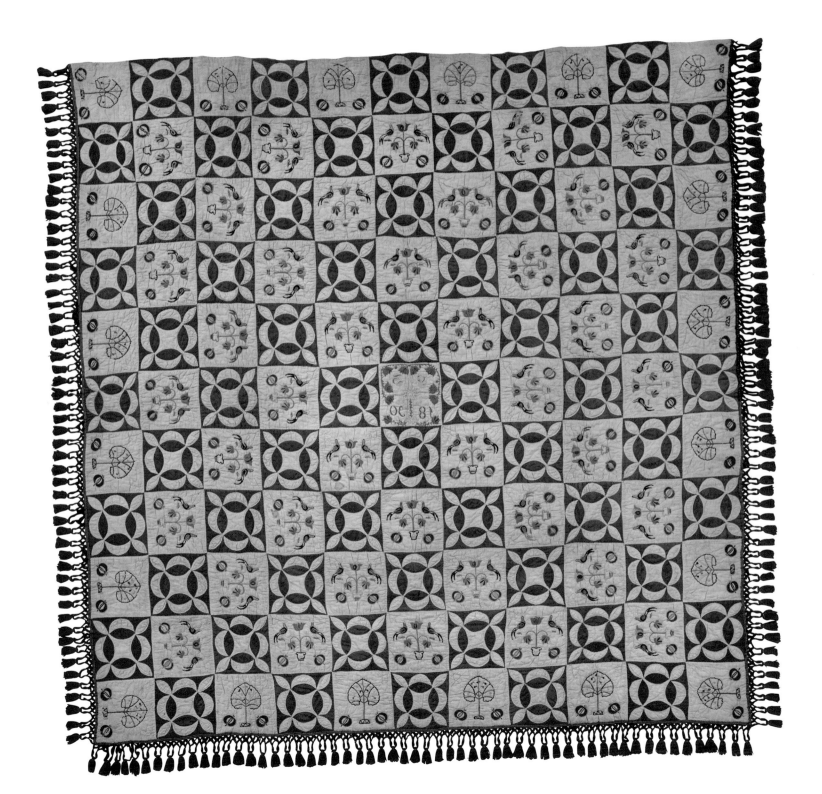

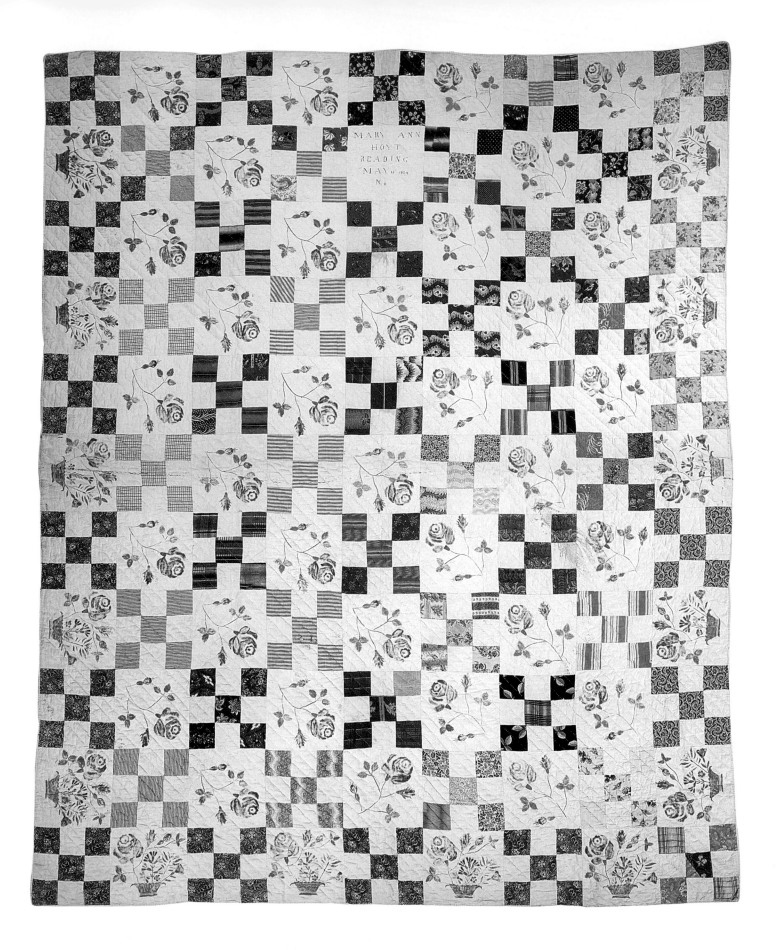

Designs found on wool wholecloth quilts made
in eighteenth- and early nineteenth-century New
England can be traced to baroque designs that were
popular in the seventeenth century.[19] A unique silk
wholecloth quilt from Philadelphia carries evidence
of its designer in a rare quilted inscription that reads:
"Drawn by Sarah Smith Stitched by Hannah Callender
and Catharine Smith in Testimony of their Friendship
10 mo. 5th 1761."[20] Most eighteenth-century quilts
from Philadelphia show a closer relation to the framed
central medallion styles prevalent in England than
to the wholecloth quilts made in New England. The
Quaker community in Philadelphia kept in close touch
with other members of their family and their faith in
England; their business as well as their religious connections were usually based on kinship networks.

A group of quilts made in Philadelphia between
1750 and 1775 have been identified, all quilted using
extraordinarily similar designs. These are all associated
with a group of wealthy Quakers including the Logan,
Norris, Trotter, Emlen, and Mifflin families. Despite their
similarities, the actual details of each design are slightly
different, confirmation that they were quilted within the
family rather than purchased as a commercial product.
Other distinctions can be seen in the choice of materials. The face of Mary Norris Dickinson's quilt is made
from a highly reflective light-blue silk satin, while
Hannah Trotter's quilt is made from dark-blue worsted
wool. Winterthur's yellow quilt, said to have been
passed down in the Mifflin family, is made from a plain-
weave silk taffeta. The deep border designs delineating
double-handled vases and large flowers link this group
of bed quilts to two surviving silk quilted petticoats.
One of these petticoats, worn by the renowned
needlework teacher Ann Marsh, is also made from a
light-blue silk taffeta.[21] The backing fabrics used for the
bed quilts are rare printed cottons, which in the mid-
eighteenth century were both highly fashionable and
expensive. The linings of both quilted petticoats and

the Trotter wool bed quilt are made from worsted
wool fabric.

The flowering tree, sometimes related to the biblical tree of life, is a motif that was fashionable in Europe
and America from the early seventeenth through the
mid-nineteenth century. This design was featured in
many appliqué quilts of the late eighteenth and early
nineteenth centuries. Clearly related stylistically to
imported Indian palampores, an example at Winterthur
that dates to between 1790 and 1810 is embedded with
traditional European iconography, including the two-
handled vase, the cornucopia, and a peacock, often the
emblem of vanity. Framed by an undulating branch of
leaves and flowers, the outer border consists of a series
of discrete motifs resembling seventeenth-century slips,
embroidered designs worked on one fabric and then
applied to another, really a form of appliqué.

Terminology about these different forms of needlework are imprecise, and even the historic use of the
word "patch" is problematic. It is thought to derive from
words that describe Indian cottons printed or painted
in many colors, designs that could only be achieved in
Europe at the time through the more expensive process
of drawloom weaving. In 1773, the *Providence Gazette*
advertised "A fine assortment of calicoes, chintz and
patches," in addition to the "best copperplate curtain
furniture" (meaning bedhangings). By 1791, a reference
from the same newspaper implies that a patch is a short
length of cloth, advertising "India Chintzes and Calicoes,
in Patches and Pieces of the newest patterns."[22] Many
examples of appliqué furniture covers survive in both
Britain and America, which may be what is sometimes
termed "patch" in inventories.[23] Whether or not the
technique used here would have been called "pieced" or
"patched" in the period, the quilted bedcover on page
74 uses a variety of earlier textiles, some of which may
have been thirty years old when it was made.

A later quilted bedcover (page 75) represents a con-
tinuation of this traditional design into the nineteenth

century. The pastoral scene underneath the flowering tree, cut from a cylinder-printed fabric from the 1810s or 1820s, is based on a literary convention that harkens back to a golden age when people lived in a rural utopia untouched by the tensions of modern, urban life. The double-sawtooth appliquéd borders here reflect a more contemporary aesthetic, but the overall framed medallion format remains formal in nature.

The design of Mary Remington's quilt is also formal, with a central medallion containing her family's coat of arms. It is closely related to the formal and state beds designed for the British aristocracy by leading architects, such as the Adam brothers, and upholsterers, such as Thomas Chippendale.[24] Little research has been done on the beds of the British gentry, the socioeconomic level equivalent to the majority of the American elite, but it must be no coincidence that the best surviving examples of bed furniture (meaning textiles at that time) from the gentry are elaborately embroidered curtains and bedcovers of crewelwork painstakingly embroidered and treasured by generations of family members. Similar examples can also be found in New England and the Mid-Atlantic region in the eighteenth century. Americans were aware of and influenced by the formal beds of Europe; Ann Bingham, wife of arguably the wealthiest man in America at the time, went so far as to bring back a state bed in the 1790s for her elaborate (some thought ostentatious) town house in Philadelphia.[25]

While formal beds certainly followed contemporary fashion, their design was overlaid with a sense of tradition. The design of their hangings and bedcovers were adapted not only from the ancient examples that inspired the neoclassical designs so fashionable in the late eighteenth century, but also from seventeenth-century Baroque styles or even from earlier Gothic motifs.[26] Many Americans found it difficult to distance themselves from the cultural preconceptions of Europe, where status was often connected with generations of family wealth, and historic houses on

large estates were furnished with inherited antiques. In terms of style, a very close correlation can be made between Mary Remington's quilt and the headcloth and counterpane dating to the sixteenth century that was made for Christian Bruce, the wife of the second Duke of Devonshire, with its central heraldic device surrounded by a scattering of slips, or needlework motifs, applied to a velvet background.[27] The compartments and strapwork elements are traditional designs that remained in use through the late eighteenth and early nineteenth centuries and were revived again in the late nineteenth century. The designer and cabinetmaker George Smith wrote in 1826 about designs influenced by the decoration of the period of Louis XIV, whose long reign spanned the second half of the seventeenth century: "The chairs, sofas, candelabra, tripods, glassframes, &c. each, and all partook of the same splendid style of enrichment; and although there might and did exist, a bad taste in the design and arrangement of many of the parts composing the whole of this style of decoration, yet it has never been surpassed by any other taste for richness and splendour of effect. It is alike suitable to the kindly palace, as it is to the mansion of the nobleman; but is no ways answerable to the dwellings of persons of small fortune."[28]

Architectural models and, more particularly, the designs for floors, can clearly be seen to have influenced the design of pieced and block-set quilts. Denis Diderot's extravagant encyclopedia, published in Paris between 1751 and 1765, includes a group of designs for marble floors, many of which resemble formats found in block-set quilts of the nineteenth century.[29] Writer and philosopher Diderot, together with his coauthor Jean Le Rond d'Alembert, was working toward a comprehensive documentation of the arts and sciences of his time. Enlightenment philosophy focused on rational thought and provided a moral and philosophical grounding to the classical taste that first became popular in Europe, and then in America after the Revolution.[30]

Above **Detail, Mifflin Family Quilt**
Rare and important examples of early block-printed fabrics survive on the back of silk quilts made by Philadelphia Quakers. This madder print is similar in style and quality to fragments that were found in sample books or used as linings for clothing during the first half of the eighteenth century.

Opposite **Yellow Silk Wholecloth Quilt**
This quilt was made by a member of the Mifflin family, a wealthy Quaker family from Philadelphia. There was not enough yellow silk taffeta available for the quilt, so a changeable silk was added, seen here at the top. Changeable silks, later known as shot silk, have different-color yarns in the warp and weft of the fabric. In this case, the warp is yellow, and the weft is pink. Changeable silks were popular Quaker dress fabrics in the eighteenth century.

Right **Appliqué Quilt**
Some of the fabrics used to create this appliqué design are printed on fairly coarse fabrics woven with linen warps. This feature is characteristic of fabrics printed in England before the 1770s. The quilt maker is unknown.

Opposite **Pieced and Appliqué Quilt**
Numerous techniques were used to create this 1815–30 quilt. The double sawtooth borders are pieced; the central medallion and floral border are appliquéd; and the open areas are embellished with stuffed work. Many of the brown-colored fabrics have been badly damaged by light.

Mosaic quilts, specifically ones made from hexagonal templates, have been identified with the Gothic Revival style, fashionable in the middle of the nineteenth century, and has also be linked with mosaic floor patterns and the contemporary fashion for marble mosaic tabletops. Underpinning this style, once again, is a Romantic movement that looked back to a golden age that incorporated concepts of manners and beliefs that were felt to be lacking in contemporary culture. This was reflected not only in the design of quilts, but in clothing, furniture, carpets, and the architecture of domestic, religious, and public buildings.[31] Hexagon-mosaic quilts have been found in Britain and America, dating from both the eighteenth and the nineteenth centuries. The difference in style is not the shape of the pieces, but rather the allover design created by differences in color that determine the relation to the fashion for Gothic styles that began in the second quarter of the nineteenth century.

Eliza Ely Bready included a Gothic bishop on her appliqué quilt from a design that featured Gothic-style stained-glass windows. The uncut fabric survives on a quilt in a private collection that features the same fabric interleaved with blue cotton stripes on the face, but in wholecloth on the back.[32] Incorporating fabrics that span the second quarter of the nineteenth century, the appliqué motifs set in large square-set blocks relate this to the heavier styles of furnishing associated with this period. Many of the blocks incorporate fabrics made specifically for use in quilts.

Geometrical designs were particularly valued in the late eighteenth and early nineteenth centuries. Geometry was the foundation for design and decoration in architecture, the decorative arts, and on many quilts. While women were certainly capable of producing many of these designs using simple household articles, like dinner plates, if they had any schooling at all, they would have been taught the elements of formal geometry using a compass and straight edge.

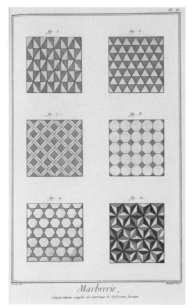

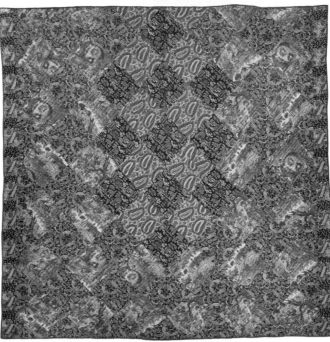

Far left, above and below Diderot Designs
Geometrical formats of contrasting colors have been used for floors over the centuries. The systematic study of ornamental patterns was popular in the early nineteenth century.

Left, above Pieced Quilt
Winterthur acquired this quilt in 1962 primarily for the plate-printed fabric in the center. The original border was made from the same fabric, but only four fragments survive. These were found tacked to the quilt, extending the plate-printed design beyond the central medallion. It is unclear whether the border was removed before or after its acquisition. The quilt was made between 1780 and 1800.

Left, below Pieced Quilt
The placement of the different fabrics in the one-patch blocks determined its configuration on a bed. Blocks set on point was a common configuration for floors, carpets, and quilts.

Opposite Mosaic Quilt
The family history of this 1825–40 quilt is unclear. It could have been made by Catherine Brobst of Reading, Pennsylvania, her daughter Fanny S. B. Jungmann, who was born in Pittsburgh in 1830, or possibly by Fanny's husband's mother. Fanny married Harry Thane Miller in Cincinnati, Ohio, in 1848. The quilt was donated to Winterthur by a descendant.

Above **Detail, Eliza Ely Bready Quilt**
The Gothic Revival style was
extremely popular in America in the
mid-nineteenth century. This bishop
was cut from a glazed-cotton fabric
and placed within an arched stained-
glass window.

Right **Eliza Ely Bready Quilt**
This quilt was made in Philadelphia
by Eliza Ely Bready, the great-grand-
mother of the donor. The fabrics
used for this quilt range in date from
about 1815 to the 1840s and include
patterns sold specifically to apply
to quilts.

Out of a total of 162 female seminaries active between 1742 and 1871, 100 claim to have taught plane geometry and four taught solid geometry, while a total of 119 listed reading in their curriculum, and only 80 specifically mentioned drawing.[33]

Geometry was an integral part of learning to draw in perspective in the eighteenth and nineteenth centuries; it was taught to girls as well as boys. In 1815, Charles Hayter, who billed himself as a portrait painter and teacher, published the second edition of *An Introduction to Perspective, Drawing, and Painting in a Series of Pleasing and Familiar Dialogues between the Author's Children*, although the language is so stilted that it is hard to believe that anyone could think it represented a true dialogue with children. Big brother George is given the task of defining geometry: "It practically teaches the methods of drawing lines, squares, triangles, circles, ovals, polygons, &c. with truth, and proportionate to any scale you may find occasions to adopt. But it may be some considerable gratification to the alarmed to inform them, that little more than a dictionary of the general figures, and a very few practical problems, will be all that is requisite to our progress in perspective."[34] This scientific approach increased in popularity in the nineteenth century, as rules governing taste and design were being codified and regulated into a series of principles, exemplified in the pronouncements of critics about good and poor design.

The kaleidoscope has been credited as being the inspiration behind so many quilts whose design is based on repeating stars or other geometric motifs.[35] Certainly the invention and the widespread popularity of this toy boosted the usage of this style of design. Sir David Brewster, its inventor, was an active writer and editor of scientific and philosophical journals, as well as an experimental scientist interested in optics. He promoted his kaleidoscope in print at every opportunity, as did some of his influential friends, like the successful decorative painter and writer on art and design David

Ramsey Hay, a fellow member of the Edinburgh-based Aesthetical Club, "a society . . . dedicated to founding a science of beauty on fixed mathematical principles."[36] Hay, a highly successful decorative painter, reinforced Brewster's promotion of the use of the kaleidoscope for designing "carpets, geometrical pavements, and paper hangings," which were all "viewed by the spectator with various degrees of obliquity."[37]

But many similar rectilinear designs, such as eight-pointed stars and diagonal and straight trellis patterns are found in weaving pattern books as early as the sixteenth century. These styles related to examples from Islamic Spain and the Middle East, while designs based on circles and ovals were found in many textbooks on geometry.[38] The templates needed to create some of these amazing masterpieces are more quickly and easily created with the use of a compass and straight edge, or their more readily available domestic equivalents, than by the projection of kaleidoscopic images. The types of designs made by kaleidoscopes, with their changing geometric form and variety of saturated colors, were unquestionably in fashion, but the role of the kaleidoscope in quilt design and production is questionable.[39]

Vibrant patterns of stars are also found on printed fabrics in the 1820s. This pattern, known as "Catherine wheel," is printed in a style of different-colored stripes known collectively as rainbow prints. Winterthur's collection includes three colorways printed on cotton cloth of fairly poor quality, one of which is cut to form stripes in a strip-quilt. The cylinder for the original of this design was supplied by Joseph Lockett to Samuel Matley, at the Hodge Printworks in Cheshire, England, and was first produced in 1824. The origin of the strip quilt is unknown, but strip quilts were popular with Quakers in the Mid-Atlantic region.

Evidence coming from the many quilt-documentation projects has provided information about regional preferences in quilt design in the nineteenth century. Winterthur's collection is not limited geographically,

Printed Samples
Said to be the best engraver and cylinder-maker, Joseph Lockett exported many of his stock of 20,000 designs to the United States after 1825. The original design is dated 1824, but it would have been in production for many years.

appliquéd all over were cut from extremely high-quality imported fabrics fashionable throughout the 1830s.

Another quilt in the collection reminds us that quilt design could also be fairly free-form and individualistic. Made in Montgomery County, Maryland, an ink inscription on the back reads: "Elizabeth Jane Allnutt to Effie M. Allnutt to Mami Poole." Elizabeth Jane was born in 1819, and married John Hanson Allnutt in 1838. Upon her death, her husband remarried and had three children, one of whom was named Mary Effie Allnutt. Effie married John William Poole II, and their daughter was Mamie Louis Poole, the final name on the inscription.[41]

The ground fabric of the face is a coarse cotton. The dark ground chintz used for the appliquéd motifs is penciled in blue. It would have been fashionable in the late eighteenth or early nineteenth century, and could possibly have been produced as late as 1820. The printed border would seem to date to the later 1820s or the 1830s. Individual motifs of flowers, leaves, pinwheels, and swastikas radiate from a small central medallion of four curved-leaf forms. The buttonhole stitches of yellow silk were executed by at least two different hands, one of whom seems to have been more experienced than the other. The ground is quilted in double rows of diamonds, but the quilting stitches do not go through the motifs, which are quilted according to each shape. Although the design is unlike any other, the individual motifs have been carefully and formally placed.

Quilts were a way of bringing color and pattern into a room. Wholecloth quilts could be purchased or made within the home. Such useful and basic examples were made throughout the nineteenth century, though they went in and out of fashion. Pieced and appliquéd examples were often public displays of their maker's skill and taste. The word "work" once referred almost exclusively to sewing and knitting, whether the end product was a mundane pair of stockings or the quilts that we value so highly today.

but many examples come from the Mid-Atlantic region. A particularly interesting example is an appliqué quilt by Sophia Myers Pearce (page 83). The diamond center set on point was a style that was particularly popular in Virginia and North Carolina, but made from fabrics found in many quilts from Maryland. Sophia was the daughter of Jacob Myers, who was a prominent tobacco merchant and one of the founders of the German Presbyterian Church that stood at the corner of Baltimore

and Front Streets in Baltimore. Her brother Samuel lived in Richmond, Virginia. She married John B. Pearce in 1832, and they lived at Clifford, considered to be one of the most beautiful estates in Baltimore County.[40] The quilt dates to around 1840, but it is possible that Sophia made it close to the time of her marriage. The blue ground fabrics used for the sawtooth borders, and the shawl pattern border framing the central medallion, date from the mid to late 1820s, while the floral motifs

Opposite **Elizabeth Jane Allnutt Quilt**
Contrasting with the sophisticated styles found in the city of Baltimore, this unusual quilt was made in Montgomery County, Maryland, in the 1830s.

Left **Miniature Quilt**
A perfect miniature, this quilt is only 27½ inches high. Purchased from a dealer in Pennsylvania, its origins are unknown, but we do know that it was made in the early 1800s.

Above **Miniature Bed and Bedding**
Complete with its original hangings, mattress, bolster, and pillows, this miniature bed is a perfect copy of a full-sized one. The miniature quilt is in perfect scale and provides a rare opportunity to see a quilt in its original context.

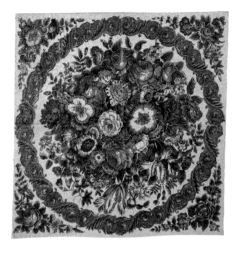

Opposite **Mary Jane Moore Eastburn Quilt**
An inscription on the back of this quilt records that it was pieced by Mary Jane Moore in 1837 at her home in Mill Creek Hundred, Delaware. She completed the quilting in 1839, after her marriage to Amos Eastburn. The couple had 10 children, 39 grandchildren, and at least 37 great-grandchildren.

Left **Sophia Myers Pearce Quilt**
The brown borders framing the central diamond of this appliqué quilt are printed in a type of design known as shawl patterns. This example can been attributed to the English firm of Bannister Hall. The quilt was made in Baltimore in 1840.

Above **Printed Quilt Center**
Fabrics were often printed to shape for specific purposes, such as counterpanes and chair covers. Some designs, such as this one, were made specifically to be used in quilts.

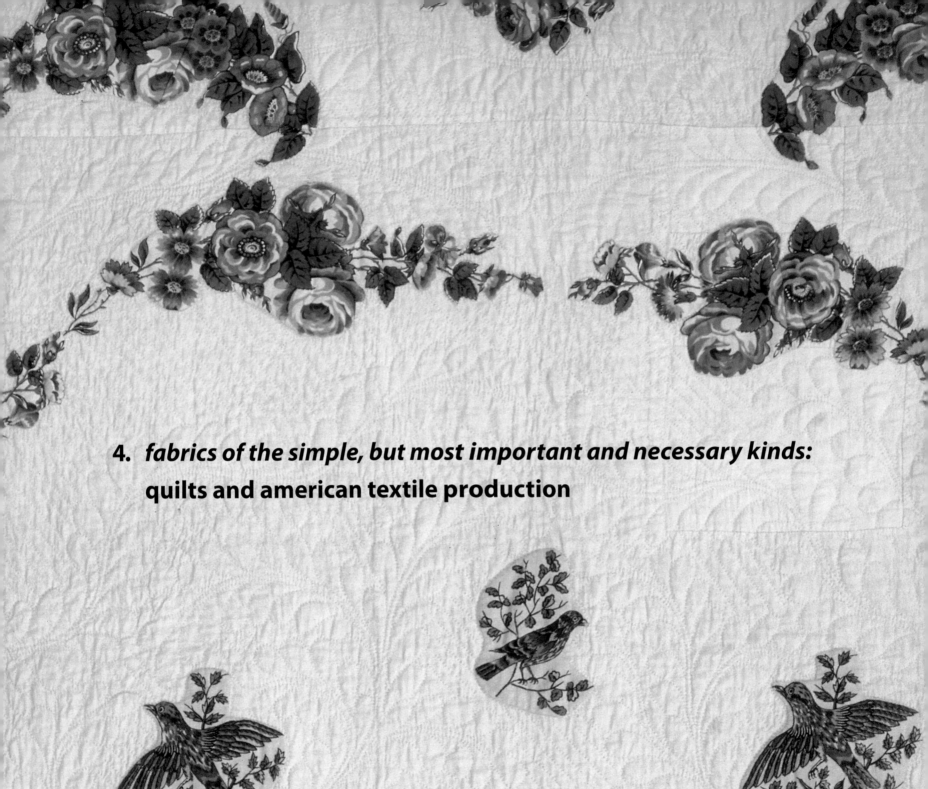

4. *fabrics of the simple, but most important and necessary kinds:* quilts and american textile production

Quilts are said to document the history of textiles. This history is often told through the beautiful imported chintzes, printed in both Europe and India, and the advances in chemistry and technology that they represent. This chapter looks at fabrics of a more mundane nature that were made in America. Some are the products of the changeover from the system of hand spinning and hand weaving to the mechanization of both processes. Others have been influenced by the related movement for "domestic manufactures." The use of the word "domestic" in this context can be confusing. It can mean textiles produced in the home within the family or by outworkers for a manufacturer, but it can also apply to objects manufactured in America, whether their origin is in a home or in a factory. Warwick, Rhode Island, was an early center for mechanized cotton spinning in factories—some of which were owned by family and friends of Mary Remington, who wrote in 1813, "Sunday morning took a ride before breakfast. I with Mr. Waterman and his little son, Catherine with the Capt. We had a fun ride Mr. W. waited on us to the cotton factory he was building."[1]

The admonition to "buy American" is not something new. It was first encouraged in the 1760s, and continues even today. In the 1700s the British government discouraged colonial manufacturing, seeing America as both a source of raw materials and a market for their own manufactured goods. But there had always been a certain amount of small-scale local textile production in both Britain and the American colonies. The definition of what is known as "homespun" cloth can be confusing, and there could be many regional variations in its production. Fibers such as linen, wool, or cotton were often spun at home. At this time, fewer people owned looms than spinning wheels, but many basic cloths could be woven in the home or could be purchased from a professional weaver.[2] The key is that the fabrics produced were very simple, basic cloths such as sheeting and blanketing. During the 1760s and 1770s, the use of

homespun fabric was seen as a patriotic act, enabling the disgruntled colonists to boycott British goods. In the late 1780s, the balance of trade was not in the favor of the United States, and the bankers and economists of the new nation realized the importance of keeping as much currency within the country as possible, in order to improve America's chances of paying her debts.

One of the early advocates of American manufacturing was Tench Coxe (1755–1824), an assistant to Alexander Hamilton, then Secretary of the Treasury. Favoring a national economy balanced between agriculture and manufacturing, Coxe encouraged English and European textile workers to emigrate to the newly founded United States, where he claimed that most of them could be assured of success. According to Coxe, however, the American market was not interested in luxury goods, a viewpoint not shared by many of his wealthy contemporaries or by present-day historians. In 1794, he wrote, "There is least opening for those, who have been used to make very fine and costly articles of luxury and shew. There is not so much chance of success for the luxurious branches, unless they are capable of being carried on in a considerable degree by machinery or water works; in which case they also will thrive if the necessary capital be employed—there is already some consumption of these fine goods in America, and as free an exportation of them (without duty of excise) as from any country in the world."[3] The production of textiles made in America was a matter of pride in the new nation, promoted extensively by newspapers and journals such as *Niles' Weekly Register*, published in Baltimore from 1811.

The first aspect of textile production to be mechanized was cotton spinning, with Rhode Island being an early and important center of this development.[4] The first large-scale production of cotton woven on mechanized looms began in Waltham, Massachusetts, between 1814 and 1817. The New England textile industry was famed for its vertical production, where

Fanny Johnson McPherson Quilt

Fanny Johnson McPherson made this quilt in Frederick, Maryland, between 1835 and 1850. A wealthy woman, she was the granddaughter of the first governor of Maryland and a cousin of Louisa Catherine Johnson Adams, the wife of John Quincy Adams. Fanny may have made the quilt for her daughter and namesake, Fanny Johnson McPherson, who was born in 1837, two years after the founding of Boott Mills. This second Fanny married George Robertson Dennis, and the quilt descended in the family of their son George. It was given to Winterthur by his daughter Barbara Brooke Dennis Avirett.

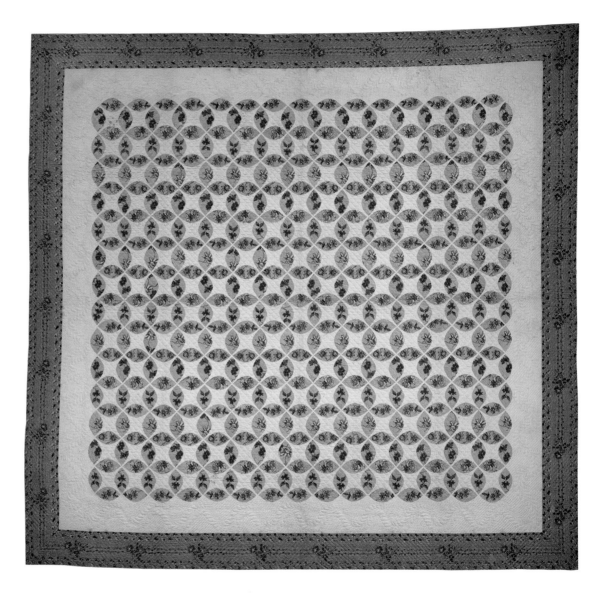

Stamp, Wholecloth Quilt

The company that produced the fabric stamped "Walkill Sheeting" has not been identified, but it was undoubtedly one of the many manufactories along the Walkill River in New York. Such plain and basic fabrics rarely survive unless used as the backing for a quilt.

cotton was spun and then woven into various sturdy and useful fabrics.[5] Much of the production of the early American mills was a coarse-quality cotton shirting and sheeting. (Drilling, a heavy-twilled cotton, is also mentioned, but was not found on any quilts in Winterthur's collection.) Documented early examples are rare, so the survival of makers' stamps on the backings of two quilts in Winterthur's collection is of significance.

A stamp on the backing of a quilt made in Frederick, Maryland, identifies its source as Boott Mills, Lowell. Looms dating from the early twentieth century still produce cotton fabric that is similar to some of the original products, known as drillings, sheetings, and shirtings. Such utilitarian fabrics are rarely saved for posterity. Few documented examples survive, and little work has been published about the distribution of these fabrics, so it is important to document the presence of this fabric on a quilt made in Frederick, Maryland. This is, in fact, a fairly high-quality cloth, with a thread count for both warp and weft of between 82 and 86 threads per inch.

In John Leander Bishop's comprehensive book *A History of American Manufactures from 1608 to 1860,* he gives a technical description of the "staple of American Cotton manufactures" as "heavy unbleached sheetings of No. 14 yarn, thirty-seven inches wide, forty-four picks to the inch, and in weight something less than three yards to the pound."[6] Taking shrinkage and a thick batting into account, this perfectly describes a second example used as a backing for a printed wholecloth quilt, stamped "Walkill Sheetings."

Cotton mills for spinning and weaving were potentially lucrative businesses. Although the most well-known of these early mills were built in New England, entrepreneurs were establishing them wherever there was a good source of water power. Such was the case with the Walkill River that runs from New Jersey, north and west through Orange County, and into Ulster County in New York where it joins the Rondout Creek before emptying into the Hudson River near the town

of Esopus. It provided power for a number of early cotton mills. One of the first was founded at Rifton, where Joseph and Benjamin Arnold established a mill in 1827, which operated until 1857. It was purchased in 1861 by J. W. Dimmick, who is listed as one of the principal cotton manufacturers in the United States in the 1860s. Dimmick used the buildings at Rifton Falls as a mill for wool and produced blankets during the Civil War.[7] Another mill was founded at the Dashville Falls, in the town of New Paltz in 1832. Known as Dashville Falls Manufacturing Company, the founders intended to make cotton and woolen goods and machinery.[8] As early as 1812, Jacob T. Walden founded cotton and woolen mills in Kiddtown, later renamed Walden in his honor. Like many of his fellow merchants, Jacob Walden switched to manufacturing as many once-prosperous shipping concerns struggled to survive the impact that the War of 1812 had on their businesses. By 1834, his cotton mill was consuming "around one hundred twenty thousand pounds of cotton, which was made up in sheeting."[9]

Unless further information comes to light, we will probably never be sure where this particular example of sheeting was made, although since one list of cotton manufacturing statistics for 1845 lists Orange County producing just over twice as much as Ulster County, the balance of probability would seem to sway it in that direction. Few discussions of the American cotton-spinning and weaving industries discuss the myriad small partnerships that formed the bulk of early American manufacturing. By systematically documenting the marks and stamps on these humble, cheap, and often poor-quality fabrics, we can come to know more about the products of the early American cotton industry.

The backing fabric is badly dyed an appalling muddy yellow color. A recipe offered by Lydia Maria Child 1833 describes a cheap but effective method of producing a yellow color that she suggests would be "very useful for the linings of bed-quilts, comforters, &c."[10] Similar recipes survive in dye books used by Pennsylvania German dyers, which have been successfully tested and shown to produce a mustard-color tone often found on linen checks produced in that region. Using such basic ingredients as rusty nails and vinegar, this recipe is a cheap way of imparting a fashionable color to an otherwise basic cotton cloth.[11]

Calico printing in America was a difficult business in which to succeed, as it was a much more complicated business than dyeing. As late as 1815, Thomas Cooper was "not persuaded that a callicoe printing establishment will be for some time an eligible speculation on a large scale."[12] Described by John Adams as "a learned, ingenious, scientific, and talented madcap" (which was generous of him—Cooper had been convicted, fined, and imprisoned for having libeled Adams in 1799), Thomas Cooper was, among many other things, an unsuccessful bleacher and calico printer.[13] Indeed, many early calico printers on both sides of the Atlantic seem to have failed during the late eighteenth century. In London, a total of thirty-six calico printers went bankrupt between 1752 and 1782. Many, but not all, were the smaller firms that are poorly documented.[14]

After the 1772 bankruptcy of the firm of Thomas Bedwell and John Gross in Wandsworth, London, Thomas Bedwell emigrated to Philadelphia, where he founded a calico printing company with John Walters, in 1775 on Germantown Road.[15] While Bedwell had experience in the cotton-printing industry, Walters's contribution to the business was probably pattern drawing and possibly block cutting.[16] This firm was not a success either, and Walters announced in the *Pennsylvania Evening Post* of June 5, 1777, that he had "intirely quitted the linen stamping business" and begged "all persons who have goods in his hands to fetch them away."[17] Walters and Bedwell were "job printers." Their clients provided "Muslin, Linen, Cotton, &c." to be "Printed at the most reasonable rates, and in every

respect equal to what comes from Europe . . . Bed Quilts and Curtains printed blue, for which Purpose Linen that has been worn will do. Ladies choosing any particular pattern may have it done, though for a single Gown."[18] Such a business required less start-up capital because the proprietors did not have to invest in stocks of plain fabric to be printed (which could account for between one-half to three quarters of the total cost of the final product), but only in the printing blocks, dye vats, dyestuffs, mordants, and other chemicals.[19] Job printers tend to be smaller businesses, individual artisans working for themselves. The only reason we know so much about Walters and Bedwell is that they undertook an exceptional advertising campaign in the spring of 1775.[20] The one example of their production that survives is printed on a heavy piece of linen with a selvage width of 40 inches, a product characteristic of the local German weavers, though an unusual type of cloth to be printed in the madder style at this time.[21]

The calico-printing business was not any easier after the American Revolution. Another job printer, Henry Royl & Co., began a "Calico Printing Manufactory" at Bakeovens Place on the Germantown Road, two miles from Philadelphia. They specified that their patterns could be seen at the manufactory as well as at "Wood and Thornely's Store in Chestnut Street" where "Goods will be taken in, and orders faithfully and expeditiously executed." It would seem that Royl and his partners, too, were refugees from the declining London calico-printing industry, advertising that "the undertakers of this work having been regularly brought up to the business, they flatter themselves capable of giving entire satisfaction &c."[22] Despite the flattery, by 1787, the minutes of the Pennsylvania Society for the Encouragement of Manufactures and the Useful Arts (PSEMUA) recorded that Henry Royl was winding up his business and intended to leave the country. He was hoping to sell his printing equipment, which consisted of "a Calinder, prints, Stamps, etc." to the society, but they declined.[23]

Design Repeat

This design repeat is from an 1825–30 printed wholecloth quilt. The top is made from a cylinder-printed cotton. The stylistic group to which this fabric belongs has been described as pillar print. The cylinder-printed versions, such as this one, come from the second phase of this fashion, dating in English sample books from 1825 to 1830. Florence Montgomery dated this design to between 1835 and 1840.

Right **Walters & Bedwell Fabric**
John Walters and Thomas Bedwell
marked the end of this piece of linen
with their names and location—the
only example of this practice in
America during the eighteenth century. Walters and Bedwell were job
printers, printing on fabrics brought
to them by their customers. This
example from 1775–77 is done on
a fairly heavyweight linen that is 40
inches wide—the characteristic loom
width of weavers within the Pennsylvania German community.

Opposite **Rowan Fabric Fragment**
Archibald Hamilton Rowan was an
exiled Irish revolutionary. He purchased a calico printing business
from William and Thomas Jordan,
whose firms in Manchester, England,
and America were unsuccessful. This
fragment from 1797–99 is one of
four surviving examples of Rowan's
production. In June of 1799, Rowan
advertised that he owned rollers for
about 150 prints.

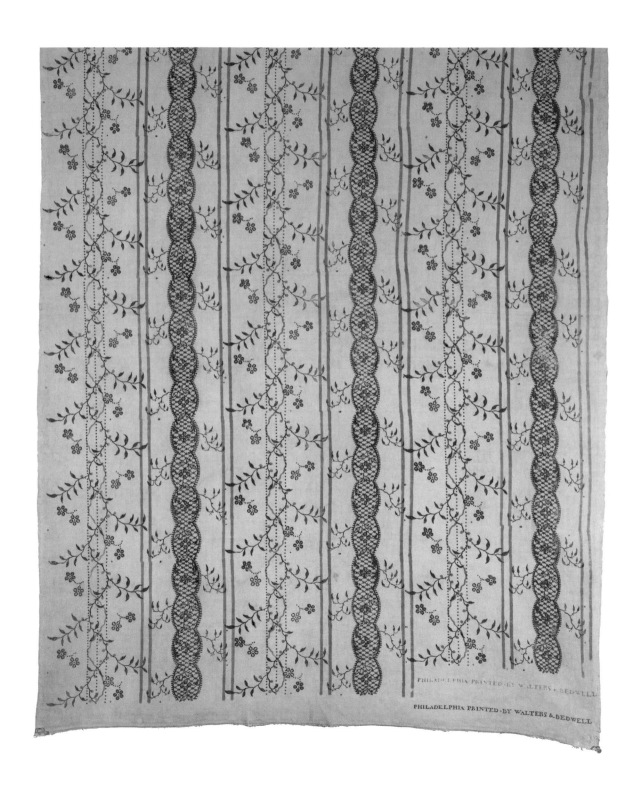

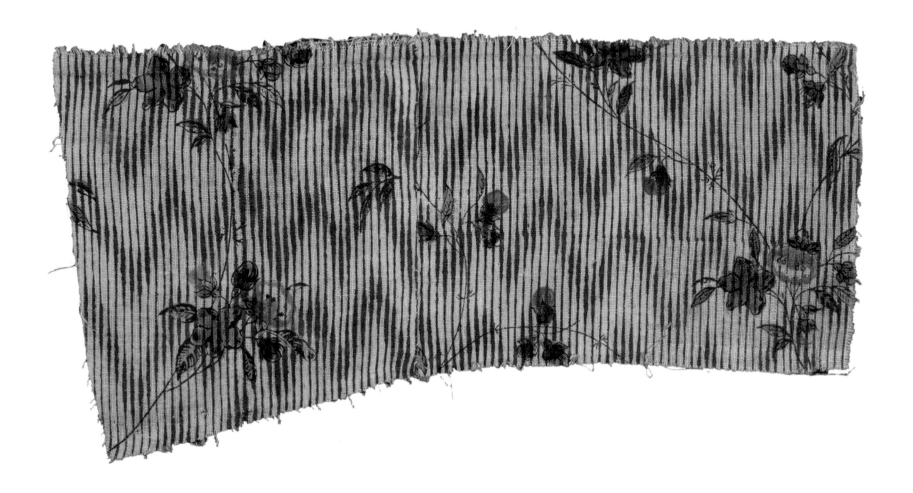

Yet another example of this depressing trend was Stephen Addington. In 1794, Henry Wansey described Addington's printworks in Springfield, New Jersey, as "a considerable business in printing callicoes, muslins, and linens, and an excellent bleaching ground; but it is as yet quite an infant undertaking and will hardly succeed for want of a larger command of capital. The difficulty of making returns of money, will for many years operate against establishing such concerns."[24] Sadly, this prognosis proved to be correct, as the *Pennsylvania Packet* advertised a sheriff's sale of Addington's tools and furniture in December of 1797. From Wansey's description, it would seem that Addington was not a job printer but was attempting to build a calico printing business along the lines of those established in Britain.[25]

Archibald Hamilton Rowan had no better luck on the Brandywine Creek in Delaware. He had purchased his business from two brothers who had been in the calico-printing business in Manchester who, "'either from indolence or extravagance' . . . had become bankrupt after expending a large sum on their establishment."[26] Rowan's business only survived for two years. When putting up the property and equipment for auction, he bitterly offered that "Any person inclined to sacrifice his property by carrying on this manufactory in America, may have the whole for one half the sum they cost, and immediate possession of the premises, from Archibald Hamilton Rowan, at the Factory."[27]

The problem was not only competition from imported British goods, which was significant, but also the complications of the business itself. Every description of the calico printing in the eighteenth and early nineteenth centuries stresses the need for a wide knowledge of chemistry, a good sense of design, the ability to keep up with rapid changes in fashions, and the high level of risk. Block printing in particular required the cooperative endeavors of large numbers of skilled artisans and unskilled laborers, which was problematic in America, where labor costs were high.

There was a delicate balance between the fixed capital of a calico-printing business and its working-capital needs, which were much higher.[28] Both large and small entrepreneurs went bankrupt in an industry where it could be difficult to achieve a decent return on the capital investment needed for the raw materials (dyes, mordants, cloth), buildings (print room, color house, etc.), equipment (large coppers, tables, calendering equipment), and land for bleaching and drying. The British firm of Livesey, Hargreaves and Co. failed in 1788, owing nearly a million and a half pounds. They are believed to have employed between 700 and 1,000 printers, and to have been "the means of giving bread to near 20,000 persons," while their bleachfields "extended for more than twelve miles." But many, if not most, of the smaller printworks also "changed hands through bankruptcy."[29] Dramatic fluctuations in prices, the upward trend in the rate of inflation, continuous crises in the availability of credit and specie, worldwide political instability, trade wars, and economic blockades made it difficult to succeed in any business in the late eighteenth or early nineteenth century—particularly one that could be deemed a luxury, only providing added value for a cloth that, discounting fashion, could be perfectly well used plain or undecorated.[30]

Within this context, it is nothing short of miraculous that John Hewson was able to establish a calico-printing business in Philadelphia that survived from 1774 into at least the early 1820s. Hewson is said to have come to Philadelphia at the behest of Benjamin Franklin, no less, because his family was worried about his loudly proclaimed republican views.[31] There was a widespread increase in radical politics throughout Europe at this time, as inflation increased and real wages fell, causing suffering and discontent among the poor and middle classes. In Hewson's case, the specific causes of his radical opinions were probably the changes occurring in the calico-printing industry in England. Not only were many of the London printworks going bankrupt, but

the center of the industry was moving to the north of England, causing unemployment and distress to the skilled artisans of London, and almost certainly resulting in decreased wages. Between 1760 and 1785, the number of calico-printing firms in London fell from more than twenty to just thirteen, while in Manchester, the number of firms grew from just one in 1760 to forty-five in 1785.[32]

Hewson seems to have been somewhat pugnacious in temperament, a character trait that was probably essential given the ruthless nature of competition among Philadelphia's calico printers at the time. Hewson's apprentice, John Douglas, ran away on June 26, 1777, and Hewson did not waste any time before advertising for his return. "He is suspected to have gone to some part of New-England with a former master of his, whom the subscribers bought his time of, a noted villain and a great cheat, goes by the name of John Walters, his right name is John Groase; he is very lame in his hands and feet with the gout. . . . Whoever secures said apprentice in any jail of the United States, and will give information thereof to the subscribers, shall have Twenty Dollars reward, if brought home thirty, and reasonable charges."[33] Hewson only posted a reward of four dollars when his own son, John Jr., ran away from home in June of 1783. He told people that he had "a hard master." Hewson's advertisement seeking his son's return combines threats ("This is to warn all masters of vessels and others not to harbour said lad, as they will answer it another day") with a touching offer of compromise ("If he returns to his parents, he will be freely forgiven. And if desirous of going to sea, he shall be provided for accordingly"). His description of the missing teenager is also poignant. John Hewson Jr. was "a lad about fifteen years of age, slender made, short light brown hair, a little pock marked, and much freckled. He had on a short brown jacket with sleeves, white tow trousers, silver shoe buckles, wears his hat close up on the sides and slouching over his face, is a remarkable modest boy,

was never before from home, and has much the appearance of a stranger."[34]

Hewson was relatively restrained when he accused two competitors, Nathaniel Norgrove and William Grant, of going to his "Factory at Kensington, while the enemy were in possession of the same" and stealing "a large wooden machine, used in the linen printing work, strongly moored and anchored at the subscriber's wharf; likewise a printing table, colour tub, a number of prints, and several other articles . . . but not finding the call for them they expected, did maliciously cut said machine to pieces and burn it, and are now retreated to Conestogo Creek, within a few miles of Lancaster, thinking thereby to escape justice: This is therefore to warn them to come and settle with the subscriber for the damages of the same, or cause it to be settled by some correspondent . . . or they will be prosecuted with the utmost rigor of the law."[35] Norgrove had come to Philadelphia with Hewson in 1773, both commended by Benjamin Franklin as being "sober industrious young Men, and very ingenious in their Business of Calico or Linen Printing."[36]

Hewson seems to have had at least two partners through the late 1780s, which can be interpreted as either opportunities for additional capital investment, or the necessity of offering partnership terms to artisans whose skills he desperately needed. Hewson's first advertisement in 1774 describes him as the sole proprietor, but the firm is designated as either Hewson and Lang or Hewson & Co by 1777. William Lang was a pattern designer and block cutter, and was still associated with the business in 1788, when he demonstrated his skill alongside the Hewson family (not including John Jr., but including his step-mother and sisters) in the Grand Federal Procession in Philadelphia to celebrate the ratification of the Constitution in 1788.[37]

At some stage, Robert Taylor, a bleacher, was also taken into partnership as Hewson advertises the dissolution of their partnership in July of 1785.[38]

George Washington Handkerchief

This handkerchief, which was used as a quilt center, has been attributed by some to John Hewson of Philadelphia. Although a convincing case has been made for dating its production to 1776–77, there is no proof that it was printed by Hewson. The print from which the central image was taken was produced in London by C. Shepherd from an original painting by Alexander Campbell. Because of the unsophisticated design and the block-printing technique, it has been assumed that the handkerchief was printed in America.

Three textile printing businesses are known to have been active in Philadelphia at this time: John Hewson, John Walters and Thomas Bedwell, and Nathaniel Norgrove, who came to this country with Hewson. No surviving handkerchiefs have any history of ownership to provide clues to the makers.

Detail, George Washington Handkerchief

The batting is wool, and the backing fabric is a coarse plain-woven cloth with a linen warp and cotton weft. Lines of chevron quilting, spaced one-half inch apart, have been stitched in linen thread.

Taylor stressed the process of bleaching when he announced that he had his own business in Lower Merion township in the *Freemans Journal* of March 14, 1786. PSEUMA seems to have considered his printed calicoes to be inferior to Hewson's work.[39] Perhaps Taylor was involved at the beginning, as Hewson's first advertisement describes the business as a "calicoe printing manufactory, and bleach yard," stating that "Linen sent for bleaching, from one yard to a thousand, shall be punctually returned in three weeks, compleatly finished, at 4d. per yard." Although not producing prints of as high a quality as Hewson, Robert Taylor operated his business successfully until his death in early 1795.[40]

John Hewson was not a job printer like Walters and Bedwell or Henry Royl, as he was clearly looking to buy cloth when he offered "the best price for any quantity of fine country made linen" in 1777.[41] He later printed on cotton "imported from India, in an American bottom [ship]." Christophe-Philippe Oberkampf and other European printers also used Indian cotton, although by this time, 1793, most British printers were using cotton woven in Britain. Hewson did undertake the bleaching of small pieces of cloth belonging to clients when he began the business in 1774, and provided this service to PSEMUA in 1789.[42] He never offered to print cloth brought in by his customers, although he did print cotton manufactured by the PSEMUA. In 1789, they, too, decided that "the stamping [of] the Bleached cottons to be unprofitable, we have requested Hewson to stop all further process in the Stamping Business."[43] Interestingly, it was in the following month, March of 1789, that the society awarded him a gold plate or medal "for the best specimen of calico printing done within this state."[44]

At this time, Hewson was clearly looking to expand his business. During the Revolution, Hewson's business had been all but destroyed by "the savage foe of Britain," as well as his former friends. The loss of materials and

equipment meant that Hewson and Lang were unable to carry out the complicated madder style of printing, involving sophisticated use of metallic salts to achieve a variety of colors from dark brown to light pink and even a buff color. Instead, they resorted to dyeing with indigo in the resist style, "printing . . . blue handkerchiefs, with deep blue grounds and white spots; also very neat gown patterns of the same color."[45] By the 1780s, Hewson had clearly built his business back to where he was once again printing with a full range of colors. Winterthur's counterpane, and other surviving examples, could well have been printed about this time.

In 1789, Hewson requested and was granted a loan of two hundred pounds from the state of Pennsylvania "for the purpose of assisting and enabling him to enlarge and carry on the business of calico printing and bleaching within this state."[46] This was a time of great change in the textile industry as a whole, and Hewson was looking for partners to bring capital into his business. He advertised that "Any person or persons willing to enter into the above mentioned branch of business [calico printing] in an extensive manner, may have further information on the subject by applying to John Hewson & Co."[47]

Hewson applied to the state of Pennsylvania for another loan in 1792, but his request was "ordered to lie on the table."[48] Two advertisements from the early nineteenth century indicate that Hewson and his son at some time had expanded their holdings to include a city warehouse and even a weaving factory, using a business strategy that is remarkably similar to that of the larger firms of the north of England.[49] In 1808, John Jr. advertises his products "For Sale, at the American Printed Callico Ware-House" at "No. 7 South Third Street," and, in 1817, he offers a reward of one hundred dollars for information about the goods stolen from his "Weaving Factory" on Green Street; a John Hewston, cotton manufacturer, is listed in a Philadelphia Directory for 1822.[50]

Opposite **John Hewson Counterpane**
One of two known counterpanes printed by John Hewson, this example is stamped "F. M." (in ink) in one corner. These are believed to be the initials of Frances Wardale Lieber McAllister, the second wife of John McAllister, who came to New York from Glasgow in 1775 and moved to Philadelphia about 1780. The counterpane has been printed to shape; the central seam was sewn before the fabric was block printed, and the design was adapted to the size of the counterpane.

Above **Detail, Hewson Counterpane**
This detail demonstrates how Hewson manipulated the type of metallic salt and the concentrations of his mordant solutions to achieve a variety of browns, reds, and pinks from madder. The uneven nature of the indigo blue is characteristic of the technique known as "penciling," where the dyestuff was brushed onto the fabric by hand—a job usually reserved for women.

After the American Revolution, Hewson seems to have been selling his work to merchants rather than individual clients. In July of 1781, he specifically targets his advertisement in both the *Pennsylvania Gazette* and the *Pennsylvania Journal* to "Merchants and Store-keepers."[51] In 1793, when offering his chintz to Martha Washington, he mentions only the wholesale price, and, in 1815, John Jr. is busy selling handkerchiefs in bulk to the Philadelphia merchant Richard Ashhurst & Co.[52] There seems to be no system of long-term credit in operation at this time, as Richard Ashhurst & Co. paid its debts almost immediately.[53] Provenanced examples of quilts made from Hewson fabric have a geographic range from Springfield, Massachusetts, to Baltimore, Maryland, providing additional evidence that Hewson's work was distributed outside Philadelphia.[54]

Hewson's business was quite small by European standards. Results from the 1810 census of manufactures, published in 1814, indicate that at that time there were eight "Muslin and Linen Printers" working in Philadelphia county, employing 122 people and producing over a million yards of "gown stuff, shawls, handkerchiefs &c., &c." totaling a value of $145,290.[55] Even allowing that Hewson might have had the largest business, employing perhaps thirty to forty workers, he can't compare to British firms like Peel, Yates & Company, who sent a considerable proportion of their output to America, and who employed 800 people in 1785.[56] Oberkampf, at Jouy-en-Josas, the largest firm in France, employed 1,327 workers in 1806. The value of the equipment, dye-stuffs and chemicals, buildings, and land are difficult to compare, but the discrepancy is apparent in the valuation of the Peel's Church Printworks from 1809 to 1811 of £42,070, while in 1822, Hewson left his son an unspecified amount of "Printing Utensils and the Printing Manufactory . . . all my prints, printing tables, sieves, blankets, brushes, Mauls, Copper Boilers and Kettles, Dye Vats, presses Calander and all the Mill work belonging thereto. Also a Horse named Dick."[57]

John Hewson Sr. retired from the business around 1810. How long it survived into the nineteenth century is unclear. John Hewson Jr. is listed as a calico printer in the Philadelphia directories until 1823, and it is uncertain whether the business failed at this time, or whether it was sold to others. Interestingly, the calico-printing firm founded by Christophe-Philippe Oberkampf at Jouy-en-Josas in 1769 went out of the control of the family in 1822, and the Peel family in England was also trying to sell their various printing concerns at this time.[58] Prices for calicoes were plummeting not only due to the increasing speed of production of roller-printed goods (it was said that one roller-printing machine "attended by a man and a boy" could produce "as much work as could be turned out by one hundred block printers and as many tear-boys"[59]), but also because the supply of textiles produced in the north of England exceeded the capacity of the international market to absorb them.[60] Although Hewson's printworks was much smaller in scale, it was clearly successful, enabling both father and son to retire comfortably. Both are described in the Philadelphia directories as "gentlemen," a term that denoted a man living on his accumulated income and investments.[61]

Quality is an issue that is mentioned in many of John Hewson's advertisements. From the start, he stated that his work would equal that of his former employer, the famous Bromley Hall printworks whose products were being extensively imported into Philadelphia by merchants like Richard Vaux.[62] Later advertisements stressed the high quality of his printing. Clearly the poor reputation of American-made goods was prevalent, as he suggests that by wearing his chintz, Martha Washington "might be a great means of introducing the like amongst the more affluent of our fellow citizens, and would help to remove the injustice, that at present too much prevails, against American manufactures." He continues, "The subscriber is willing to risque his reputation on the piece herewith presented, as the

Appliqué Quilt
The maker and origin of this quilt are unknown, but it can be dated stylistically to between 1830 and 1850. The quilt was purchased by Henry Francis du Pont before 1935.

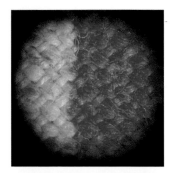

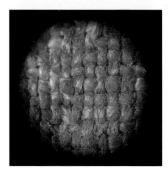

Top **Photomicrograph, Printed Cotton**
This photomicrograph, taken at 50x magnification, shows how the traditional technique of mordant printing results in fibers that are dyed. The color has soaked right into the fibers and appears somewhat translucent, like a stain.

Above **Photomicrograph, Stamped Cotton**
Contrasting with the above image, this example from the Waterman quilt shows how pigment sits only on the surface of the fibers and has an opaque appearance. Some of the original pigment has worn off, resulting not in a fading of the color but in the abrasion of the surface of what is essentially paint.

best performance ever exhibited on this continent to the present day. The wholesale price is nine shillings pr. Yd. and upon strict enquiry, will be found that no importer in this city can present a piece of equal fabrick and workmanship, from any part of the world at a less price."[63]

Why was Hewson so defensive? An examination of examples of his work at Winterthur shows that he was employing the standard mordant printing processes described by Thomas Cooper, who, in turn, took his information from a variety of French and English sources.[64] Hewson manipulates the composition and concentration of the mordant solutions to produce three shades each of reds and browns, with the indigo blue penciled in by hand. The typical technique of preparing the cloth, printing the mordants, aging the mordanted cloth, washing it in dung, dyeing, clearing, scouring, and finishing was time-consuming and required considerable knowledge and skill.

Scientific analysis of the coloring matter found on a group of quilts and related printed textiles in Winterthur's collection has identified an unusual technique for printing textiles in America that might account for the poor quality of calico printing and the reason purchasers were hesitant to buy American-made fabrics. The term "stamped" has often been used to describe these unsophisticated printed fabrics, although it is unclear whether the period use of the words "stamped" and "printed" denoted any differentiation of technique in the late eighteenth or early nineteenth century.

There are two methods of printing what are called "fugitive" colors, or *petit teint* in French. One method is to use dyestuffs that are known to fade from exposure to either water or daylight, such as brazilwood for red or *grains d'Avignon* (also known as Persian berries) for yellow. These fugitive dyes were also often used to strengthen or shade other more lightfast dyes. The other method involves grinding pigments in oil and printing them onto the surface of a fabric.

Opposite **Waterman Family Quilt**
It is believed that the designs on this quilt, which dates to 1780–1815, were stamped by a member of the Waterman family of South Scituate (now Norwell) Massachusetts. The family lineage is traced from Ebenezer Copeland, who married Sarah, the widow of Thomas Waterman; their daughter Huldah, who married James Waterman; their son Ebenezer Copeland Waterman; to his son James C. Waterman, who sold the quilts and stamps to Winsor White, the dealer who in turn sold them to Henry Francis du Pont. At least one of the Waterman quilts was displayed in an exhibition held in 1927 in Hanover, Massachusetts, to celebrate the 300th anniversary of the town's founding. The committee that organized the exhibition was chaired by Sarah L. Waterman, wife of James C. Waterman.

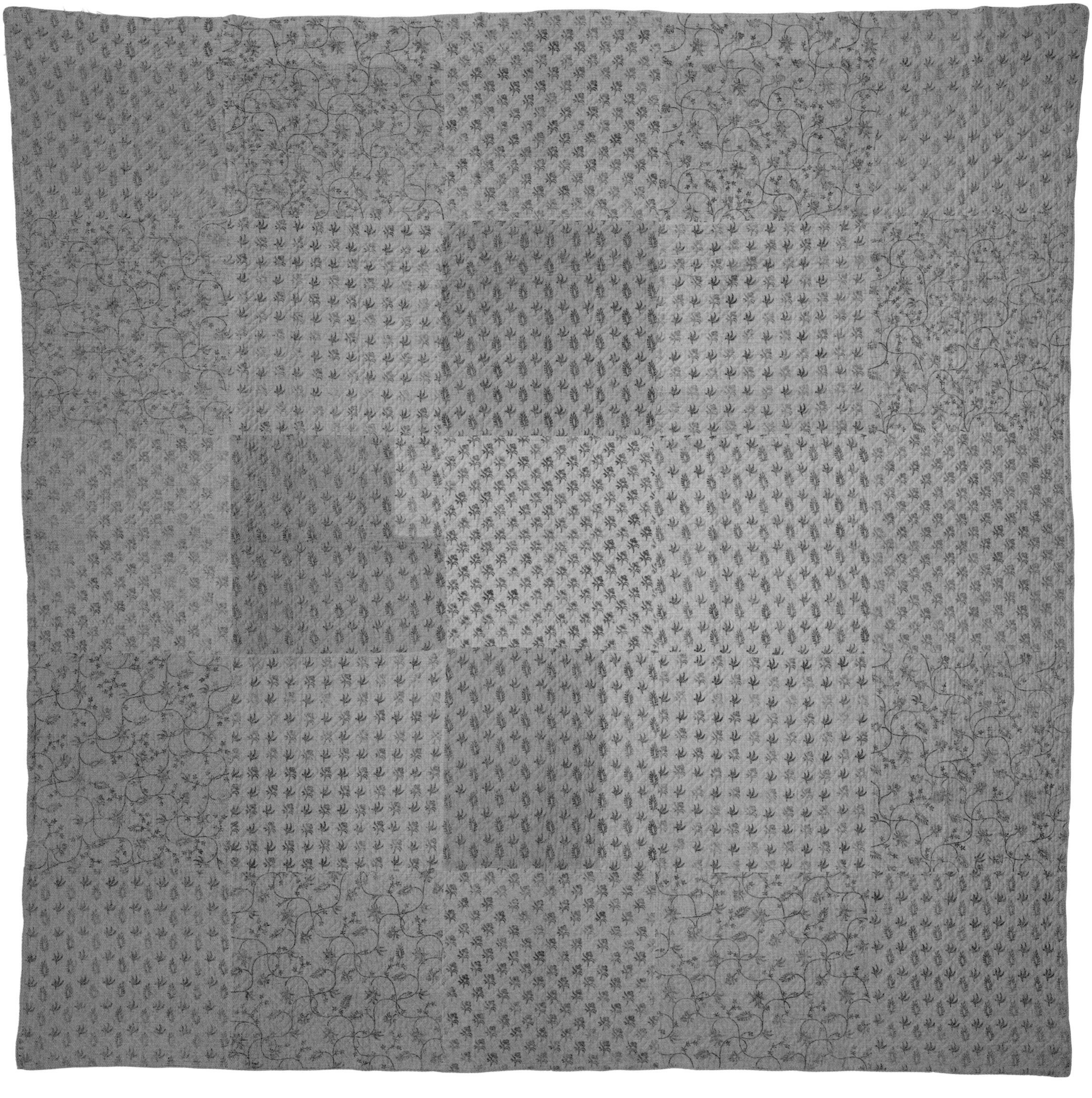

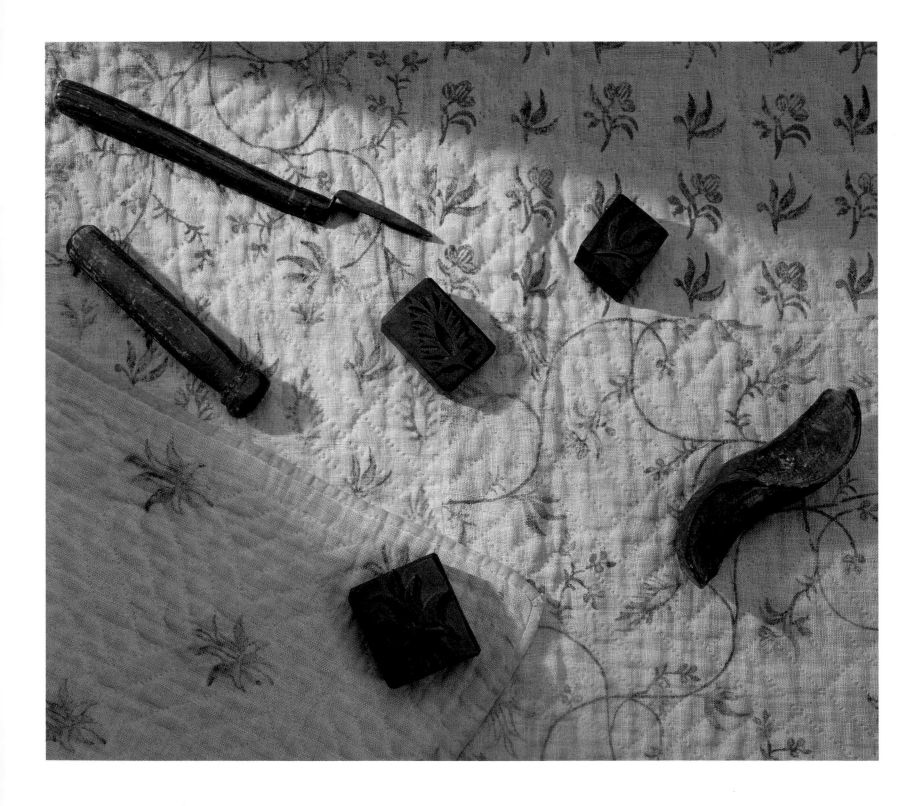

This method is quicker, easier, and far less expensive than the traditional mordant process. Rarely cited in instruction manuals of the period, this is most clearly explained in a French book, *L'Art de Peindre et d'Imprimer les Toiles en Grand et Petit Teint*, published in 1800. After describing dyestuffs like brazilwood, used for a red that is less fast than the traditional madder, the author briefly describes a technique using colors "ground in oil" (*broyées à l'huile*). These are considered fast, and will not come off unless boiled and scrubbed, but they are easily abraded.[65] It is these pigments in oil that have been identified on examples in Winterthur's collection.

Applying pigments in an oil medium directly onto a fabric is a variant form of what is termed the "direct style" of textile printing, characteristically different from the madder style, which involves printing a mordant and then immersing the cloth in a madder dyebath. This process also differs from the dyes known as mineral or steam colors, a complicated type of direct-style printing that was developed by sophisticated chemists and colorists in the early nineteenth century, using chrome, manganese, and various other metallic substances to apply color directly to the cloth.[66] It is also different from what is known as the pigment style of printing, developed later in the nineteenth century when albumen was most commonly used as the binding medium.[67] Textiles decorated with the pigment-in-oil technique most closely resemble the European printed fabrics and the painted or stained cloths imitating tapestries that have been dated to the fourteenth through the sixteenth centuries. According to Walter McCrone, the image of Christ on the Shroud of Turin was also probably made using this technique.[68] This form of low-quality printing was probably used continuously in Europe from the Middle Ages through to the period of the early American republic. Because most examples were of poor quality, they were probably almost all discarded until the significance of the few examples left was recognized and they began to be treasured as relics of early American manufacture.

Pigment-in-oil printing was first identified on two quilts in Winterthur's collection that have survived together with the wooden blocks used to print them. They were purchased by Henry Francis du Pont from the well-known dealer Winsor White in 1947. White had, in turn, purchased them from James Copeland Waterman, in whose family they descended.[69]

Many quilts have family histories of being made from linen that was raised, spun, and woven on the family farm, and in this case the story may well be true. Superb detective work by local historian Barbara Barker has located the farm in what is now Norwell (at the time, it was part of Scituate). The original owner of the property was Captain Benjamin Tolman who, not surprisingly, is said to have operated a tannery that was continued by subsequent generations.[70]

The North River divides the towns of Hanover and Scituate, which was a center of shipbuilding in the eighteenth and early nineteenth centuries. It is reported that 115 vessels were built there between 1799 and 1804.[71] Local histories mention that sailcloth was also woven in the area, and equipment for processing flax survives in the collection of the Hanover local history society. Other major local industries include a tack- and nail-making firm, whose owner patented various inventions and improvements to mechanize the production methods.[72] But no written records have been found of a linen-stamping business in the area.

The top of the quilt illustrated on page 99 is made from a variety of handspun and handwoven linen fabrics printed in five different patterns in red, dark blue, or a combination of the two colors; its wholecloth backing was printed with a different dark blue design. The quilt shown on pages 102–3 is made of two different linen fabrics, the front and back being printed with different motifs. A third quilt, in the collection of Old Sturbridge Village, has a border printed in motifs made from a complex grouping of five of the small blocks used on the backing of the quilt just cited.[73]

Right **Detail, Wholecloth Quilt**
A member of the Waterman family used a variety of small stamps to create this pattern of undulating stems and florets in imitation of fashionable British printed cottons. The main component of the dark blue/black pigment is lead, with small amounts of tin and iron.

Opposite, left **Detail, Wholecloth Quilt**
The reverse of the quilt at right is made from a fabric with a repeating floral design printed using a combination of blocks.

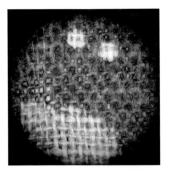

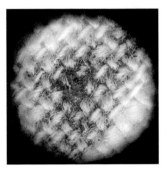

Top **Photomicrograph, Indigo Resist**
Indigo is a vat dye that is not printed using a mordant. To obtain a printed pattern, areas that are to remain white are covered in a paste. Then the fabric is dipped into the indigo. When the paste is removed, the protected area is white, but the remainder is dyed blue. Indigo soaks into the fibers like mordant dyes.

Above **Photomicrograph, Prussian Blue Pigment**
Prussian blue pigment particles sit on the surface of this fiber, distinguishing them from a dyestuff. The color loss is from abrasion of the surface rather than from light fading.

Wholecloth Counterpane
This cotton counterpane was made using Prussian blue and vermilion pigments. Formal in design, like other examples of pigment- printed fabrics, the motifs are made up from a variety of fairly small blocks.

Analysis undertaken by Janice Carlson in Winterthur's Scientific Research and Analysis Laboratory (SRAL) of the colored residue on the printing blocks identified the standard pigments employed in the late eighteenth and early nineteenth centuries, namely vermilion, Prussian blue, a copper-based green (probably verdigris), and lead white. Analysis of the pigments on the quilts was more difficult as they could not be sampled, but seemed to point to similar pigments as found on the blocks.[74] The presence of lead together with small amounts of iron and tin in the second quilt (above) indicates that the blue color was not obtained from Prussian blue. It was thought that this pigment could be a relatively rare pigment known as vivianite, blue ocher, or native Prussian blue. This pigment is a "blue phosphate of iron found in Cornwall and North America," and occurs as a secondary mineral in association with tin.[75] Further analysis, however has not confirmed this; the pigment remains unidentified.[76] Analysis of the binding medium on the blocks showed that it was probably linseed oil, a drying oil often found in paints. Visual examination of both Waterman quilts shows quite clearly, particularly under magnification, that bits of particulate color sit on the surface of the fibers and do not saturate it in the way that a traditional dyestuff does.

Having identified this pigment-in-oil technique of printing, the search was on for other examples. One was found on an older linen fabric that was reused for the back of a tied comforter. The top is made from a red roller-printed fabric that dates to the 1830s. Once again the colors printed on the plain woven linen were found to be Prussian blue, lead white, vermilion, and a copper-based green. Although the medium would seem to be oil-based it was not possible to confirm this because samples could not be removed from the quilt.[77] The design was again produced with a number of smaller-size blocks. All three of these quilts are stamped with

repeating patterns that relate closely in design to more traditional printed calicoes of their time, and would therefore seem to date stylistically to between 1790 and 1820. Sadly this comforter has no known provenance.

Winterthur's collection contains two examples of blue printed on cotton rather than linen fabrics, where the appearance of the printing technique does not resemble traditional printing processes. Unlike the previous examples on linen, the color on the following examples has soaked into the cloth substrate more completely. Analysis indicates the use of a Prussian blue pigment with an oil binder.[78] The first is a fragment cut from a larger cloth, depicting the eagle and shield of the Great Seal of the United States. Although not itself a quilt, a second version of this cloth forms part of a quilted counterpane in the collection of the National Museum of American History at the Smithsonian Institution. The only difference between the designs of these two fabrics is that Winterthur's example has stars surrounding the central motif while the example at the Smithsonian has a series of motifs consisting of a flower on a stem with two leaves; otherwise, they were printed using the same blocks. Winterthur's fragment has no provenance, but the Smithsonian counterpane is said to have been printed in Kentucky for a Mrs. Farris, whose daughter Elizabeth C. Nunn is said to have lined and quilted it.[79] Both have been dated to between 1812 and 1816, on the basis of the eighteen stars that appear on Winterthur's example, as the eighteenth state, Louisiana, was admitted to the Union in 1812, while Indiana was admitted as the nineteenth state in 1816.[80] It is probably no coincidence that Kentucky is the home of one of the most famous supporters of American manufactures, Henry Clay. In 1789 the Kentucky Society for the Encouragement of Manufactures was organized with the intention of building a cotton mill, which was producing fabrics by 1790. But little is known about this early industry.[81]

Above **Detail, Wholecloth Comforter**
Printed in a pattern with a half-drop
repeat, the designs on this fabric
were made using small blocks for
individual motifs.

Right **Backing, Wholecloth Comforter**
Purchased from the Andrews sisters
of Rhode Island, the origin of this
tied comforter is unknown. The face
(made from the fabric seen above)
is a red roller-printed cotton from
the 1830s. The backing is made of an
older linen fabric, block printed with
the pigments Prussian blue, vermilion, lead white, and copper green,
probably in a medium of linseed oil.

Left Elizabeth C. Nunn Quilt
This quilt from the collection of the National Museum of American History at the Smithsonian Institution is made from a counterpane printed with the same blocks as those used for Winterthur's fragment above. The blue pigment has turned to a greenish gray, indicative of considerable washing; the Prussian blue is known to turn this color in alkaline conditions.

Above Quilt Center
Printed with Prussian blue in an oil medium, the pigment particles have soaked into the cotton. This fragment was cut from the center of a counterpane.

The origin of the second example is unknown. The stamped counterpane also depicts the Great Seal of the United States: in this case there are fifteen stars above the eagle, which may indicate a date of between 1792, when Kentucky was admitted, and 1796, when Tennessee was admitted. However, the number of stars does not necessarily indicate the number of states in the Union at the time of manufacture, but could just be the number needed for their decorative placement. More awkwardly placed are the twenty-four eight-pointed stars in the center field, which could indicate a date between 1821, when Missouri was admitted, and the 1836 statehood of Arkansas.

A case could be made for both the earlier and later dates from the stylistic elements of the bedcover. The motif of a bird on a branch, repeated four times in the central field, is very similar to those printed by John Hewson, a fashionable motif found during the second half of the eighteenth century. The fleur-de-lis motif that is repeated inside the outer border could signify France under the rule of the Bourbon kings, remembering that Louis XVI was executed in January of 1793, but it could also be interpreted as an anthemion, a classical motif popular in the nineteenth century. The repeated star-medallions in the outer field resemble designs popular in the second quarter of the nineteenth century, as does the central, lobed medallion. This piece was purchased from the influential dealer J. A. Lloyd Hyde, who claimed that it came from Rhode Island, but provided no information to confirm this attribution. Analysis has shown that this counterpane was printed using a Prussian blue pigment in an oil medium.[82]

Although the trade in dyestuffs and mordants was international in nature, the Prussian blue pigment may well have been made in the United States. One of the growing industries in the early American republic was the manufacturing of chemicals and pigments. Pearl and potash, important sources of alkalinity for the dyeing industry, was always in demand and formed an important export to Britain. Paints, pigments, mordants like copperas and alum, dyestuffs, and other coloring materials, as well as chemicals of various sorts were increasingly produced in America after the Revolution, and growth was particularly strong in the early nineteenth century. It became noteworthy in period advertisements to denote items of American manufacture. Prussian blue, it was said, could be manufactured more cheaply in the United States than in Europe.

American domestic manufactures, also known generically as homespun, were first promoted in the 1760s to protest the imposition of taxes on the colonies. After the Revolution, American-made products continued to be advocated by Benjamin Franklin; by economists like Tench Coxe in Philadelphia; by publications such as *Niles' Weekly Register*, published between 1811 and 1849; and later by Henry Clay with his American system. His plan called for using protective tariffs to boost the development of American industries. A popular political figure, Clay ran for president five times but never won. He was reputed to have been even more popular than George Washington. Henry Remington, Mary's father, named his first son Henry Clay Remington, and the name has descended as a tradition in many other American families.

Detail, Wholecloth Counterpane
The eagle and shield depicted on the Great Seal, adopted by Congress in 1782, was one of the most popular images in early America. It was found on European fabrics printed for the American market as well as on American-made fabrics, furniture, silver, ceramics, and glass.

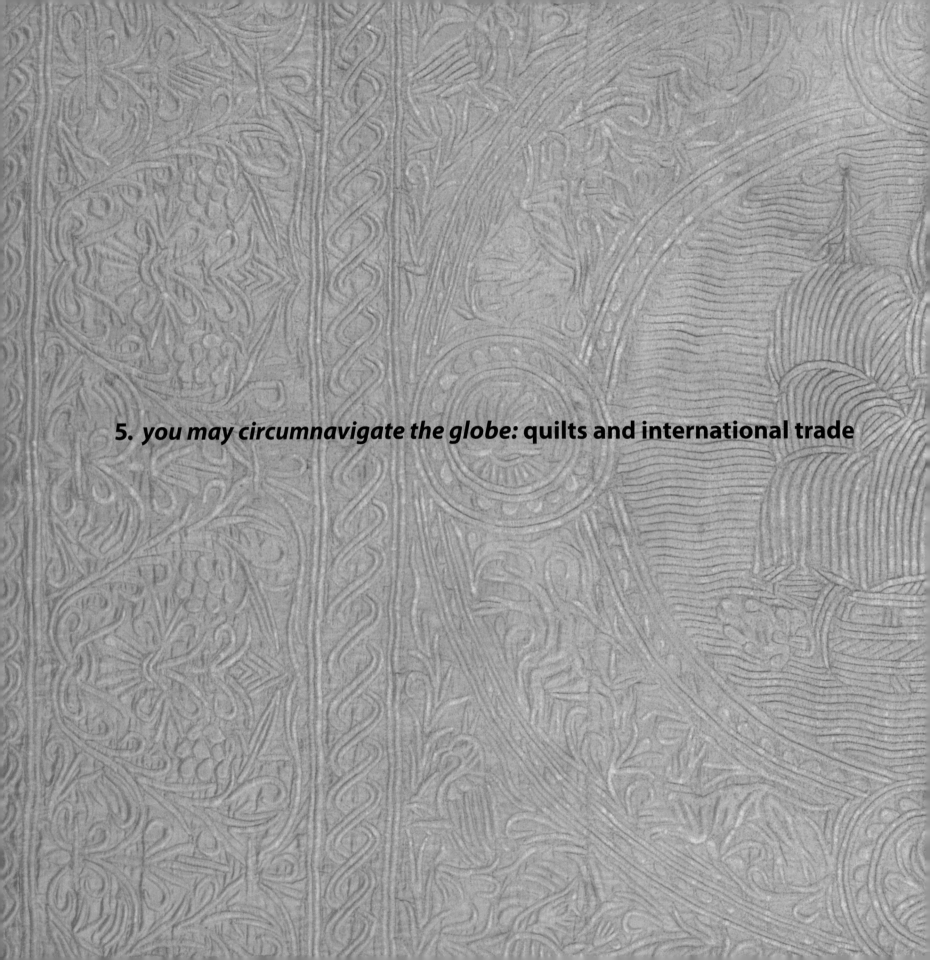

5. *you may circumnavigate the globe:* quilts and international trade

Previous pages **Detail, Wholecloth Quilt** Scholar and dealer Elinor Merrell sold this quilt to Henry Francis du Pont in 1943. A similar example, possibly its pair, survives in Cornwall, England. Other related quilts have provenances that connect them to Italy. Dye analysis and iconography confirm a European origin, but exactly where it was made remains unknown.

Opposite, left **Detail, Wholecloth Quilt** The sailing vessel depicted on this seventeenth-century quilt resembles a carrack—a type of ship originally designed by the Portuguese but copied by other European countries. Its presence explains why early catalogue records describe this quilt as Portuguese.

Opposite, right **Detail, Wholecloth Quilt** The bright yellow dye in this quilt has been identified as weld, also known as dyer's rocket, an ancient European dyestuff often used on silk and wool. The pink is probably from brazilwood, whose color shifts with changes in pH. Although widely used, it was not fast to light or washing.

uilts, as well as the textiles from which they were made, have always been associated with world trade. Advertisements in the *Pennsylvania Gazette* throughout the eighteenth century list fabrics and quilting from Persia, India, Flanders, Turkey, Hamburg, Holland, Russia, Scotland, England, France, and more specifically Marseilles.[1] Despite the fact that she never traveled farther than Connecticut, Mary Remington was personally connected to the worldwide trade in goods. Apponaug Cove was quite deep, and "sloops of fifteen tons burden" offloaded at the dock of Jacob Greene & Co., visible from the back windows of Mary's home.[2] The Greenes were part of the large and tightly knit merchant community that involved many Rhode Island families, including Mary's own cousins, the Holdens. Mary's fiancé, Peleg Congdon, wrote to her about his experiences crossing the Atlantic and described his travels in Sweden and Denmark.

Mary was not unique in her personal connections to people engaged in world trade. The wives, sisters, daughters, cousins, and friends of merchants and sailors also had connections to international ports through direct contact with people who had been there. Sailors tended to be relatively young men, many of whom later came home to become artisans or shopkeepers, and who no doubt recounted their adventures for their less well-traveled friends and clients.[3] While some wealthy women, often the wives or daughters of merchants or diplomats, had direct experience of living in exotic foreign ports, knowledge of the world was usually obtained secondhand, but was a common topic of everyday conversation in coastal New England. Mary's son, John Remington Congdon, became a ship captain like his father. His wife, Cynthia Sprague Congdon, traveled the world with him from 1852 to 1854, and kept a diary of her experiences.[4] Winterthur's quilt collection documents international trade from the seventeenth to the nineteenth century.

The earliest known quilt was made in Sicily around 1400, depicting scenes from the legend of Tristan. Similar quilts formed part of the trade in luxury goods that came into Europe through Genoa and other Mediterranean port cities.[5] Few others have been identified that predate a group of related reversible silk wholecloth quilts from the seventeenth century. The example from this group in the collection at Winterthur, designed and executed in the opulent style of the early baroque period, exemplifies the continuing trade in luxury goods. These quilts were once thought to have been made in either India or Portugal. Winterthur's example was purchased in 1943 by Henry Francis du Pont from Elinor Merrell, who did not ascribe a country of origin to it.[6] This was wise, because recent research has clearly shown that the origin of these quilts was neither India nor Portugal. They were possibly made on the Aegean island of Chios, which was controlled by Genoese merchants and occupied by the Ottoman Turks after 1566.[7]

Dye analysis undertaken by the Koninklijk Instituut Voor Het Kunstpatrimonium in Brussels also confirms a European origin for this quilt.[8] The striking yellow silk on one side of the reversible quilt was obtained from weld (*Reseda luteola L.*), the most frequently used yellow dyestuff in Europe during the seventeenth century, but not one encountered in a study of dyes on early Indian silks.[9] The other side, now pink in color, was dyed with a redwood, probably brazilwood. Because of the poor lightfastness of redwood dyes, it is believed that the original color of the back would have been a deeper red. The use of redwood dyes is only mentioned once in an extensive study on the natural dyes used in India.[10] The silk itself is a lightweight plain weave, with a selvage width of approximately 29 inches. Silkworms were raised on Chios as early as the fourteenth century, and the silk woven into fabrics of this unusually wide width that were said to be comparable to the silks produced in India, Persia, and Lyons.[11] The quilting has been done in a two-ply yellow silk thread, a standard European

embroidery silk, in a running stitch. Loose rolls of cotton, a fiber also known to have been grown on Chios, create the three-dimensional imagery, while spaces between the quilted motifs have no filling.

Early quilts, like blankets, were sold in pairs, and it is intriguing to speculate about whether the mate for Winterthur's quilt has survived in England.[12] It has been suggested that the iconography of the quilt sets up a dichotomy between the East and West at a time when exotic imports were coming into Europe in increasing quantity via the recently discovered sea routes to the Far East. The quilt in England has a wide border filled with hunters and game rather than the triangular flowers found on the Winterthur quilt. Instead of men in turbans and cloaks, its corner blocks contain Hapsburg double-headed eagles. The men in the portrait medallions on the inner ring of the British quilt wear high-crowned narrow-brimmed European hats, while those on the Winterthur quilt wear turbans.[13] The earlier attribution of the Winterthur quilt to Portugal was probably made on the basis of the central image of a ship. Many early twentieth-century sources identify the vessel as a specific type of merchant ship originally designed by the Portuguese. In the seventeenth century, ships represented the political and military might of nations intent on building empires. One famous ship, called *Sovereign of the Seas*, was built in 1637 for Charles I of England at enormous expense, and was refitted in 1660 at a time of increasing tension that led to the second war with the Dutch in 1665.[14] Margaret Renner Lidz relates the ship and its iconography to the famous Battle of Lepanto in 1571, when a "multinational flotilla shattered the Turkish navy in what was the first major victory by European forces against the Ottomans. A psychological turning point for the West, the victory was celebrated during the next century in many art forms, including tiles, paintings, and tapestries."[15]

H. F. du Pont purchased the quilt with the intention of putting it in the Hart Room, the earliest period room

at Winterthur. Many American collectors at the turn of the twentieth century were using the sumptuous furnishings found in the stately homes and palaces of Europe to interpret more modest American interiors. This was particularly true for seventeenth-century interiors, a period from which few textiles survive that were actually used in America.

The architecture in Winterthur's Hart Room came from a house built by Thomas Hart in Ipswich, Massachusetts, around 1640. The Metropolitan Museum of Art purchased two of the original rooms from the house in 1936, using one to replace their earlier reproduction of the downstairs chamber. The museum sold the second room to Henry Francis du Pont the following year, and he had it installed in the old squash court in the basement at the north end of Winterthur. The quilt was probably used in the Hart Room until 1948 when a furnishing plan, which was created as du Pont began to work with professional curators to determine more historically accurate interiors, did not include a bed. A low post bed was installed in the Hart Room in 1978 and was covered with an equally inappropriate red brocatelle bedcover. Although the Puritans owned many elegant textiles and viewed material wealth as a sign of God's blessing, it is highly unlikely that Thomas Hart could have afforded such an exotic and expensive quilt. Hart came to America as a servant and later became a tanner by trade. We know from his probate inventory that he did own a fully furnished bed that probably had wool hangings, as well as a flock bed with a bed rug.[16]

Sea routes to China and India were discovered by explorers in the early sixteenth century, changing the nature of merchant activity around the world. In the late sixteenth and early seventeenth centuries, European traders took Indian textiles to the Spice Islands where they were exchanged for spices that were shipped back to Europe together with a few cheap, coarse cottons. Higher-quality silks and hand-painted cottons, some of which were quilted, trickled into Europe in small quantities in the early seventeenth century, but by the end of the century, this commerce had become a flood that threatened the silk, wool, and linen industries of Europe. The demand that fueled the mechanization of European cotton spinning, weaving, and printing industries, and played a central role in the Industrial Revolution, originated with these imported goods. This so-called "China trade," much of which was in fact with India, forever changed the world of textiles.

Winterthur's collection includes an early example from this trade which is extremely rare. Its rarity is due to the materials from which it is made. Many embroidered bedcovers, known as quilts in the period, survive. Made with polychrome silk embroidery on a white cotton ground, they are thought to have come from Satgaon, near the modern Calcutta, once the merchant capital of Bengal. Evidence of only two other examples like the one in Winterthur's collection has been published. One is a fragment in the Tapi Collection in India, and the other is in the Palazzo Venezia in Rome.[17]

The other examples, whose iconography depicts a variety of figures within a formal structure of compartments and borders, have been attributed to the Indo-Portuguese trade. The exclusively floral motifs and the provenance of Winterthur's bedcover suggests that it was part of the early trade of the English East India Company. Donated by David and Emita Stockwell, it was acquired by them at the famous auction of household furnishings at Ashburnham Place in Sussex, England, that took place in 1953 after the death of Lady Catherine, the last representative of the family that had lived there for more than 800 years.[18]

The Ashburnhams were wealthy courtiers and patrons of the arts, and the auction included important paintings, silver, jewelry, furniture, carpets, and historical relics.[19] It may well have been Sir John Ashburnham (1602/3–1671), known as the Cavalier, who purchased this quilt. The family's fortune was originally built on iron, but lucrative appointments at court, advantageous

marriages, and the acquisition of property were the basis of the family's wealth in the seventeenth century. As Groom of the Bedchamber to Charles I, Ashburnham found many opportunities to enrich himself and his family, but he suffered both personally and financially after the king's execution. Having helped to finance the Royalist forces during the English Civil War, Ashburnham was fined and imprisoned. Accused of having betrayed Charles I on the Isle of Wight, which resulted in the king's capture and execution, Sir John was later vindicated and served again as Groom of the Bedchamber after the restoration of Charles II to the throne.[20]

The high point of the Ashburnham fortunes in the seventeenth century was from the 1620s through the 1640s, just when the United East India Company of England was beginning to trade in Hugli, an area of Bengal previously controlled by the Portuguese.[21] Technique, materials, and design would indicate a date for this bedcover from the first half of the seventeenth century, just at the time that the Ashburnhams had money to spend, and quilts from this part of India were being imported into London as exotic luxuries.

The first mention of these embroidered quilts is an auction in London in 1618.[22] Shortly afterward, Robert Hughes, a factor for the East India Company, attempted to set up a new factory at Patna and wrote on November 11, 1620, that he had sent specimens of "Sutgonge" quilts "bought at such reasonable rates that wee expecte good muzera for them from the Companye. Theye are not made here, but brought from the bottom of Bengala. . . . Other sortes of quiltes are not here to bee gotten of any kinde."[23]

The white cotton chain-stitch embroidery is done through the golden muga silk and then lined with a coarse, plain-weave cotton. The two fabrics are tacked together with cotton thread, following the embroidered motifs. Although now somewhat soiled, originally the bright, white cotton would have contrasted with the

Stamp, Wholecloth Quilt

Various stamps were used on the back of palampores, and they often bled through to the front. The square mark seen here contains the initials of the United East India Company. The circular stamps are known as tamil marks. They are often found on palampores, but their purpose is unknown. Similar tamil marks appear on a palampore in the collection of the Royal Ontario Museum that has been dated to the mid-1700s.

glittering, golden muga silk to create a subtle but luxurious and beautiful bedcover.

By the late seventeenth century, the majority of the quilts imported into Europe from India were made from painted or printed cottons, decorated to shape for bedcovers and in repeating patterns for dress goods. Unlike anything seen before in Europe, these fabrics were lightweight, easily cleaned, and brightly decorated in patterns of many colors.

The heavy trunk and branches of the central flowering tree; large, heavy blossoms; and lack of fussy filling motifs date Winterthur's quilted palampore stylistically to the first half of the eighteenth century. The word "palampore" was not widely used in the period—it does not appear in either Samuel Johnson's dictionary of 1755 nor Noah Webster's American dictionary of 1806, but it does occasionally show up in government export records and period advertisements. In 1886, the word palampore was defined as being "A kind of chintz bedcover," thought to have been derived from the Persian and Hindi word palangposh.[24] Although its original owner remains elusive, the palampore was inherited by Anna Maria Boyer, who died in 1884 in Middletown, Delaware, at the age of eighty-eight. Her Boyer, Rumsey, and Rigbie ancestors were wealthy Maryland landowners, many of whom were active in public affairs in the early eighteenth century.[25]

Available in a wide range of prices and quality, it was not these hand-painted palampores but rather the middle range of chintzes for clothing that threatened the cheaper products of the British wool and silk industries—half-silks, slight silks, and lightweight worsteds were major sources of that country's wealth.[26] They became popular and widely available at a time of great social change, as the middle classes, particularly merchants and master artisans, were acquiring wealth that rivaled the upper class and nobility, whose income had traditionally been based on land ownership, agriculture, and remunerative positions at court. This social and

political instability exacerbated the furor surrounding the introduction of these new fabrics into Britain, making the propaganda war waged by pamphleteers all the more vituperative. Such "a tawdery, pie-spotted, flabby, ragged, low priz'd Thing call'd Callico, a Foreigner by Birth, made . . . by a parcel of Heathens and Pagans, that worship the devil and work for a Half penny a Day." was said to be putting the wool and silk weavers out of work.[27] Before the first acts that banned its importation into Britain in the late seventeenth century, the extravagant use of Indian printed and painted cottons was said to be the cause of excess as "Ladies converted their carpets and quilts into gowns and petticoats and made the broad and uncouth Bordures of the former serve instead of the rich laces and embroideries they were used to wear, and dressed more like the Merry-Andrews of Bartholomew Fair than like the Ladies and Wives of a Trading People."[28] The fuss was about the chintzes for clothing, rather than quilts and other furnishings, and it was felt by at least one anti-calico propagandist that "if printed calicoes were only used for aprons, frocks and quilts then no great harm would be done."[29]

Quilts are known to have been stitched in India before export, but Indian fabrics were also professionally quilted in England. A broadsheet entitled "The Case of the Makers of Quilts for Beds Only" argued that using "printed callicoe carpets" to make bed quilts was not detrimental to the manufacturers of wool, "there being great Quantities of Norwich, Kidderminster, Kendal, and other Stuffs, used for the Backsides of Quilts; beside abundance of Ordinary Wooll, which must otherwise be thrown away; it being too short for Spinning, and fit for no Other Use."[30]

Winterthur's palampore was quilted in Britain or America. Although it is filled with cotton batting, the quilting thread is two-ply linen, a type of thread not used in India. The backing is a coarse plain-weave fabric made mostly from cotton but with some linen fibers spun in the same yarn. This mixture of fibers has only

Overleaf, left **Wholecloth Quilt**
This wholecloth quilt, called a palampore, is one of the few known to have been used in America before the Revolutionary War. It was given to Winterthur by Gertrude Brincklé, the personal secretary to Brandywine Valley artist and illustrator Howard Pyle. She had inherited it from her aunt, Susan Rumsey Brincklé, who in turn had received it as a gift from her cousin Anna Maria Boyer.

Overleaf, right **Appliqué Counterpane**
Indian palampores influenced the design of American quilts in the early nineteenth century, the high point of the direct trade between India and the United States. This counterpane from the early 1800s has birds and a butterfly cut from fabrics printed by John Hewson, the Philadelphia calico printer who learned his trade at Bromley Hall, a Quaker printworks on the River Lea, on the east side of London.

Left Embroidered Quilt
Silk-embroidered bedcovers decorated with flat quilting were made by professional embroiderers in England from the late 1600s to the mid-1700s.

Opposite, above Quilted and Embroidered Cushion Cover
Quilts made in the late 1600s and early 1700s often had one or more matching cushion covers. Cushions could be placed against the bolster at the head of the bed or on top of one another at the foot. The covers were also sometimes used on cushions for seating furniture in the room.

Opposite, below Photomicrograph
The red design for the background quilting was drawn on both the quilt and cushion cover in red ink. The design for the embroidery, drawn in black ink, was done after the quilting was completed. This was the work of more than one needleworker (who could have been either a man or a woman). The quilt and matching cushion cover are the products of a commercial workshop in England.

recently come to the attention of textile historians, and has been found in sixteenth-century laces as well as indigo-resist fabrics made in Britain and other parts of Europe.[31] It is now being found on other eighteenth-century printed fabrics at Winterthur that had been identified as all cotton in the past. The presence of linen spun into the yarns indicates an origin in Europe or America and not India. At some stage before being quilted, the palampore lost its upper border, originally the wide border of undulating stems and flowers would have been present on all four sides. The palampore itself carries the characteristic lozenge-shaped stamp of the United East India Company on the back, which can be clearly seen in reverse from the front. This type of stamp appears on textiles produced for the company throughout the eighteenth century. The other two circular marks are sometimes known as "tamil" marks, but their purpose remains unclear.[32]

The import of Indian painted and printed cottons was hit with a heavy tariff of fifteen percent from 1695 to 1696, and was banned in Britain in 1701.[33] This ban was unsuccessful in stemming the flow, and both the import and wearing of Indian cottons was outlawed in 1721. It was still legal to import Indian cottons into London for subsequent export, but smuggling was rife.

The French, also in protection of their silk and wool industries, had banned both the import and the manufacture of printed or painted cottons in 1686, an attempt that proved to be as unsuccessful as the English efforts. French-made imitations were allowed in 1752, and, in 1760, taxes were levied on imported goods to protect the growing French textile printing industry.[34] The American colonies were one of the fastest growing export markets for Indian furnishing and dress chintz. An inscription on a quilted palampore in the collection of the Smithsonian Institution reads "This Quilt was purchased 1736 of a Smuggler of East India goods in the Isle of White [sic], England. Belonging to my late friend Miss Bradford. Elizabeth Smith, Charles-

ton." Elizabeth Smith's friend must have been English, for there would have been no need for an American to buy smuggled goods.[35] It is ironic that most surviving examples are from the period when they were banned.[36]

Most discussions of palampores and Indian chintz concentrate on the early period, during the seventeenth and eighteenth centuries, when small numbers of very high-quality hand-painted cottons were acquired by the wealthy. The majority of the few surviving palampores in American collections with American provenances, however, date from the very late eighteenth and into the nineteenth century. These are periods for which some scholars consider the designs and executions to have become debased, and when cotton fabrics of all types had become cheaper and more widely available.[37] The first American ship to trade directly with India, the *United States*, sailed from Philadelphia in the spring of 1784 and returned home the following year with a cargo that included "Patampores, or Bed Covers."[38]

The first self-made American millionaire, Frederic Tudor of Boston, took part in a little-known aspect of the lucrative trade with India, earning vast profits by shipping ice from the ponds and lakes of New England to the hot, humid India. In Calcutta, "everybody invited everybody to dinner, to taste of claret and beer cooled by the American importation." Evidently, American ice contained less grit than ice from the much closer Himalaya mountains to the north of India.[39] The flowering tree found on these palampores, an exotic motif that was a fusion of influences from both Eastern and Western cultures, clearly influenced the design of many quilts made in America in the early nineteenth century.

Records in the port books indicate that a large number of quilts made in Britain were exported to America in the eighteenth century, but it is unlikely that any resembled a second extraordinarily fine and costly quilt purchased by the Stockwells from the 1953 Ashburnham Place sale. Dating to the 1720s, it is one of a group

of similar quilts in various collections including the Victoria and Albert Museum, the Metropolitan Museum of Art, and the Art Institute of Chicago. It was probably acquired by another John Ashburnham, a great-grandson of John Ashburnham the Cavalier. His father, yet another John, inherited Ashburnham Place together with many other family properties, on the death of the Cavalier and was made a baron. This third John was a second son, but he inherited the title and estates when his older brother and sister-in-law died of smallpox in 1710. The third John, named the first Earl of Ashburnham and Viscount St. Asaph in 1730, had three wives. It may have been around the time of his third marriage in March of 1723/4 to Jemima, the daughter and co-heir of Henry de Grey, the first Duke of Kent, that this embroidered and quilted bedcover was acquired.[40] One matching cushion cover survives, which would have been displayed propped up against the bolster at the head of the bed.[41]

The quilt is made from a very fine cotton face and embellished with elaborate gold silk embroidery in a design of strapwork and flowers. Made by professionals as a commercial product, the quilting is done with a very fine backstitch (the number of stitches per inch ranges from 18 to 28 in different areas) in yellow silk that was sewn on a design drawn on the cotton in red. This ink has been found to contain both mercury and sulfur, suggesting vermilion, a pigment sometimes used in inks as well as paints.[42]

Little is known about the materials used to create designs on fabrics for embroiderers to follow. Charles Germain de Saint-Aubin, the son of an embroiderer and a designer to King Louis XV of France, does not mention the use of red ink for drawing embroidery designs in his book *L'Art du Brodeur*, published in France in 1770, but only India blue ink or white lead.[43] The red lines are clearly visible on this quilt, so the choice of color must have been deliberate, possibly with the intention of enriching the gold color. Gold leaf was usually applied

on top of a red bole for the same reason.[44] Red ink was only used for the geometric quilting. The design for the embroidery was done in black ink on the already quilted fabric. This style of quilting was fashionable from the late seventeenth century through the early eighteenth. Many examples were embroidered in polychrome silk, but the golden yellow monochrome embroidery was the height of fashion in the 1720s. Because there is no batting, cording, or stuffing, this type of quilting is sometimes known as "flat" or "false quilting."

Great quantities of British-made quilts were imported into the American colonies during the eighteenth century. Quilts were also made in America from imported British cloth, both high-end glazed, worsted calimancoes, and the printed cottons manufactured first in London and later in Manchester and other areas of the north, including Scotland. The policies of the British government intended that their colonies theoretically provide raw materials in exchange for the manufactured goods, a fair proportion of which were textiles; this formed an increasingly important part of the national economy. Fortunes were certainly made in the textile-printing industry, initially in London but, as the Industrial Revolution took hold, the center of production moved north. Merchants who shipped these products to the American colonies also made sizable profits.

Many examples of English plate-printed furnishing cottons survive in America. Enormous quantities were made, but relatively few can be positively identified through period sample books in collections in England and France.[45] A number of designs that can be attributed to the firm known collectively as Bromley Hall have been found in America, and evidence of the importation of their fabrics into Philadelphia and Baltimore survives in the records of Quaker merchant Richard Vaux, their largest distributor.[46]

Bromley Hall was in business by 1712, and operated in a series of partnerships between closely related

Quaker families through the early nineteenth century. Between 1763 and 1783, the firm was known Ollive & Talwin, then as Talwin & Foster until 1790, and finally Foster & Co. until 1823.[47] The Ten Eyck family of Albany, New York, owned a quilt with matching bedhangings made from a Bromley Hall design called "Ducks." Evidence of this pattern survives in a sample book at the Victoria and Albert Museum. The sample book also includes a number of designs with grasses and ferns, and a variety of birds from the 1770s and 1780s.[48] The few sample books that remain intact represent only a small number of textile printers active in the late eighteenth century; many others whose products have yet to be identified have been discovered through the documents kept by insurance companies whose records include descriptions of both large and small manufacturers.[49] With no copyright law in place, many designs were copied indiscriminately by other firms, and many similar designs remain frustratingly anonymous.

Both Peter Floud and Florence Montgomery have attributed the fabric on one of Winterthur's wholecloth quilts, similar to the ferns and grasses of Bromley Hall, to a slightly later date because of the lesser quality of the engraving. The early 1790s was a period when British fabrics were flooding the American market, as the continental markets were closed to them because of the war with France. The plate-printed design of small birds perched on thistles and ferns anchored to a meandering vine is from this period.

The same design, adapted to the shorter repeats necessitated by the diameter of rollers, or cylinders, is printed in blue on a second quilt at Winterthur. The 1780s and 1790s were a time of great technical developments. A Scotsman, Thomas Bell, is credited with inventing the first functional roller-printing mechanism in 1783, and this machine was being used by Christophe-Philippe Oberkampf in France by 1797.[50] Few examples of early roller-prints can be precisely dated, and most are

Left Wholecloth Quilt
Now brown in color, this plate-printed design was probably once purple. The color has shifted due to the aging of the iron mordant and the action of alkalies used in traditional laundry washing.

Above Design Repeat
The production of plate-printed designs was overtaken by the faster technology of cylinder printing by the second quarter of the nineteenth century. These two quilts represent one of two designs at Winterthur that exist in both a plate- and roller-printed version.

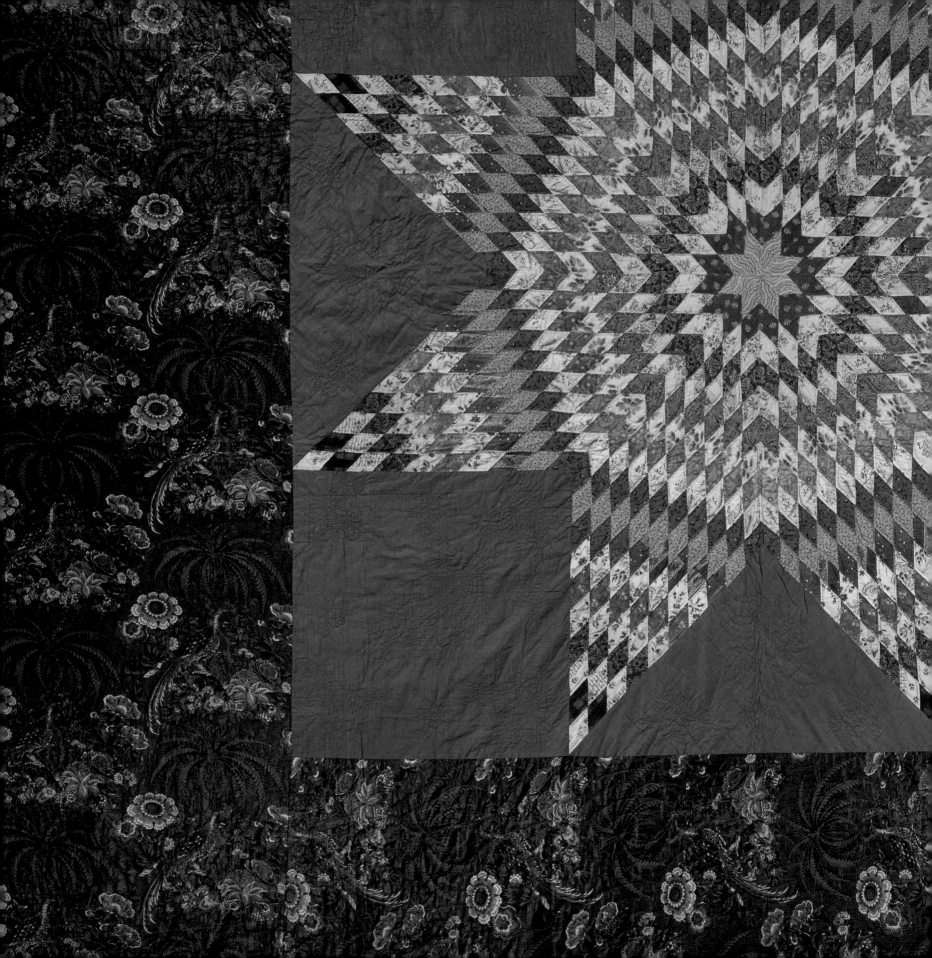

Opposite **Detail, Pieced Quilt**

Found in an attic, this quilt was probably made in the Mid-Atlantic region, possibly in Wilmington, Delaware. Analysis of some of the figured fabrics that make up the central star has shown that many were printed with early mineral dyes, which were fine pigments fixed to the cloth by chemical means. They were often bright in color.

Right **Colorways**

Popular fabrics were available in different colors. Five colorways of this English fabric, dumped on the American market after the War of 1812, survive in Winterthur's collection. Different technologies were used to print these fabrics: the example with the light-brown ground is block printed while the others are a combination of block- and cylinder-printing technology.

ascribed to the early nineteenth century because of the lesser quality of the engraving. It was the cylinder-printing machine that jump-started the American calico-printing industry in the 1820s.

A second period when great quantities of British printed cottons were dumped on the American market was after the War of 1812. Because the United States was a large and still expanding market for British goods, the embargoes and blockades that hindered international trade in the early nineteenth century had a detrimental impact on the British economy, but boosted the nascent American textile industry. Reports of the difficulties of the British manufacturers and their petitions to Parliament were reported in *Niles' Weekly Register*, one of the great promoters of American manufactures at this time. When the American markets opened up again at the end of the war, many American textile manufacturers, particularly cotton-spinners and weavers, suffered dramatically. In June of 1815, Mary Remington wrote that her friends "Mr. Smith, Mr. Westcott, Mr. Mullins, and Col. A. Harrison have all done with the Manufactory business," and many American cotton manufacturers failed.

Evidence in surviving sample books indicate that the fashion for block-printed cottons depicting game birds was strong between 1814 and 1816, and the large number of examples in American collections provide convincing proof that this style was imported into the United States in huge quantities at the close of the War of 1812.

One particular design, represented in Winterthur's collection in five colorways, was originally printed by Charles Swainson at Bannister Hall in Lancashire in 1815. Bannister Hall was noted for its high-quality blockprints and exported a large proportion of their printed cottons to America. The same pattern is also found in a stippled roller-print, with additional colors added either by surface rollers or blocks. It has been dated to the mid-1830s from the wild color com-

binations obtained through experimentation with developments in printing mineral colors.[51]

Perhaps the largest, longest, and most well-known aspect of the international trade in quilts was the type of quilting known as Marseilles work. Although a wide variety of materials in many different colors were used to make quilts in Marseilles and the wider area of Provence, the term has become associated primarily with whitework cotton quilts, like Mary Remington's, and has also been connected with woven imitations of hand-quilted whitework. Three different techniques were used in this type of quilting, which can be used together or separately. Corded quilting (sometimes also known as Italian quilting) is made by stitching a design in parallel rows of either running stitches or backstitches to form channels joining two layers of cloth. Cording, usually of cotton, is then inserted from the back to create a three-dimensional effect. The second method is known as stuffed work. Designs are stitched through two layers of cloth, and subsequently shaped by inserting some type of stuffing from the back. In the twentieth century, this came to be known as trapunto, a term that has not been found in period sources. The final type of quilting, known in France as *toiles piquées*, was made using the method most frequently employed by quilters today, where two layers of cloth are interleaved with a layer of batting. The quilted design, which may be either a simple grid or an elaborate set of figural or floral motifs, is then stitched through all three layers.[52]

Associated with the city of Marseilles, where enormous quantities of quilting was made in professional workshops and exported to many parts of the world (at least from the 1680s and probably also earlier), quilts produced using these same methods were also made in other countries throughout Europe. Winterthur's collection includes a wide range of these types of quilting from the seventeenth, eighteenth, and early nineteenth centuries, that have been attributed to both France and

Opposite, above **Dressing-table Cover**
The closely worked, curvilinear design on this broderie de Marseille dates it to the seventeenth or early eighteenth century. This type of high-quality professional work became famous throughout Europe and America, where any type of quilted or woven whitework came to be known as Marseilles quilting.

Opposite, below **Detail, Wholecloth Quilted Petticoat**
Purchased by the museum in 1963 from antiques dealer Doris Thacher, this quilted petticoat was described by her as late seventeenth- or early eighteenth-century "stuffed Indian petticoat material." There is no indication of where the piece originated, but it may have been used in America.

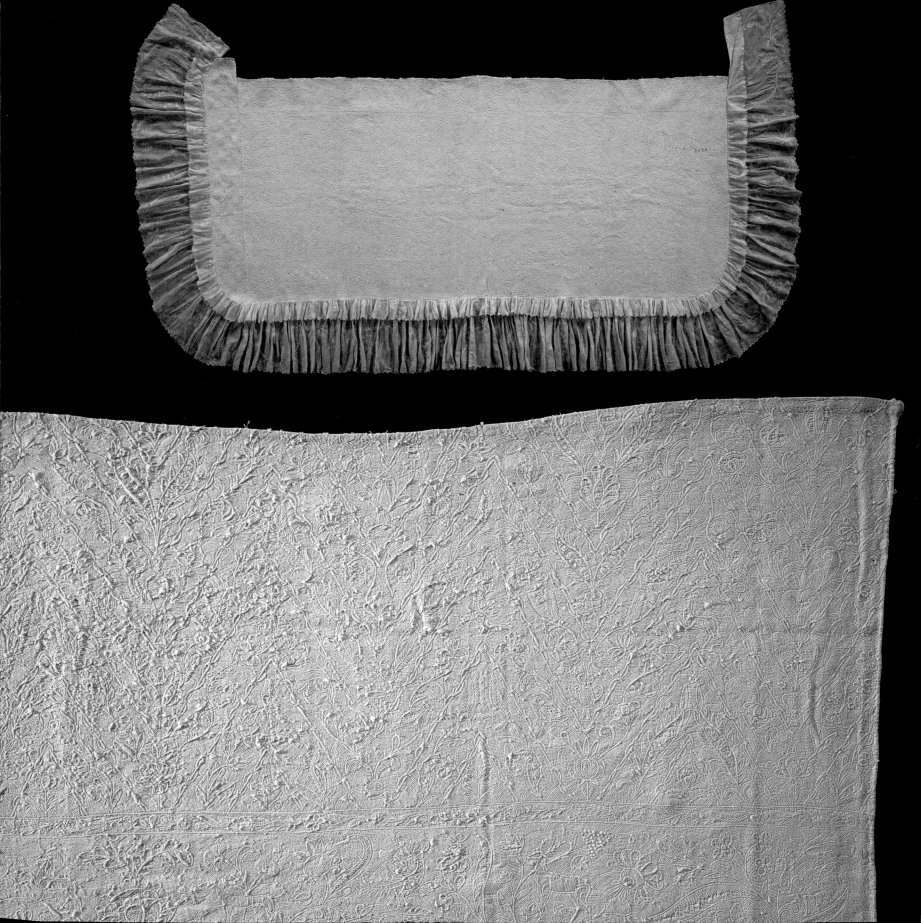

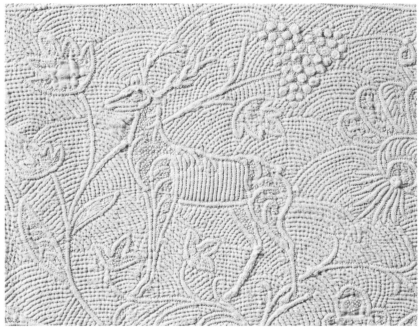

Left **Detail, Wholecloth Quilted Petticoat**
The quilted design on this petticoat repeats every 54 inches, and although the complete petticoat has not survived, it does include two figures of a soldier wearing the distinctive cap of a grenadier. The background quilting is worked with a running stitch; the figures and other main design elements are done using a backstitch.

Above **Detail, Wholecloth Quilted Petticoat**
A variety of embroidery stitches worked in white linen embellish this petticoat, indicative of its high quality and cost.

England or America. These are in the form of petticoats, bedcovers, foot-covers (known in French as *couvre-pieds*), and cushion covers. Some survive in their original form, while others have been altered and adapted for different uses in the nineteenth or early twentieth centuries.

Large numbers of French white-corded quilting has survived the centuries, but they are only a fraction of the enormous quantity of Marseilles quilting that was made. Corded quilting produced in Marseilles can be identified by the materials and, to a lesser extent, the designs. In France, the white-corded quilting is generally made from fine cotton fabrics, whereas examples attributed to Britain are often made from linen cloth.[53] Cotton was spun and woven in both Britain and France, but the primary port for the early importation of cotton from the Levant was the free port of Marseilles, where this form of cotton quilting was known to have been produced as early as the seventeenth century.[54] Cotton, whether from the Levant or the East or West Indies, was preferred to linen because it was lighter in weight, easier to process, did not require extensive bleaching, and was relatively cheap. The quality of these cotton fabrics varied widely, ranging from the coarse cloths used to clothe enslaved Africans in the West Indies and America to the fine materials found in the luxurious quilted clothing and furnishings for the nobility of Europe. Stylistic differences between French and English corded quilting are more difficult to describe. Formats and motifs vary over time and relate closely to fashionable designs in silks and other types of embroidery. From surviving examples it would seem that the French designs are fuller, more curvilinear, and often more closely worked. It is dangerous, however, to extrapolate from surviving examples as they may not represent a good cross-section of what was actually made; often they represent only the highest-quality examples.

Examples of corded quilting made in London were examined and described by Clare Rose. Most are in the form of infant's gowns and women's bedgowns—informal clothing worn at home that are similar to unquilted garments known in America as short gowns. Rose has also searched collections of eighteenth-century trade cards, discovering references to both amateur and professional "French quilting" in London.[55] In England, as in France, bed quilts seem to have been distributed through "upholders" who sold furniture and other types of furnishing textiles, whereas clothing was sold through mercers, linen drapers, haberdashers, or milliners.[56]

Three examples of British-style corded quilting survive at Winterthur, two quilted petticoats and a bedcover. All three can be dated stylistically to the eighteenth century. The earliest is a quilted linen petticoat of about 1720 to 1760. The format of repeating chevrons found in the upper portion of this petticoat can be compared to a similar example in group portrait *An English Family at Tea* by Joseph van Aken from around 1720, which depicts a quilted petticoat of white satin, filled with batting rather than cording, with a similar chevron design as a lower border.[57] Quilted into two of the chevrons on Winterthur's petticoat is a soldier wearing the characteristically shaped cap worn by grenadiers, "elite storm troops of the 1690s who originally carried grenades (bombs thrown by hand)." Instead of bombs, however, the soldier on the petticoat is carrying flowers.[58] It is made from a finely woven linen top, backed by a much more coarsely and loosely woven linen backing. The curving lines of the background, in a fan or shell pattern, are worked in running stitches with a two-ply linen thread. The decorative motifs, including stags, hounds, goats, and various birds, in addition to the soldier, are worked in backstitches. The pattern repeat in the quilted design measures approximately 54½ inches. The quilting is further embellished with areas of additional embroidery that includes French knots, eyelets, satin, and other decorative stitches. The petticoat has been altered and

repaired, and the original length and width cannot be determined. A quilted stomacher with similar embroidered embellishments is in the collection of the Victoria and Albert Museum in London. Two waistcoats with similar decoration are in the collection of Colonial Williamsburg in Virginia.[59]

Winterthur's second English-style quilted petticoat, like so many others, was later made into a bedcover. The original petticoat dates to the third quarter of the eighteenth century. The upper section is quilted in a shell pattern, and the lower border has a widely spaced floral design in corded quilting, with the areas between the raised motifs stitched in close diagonal rows of running stitches. A similar petticoat is in the collection of Colonial Williamsburg.[60] Less heavily quilted, and therefore much lighter in weight than the previous example, this design reflects the neoclassical style in fashion at that time.

Yet another example of English-style corded quilting at Winterthur is a bedcover. It is traditional in format, with a central cartouche containing a basket of flowers, surrounded by a field of floral springs within compartments, a design resembling strapwork embroidery. A similar example of the style of corded quilting can be found on an infant's gown in the collection of the Museum of London, believed to date between 1760 and 1790.[61] An example of a bedcover made from corded quilting and later made into a gown in the late 1770s is in the collection of the Victoria and Albert Museum. It is more finely worked than Winterthur's bedcover, which is worked in two-ply linen thread, with approximately ten running stitches per inch.[62] The quilted bedcover has great expanses of unquilted linen, making it relatively light in weight and open in design, characteristic of the neoclassical designs of the second half of the eighteenth century. The comparatively small diameter of the cotton cording makes the design appear subtle and is therefore difficult to see when laid flat.

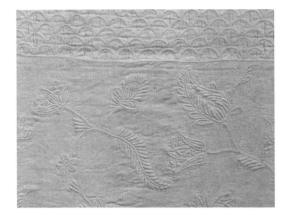

Above **Detail, Wholecloth Quilted Petticoat**

Many quilted petticoats were later cut in two and sewn together at the waist to create quilted bedcovers. In this case, the plain, unquilted section that would have been pleated into a waistband was cut off. The origin of this petticoat is unknown.

Below **Wholecloth Quilt**

English corded quilting is much rarer than French examples. The materials and technique on this quilt suggest that it could have been made in England or America. The quilt was used by Henry Francis du Pont during the summer months in the Patuxent Room.

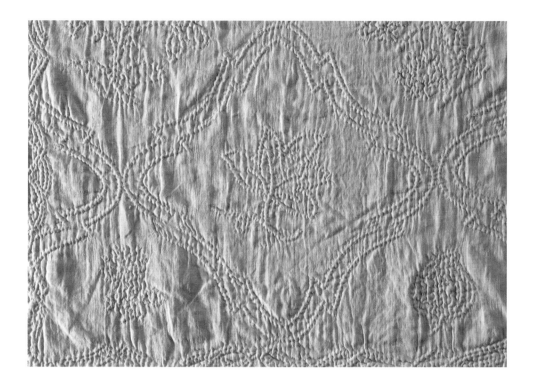

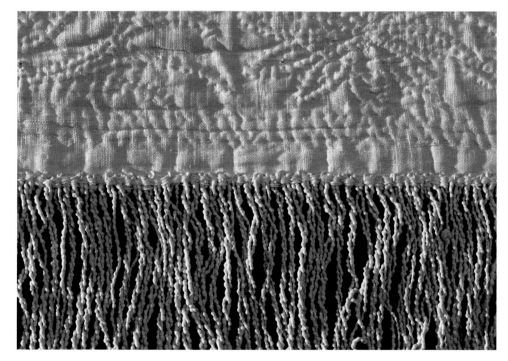

Detail, Wholecloth Quilt
The design in the center of this
quilt is composed of a series of
formal compartments with floral
motifs. Although fashionable in the
late 1700s, this type of strapwork
design is traditional and was
heavily influenced by fashions
of a century before.

Detail, Wholecloth Quilt
Knotting a fringe was a fashionable
activity for wealthy women in the
eighteenth century, and it was done
with a shuttle. There are approximately 700 knots per linear inch in
the fringe, accounting for an esti-
mated 237,000 knots in the fringe
on three sides of this quilt.

Loom-woven imitations of hand-stitched quilting were also used for bedcovers and for clothing. A rare example of woven silk "quilting," probably cut from an old waistcoat, has survived in a silk patchwork quilt made by Martha Agry of Hallowell, Maine, around 1805, the time of her marriage to Benjamin Vaughn. Martha's quilt contains more than one hundred examples of dress silks imported from Europe and China that range in date from the 1720s to the early 1800s. They include brightly colored damasks and brocades, as well as a plethora of black pieces. The strong colors of many of the silks are quite different from those of surviving examples of New England dresses from this period; eighteenth-century portraiture has more representations of somber colors, said to be for serious ladies.[63] Another unusual fabric is an orange-colored cotton velvet, printed with metallic spots that imitate the silver spangles found on fashionable waistcoats from the 1790s.

While Martha's quilt is an extraordinary collection of imported fabrics, it is made in an unusual manner. As the paper templates survive in place, our expectation would be for Martha to have used these templates to stabilize the pieces that she would join with overhand or whip stitches, as found on most examples of template or mosaic piecing. Instead, Martha seamed her triangular patches together with backstitches to form squares. These larger "blocks" were then backed with paper templates. The blocks were placed face to face and seamed with fairly large backstitches, which, like regular seams at that time, were folded or pressed to one side, making the joins of each section somewhat lumpy. The lozenge-shaped panels that form the central medallion and a second medallion at the foot of the quilt are made from appliquéd motifs cut from brocaded dress silks embellished with additional embroidery. The quilt has no batting, and is backed with dark-green glazed worsted wool. There is no particular pattern to the quilting. In some places there are diagonal lines of stitching, approximately three stitches to the

inch, but, in other places, the quilting follows the piecing pattern of the template blocks.

It is always possible that quilts found in America were made in another country. Such is the case with an appliquéd but unquilted counterpane made by Eliza Bennis.[64] Eliza Patten was born in Limerick, Ireland, in 1725 to a Presbyterian family, and married Mitchell Bennis when she was twenty years old. After hearing Robert Swindells, the first Methodist missionary to visit Limerick, she became closely involved in the Methodist Society, organizing classes and prayer meetings. She became one of the leaders of the Methodist Society in Ireland, and frequently corresponded with John Wesley, the founder of Methodism. After 1768, Eliza spent much of her time in Waterford, and finally moved there around 1773, after her husband suffered some unspecified "trials" that affected the family's fortune. After the death of her husband in 1788, Eliza emigrated to Philadelphia with her son, and died there in 1802.

While living in Waterford, she made an appliqué bedcover that she brought with her to Philadelphia, but its subsequent history is unknown until it was sold to Henry Francis du Pont by Robert H. Palmiter, a dealer from Bouckville, New York, in 1945. Clearly it had been highly valued, as someone has carefully restored areas of damage by applying new fabrics over the original. Eliza Bennis's spiritual diary survives, as do many of her letters to John Wesley, but no written reference to her needlework has yet been found.

Sometimes quilts were imported into America through personal connections rather than through the business of international trade. According to family tradition, a beautifully stitched hexagon or medallion cotton quilt was made by Sarah Moon Cadbury (1736–1811. It was more likely made by her daughter and namesake, Sarah Moon Cadbury Cash (1778–1866). Known as Sally, she moved from Exeter to London to keep house for her brother Joel Cadbury Jr. (1763–1811) after his wife and children died. Joel was a prosperous

Above **Portrait of Eliza Bennis**
Eliza Bennis had her portrait rendered in pastels while living in Philadelphia. She was an important Methodist leader in Ireland, and many of her letters and spiritual diaries survive, though they make no mention of her quilts.

Opposite **Eliza Bennis Counterpane**
Made by Eliza Bennis in Ireland in 1782, this appliqué bedcover traveled with her when she emigrated to Philadelphia about 1788. It is made from fabrics similar to those imported into the United States. The patches of lighter-color fabrics are restorations (new fabrics stitched over the old) that were done before the bedcover came into the Winterthur collection.

Right **Martha Agry Vaughn Quilt**
Only four examples of early silk
patchwork quilts made in America
are currently known. This example
was made around 1805 in the port
city of Hallowell, Maine, by Martha
Agry Vaughn, the daughter of a
prosperous sea captain who owned
several shipyards.

Below **Detail, Martha Agry Vaughn
Quilt**
The pink silk "quilting," woven in imitation of hand quilting, is quite rare.
Far more examples of woven cotton
imitations survive. This fabric could
have been used for waistcoats or
women's clothing.

Bottom **Detail, Martha Agry Vaughn
Quilt**
Silk painted in China for export to
Europe was a fashionable fabric for
women's gowns and for bedhangings
in the eighteenth century.

Below **Detail, Martha Agry Vaughn Quilt**
European painted silk can be distinguished from Chinese painted silk by differences in material and technique. Europeans did not use a white ground layer, and they painted with pigments that soaked into the fabric. The Chinese often outlined their motifs in silver.

Bottom **Detail, Martha Agry Vaughn Quilt**
Another fascinating and rare fabric found on Martha Agry Vaughn's quilt is a cotton velvet that is printed with silver-colored imitation spangles. Spangles, highly fashionable in the late 1700s, were found on women's dresses as well as men's coats and waistcoats. This fabric was probably once a waistcoat.

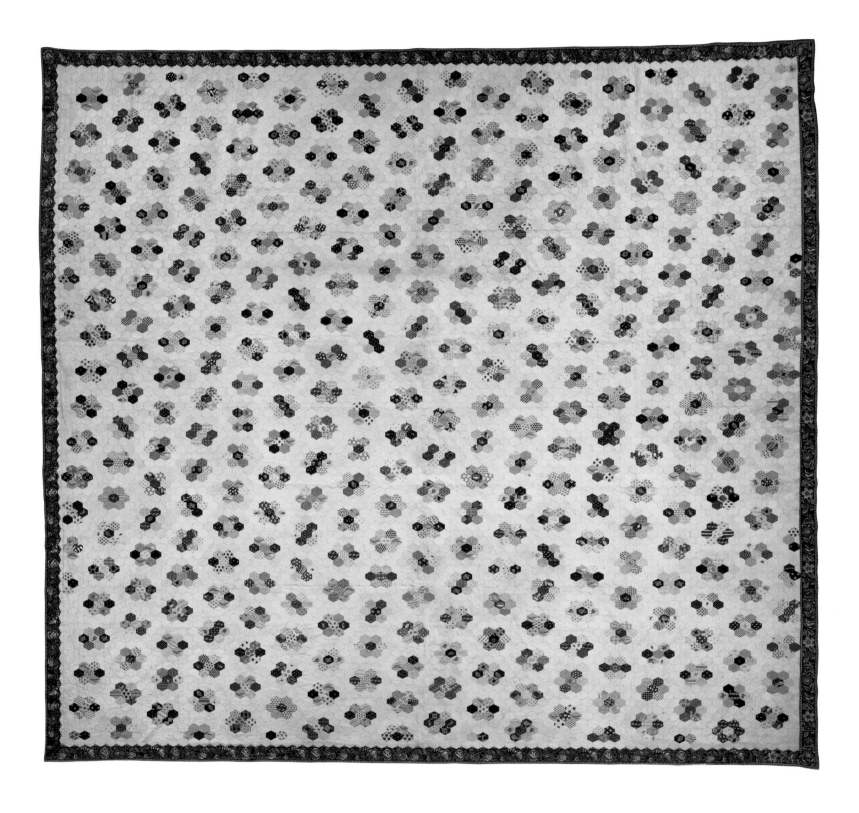

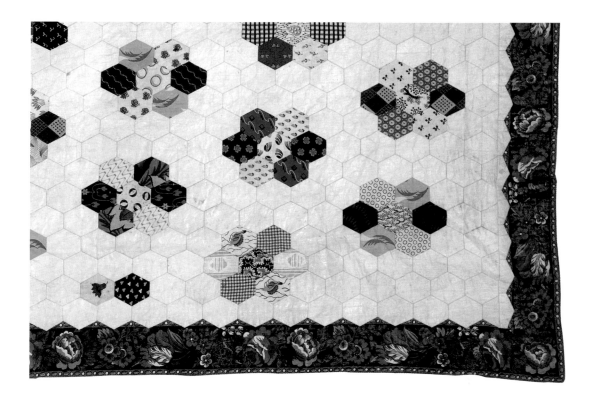

Opposite **Sarah Moon Cadbury Cash Counterpane**

This mosaic-pieced bedcover was made in London by Sarah Moon Cadbury Cash and given to her three great-nieces who lived in Philadelphia. Treasured by the family and on display in Independence Hall in Philadelphia for many years, the bedcover was donated to Winterthur in 1983 by a descendant.

Above **Detail, Sarah Moon Cadbury Cash Counterpane**

The fabric patterns in this quilt are similar to those found in sample books from between 1802 and 1811.

silk mercer with a shop on Gracechurch Street. When her brother became ill and died in 1811, Sally took over the business, which Joel had left jointly to her and her other brother, Richard, who lived in Birmingham. The following year, Sally married Richard Cadbury's former apprentice, Samuel Cash, who was thirteen years younger. They had three daughters, one of whom was Mary (1820–1886), who married Joshua Talwin Shewell of Deptford in 1844.[65] It was Mary Shewell who gave the quilt to her mother's great nieces, Elizabeth (1829–1915), Sarah (1840–1918), and Emma (1843–1923) Cadbury when they visited her in England. Sally's brother, who was Elizabeth, Sarah, and Emma's grandfather, Richard Tapper Cadbury (1768–1860), had moved from Exeter to Birmingham, where he was active in both the Society of Friends (Quakers) and in local politics. He went into business in Birmingham with Joseph Rutter as wholesale and retail drapers, mercers, and hosiers.

According to a bill dated 1794, they also sold "Curious India Muslins." From 1798, Richard was on his own, and a bill from 1808 lists the goods he sold as including a "Great Variety of Printed Calicos, Bed Furnitures, India and British Muslins, Dimities &c, silks, Poplins & Stuffs."[66]

Today we think of modern modes of travel and communication as having created the global economy. We forget that although it took longer to move around the world, and the sending and receiving of goods was sometimes precarious, the history of quilts and the textiles from which they are made is based on a global economy existing for more than four hundred years. When Mary Remington wrote to her fiancé in 1815 that he "may circumnavigate the Globe" before she would ever finish her quilt, she was entirely accurate. She worked on her quilt for about a year, approximately the same amount of time that it would have taken a merchant ship to travel to China and back.

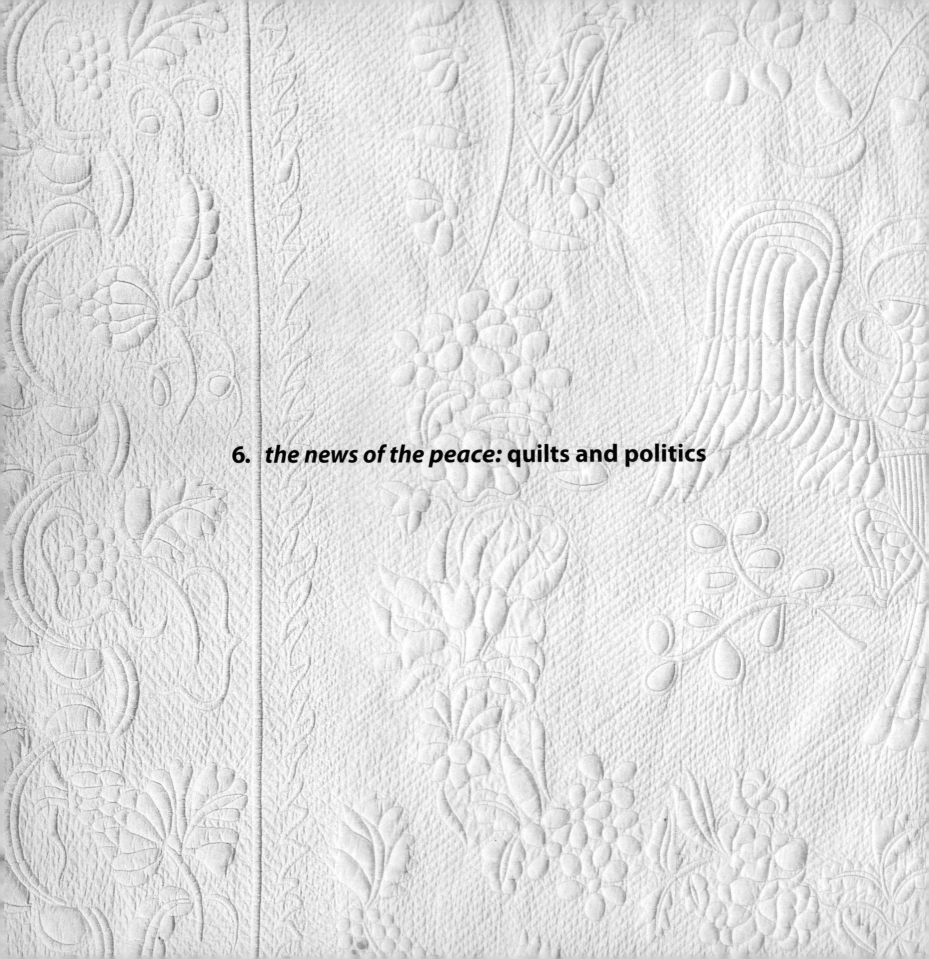

6. *the news of the peace:* **quilts and politics**

In the spring of 1812, after discussing the political affairs of wartime Europe and the American party allegiances of himself and his acquaintants, Peleg Congdon wrote to Mary Remington, "Perhaps you will think Mary from the above that I have forgot myself, or that I am writing to a Male Politician, not a Female Friend or Sister . . . "[1] In fact, it was not unusual for men to include discussions of political issues in their letters to women. Mary kept herself up to date with current affairs through newspapers and personal conversations, like so many other women of her time, and was acutely anxious for news during the War of 1812. Research using women's letters and diaries as primary sources has shown that many women were actively involved in political debate despite their lack of voting rights, although these rights were not entirely lacking. Taking the revolutionary cry of "no taxation without represen-tation" at face value, unmarried women and widows, with enough wealth to make them liable to taxation, were entitled to vote in the state of New Jersey between 1776 and 1807, when this right was taken away. Married women were not allowed a vote because their property and tax liability was held by their husbands.[2]

By the early nineteenth century, women were frequently organizing benevolent associations, temper-ance societies, and missionary organizations, yet only recently have historians discovered their wider role in politics. Added to the growing body of written evidence of the involvement of women in political discourse are the household furnishings, furniture, glass, silver, ceram-ics, and fabrics that were decorated with political and patriotic iconography. Unlike these other items, most quilts were made by the women themselves. While it can be argued that consumer choices and the domestic use of household furnishings decorated with patriotic imagery demonstrates political awareness, the time and skill required to actually produce a quilt speaks to a more personal and deeply felt involvement in political discourse. This chapter looks at a group of quilts with

political iconography in Winterthur's collection that date from the late eighteenth through the late nine-teenth century.[3]

"My chamber is a spacious and elegant one and prettily furnished. I now write in it, and which way soever I turn my eyes I find a triumphal Car, a Liberty Cap, a Temple of Fame or the Hero of Heroes, all these and many more objects of a piece with them, being finely represented on the hangings."[4] Tommy Shippen was describing a bedroom in the president's House in New York, when he wrote this to his sister Nancy in Philadelphia in 1785. He was staying with their uncle Richard Henry Lee, at that time serving as President of the Congress. Writing in 1807, the English poet Robert Southey, in the persona of a Portuguese traveler, more fully describes the same fabric, ostensibly being used for bedhangings in an inn at Carlisle: "My bed curtains may serve as a good specimen of the political freedom permitted in England. General Washington is there represented driving American independence in a car drawn by leopards, a black Triton running beside them, and blowing his conch—meant, I conceive, by his crown of feathers, to designate the native Indians. In another compartment, Liberty and Dr. Franklin are walking hand in hand to the Temple of Fame, where two little Cupids display a Globe, on which America and the Atlantic are marked. The tree of liberty stands by, and the stamp act reversed is bound round it. I have often remarked the taste of the people for these coarse allegories."[5]

These two references neatly define a period of twenty years, the time period during which designs for furnishing textiles remained in production. Within that space of that time, however, the fabric has slipped down the social scale from the highly fashionable house of a prominent politician in a major city to an inn located in an unfashionable provincial town in the north of England.

Some people find it odd that the British, who had just lost most of their American colonies in an expensive

Previous pages **Detail, Helen Mar Ferguson Quilt**
One of two white stuffed-work quilts depicting the Great Seal of the United States in Winterthur's collec-tion, this quilt was made in 1852 by Helen Mar Ferguson of Harpersfield, New York.

and protracted war that ended with the defeat of their army, should produce textiles joyously commemorating the success of their enemy. But just as there were loyalists in America who were against the Revolution, there were many people in Britain who supported the colonists in their bid for independence—or at least found their cause or the underlying philosophical principle of republicanism to be righteous, although Southey was evidently not one of them. Many of the areas of English textile production, such as the East End of London, Norwich, Manchester, and Carlisle, were hotbeds of radical politics. But even if the manufacturers in Britain did not share the delight in America's victory, they soon flooded the new republic with patriotic images on fabrics and ceramics with the purpose of restoring and increasing their profits from the American market, which had been disrupted by war. In the period just before the Revolution, the American colonies had become one of their largest and most lucrative markets. It is said that after the Revolution, many coins and medals featuring a portrait of King George III identified as George Washington also made their way into the United States. It is unclear whether this was done through intentional irony or careless haste, but the purpose was unquestionably for profit.[6]

Winterthur's collection includes examples of the fabric described by Shippen and Southey, known as "The Apotheosis of Franklin and Washington," in red, brown (possibly once purple in color), and blue. That so much of this design survives in American collections attests not only to the widespread popularity of its iconography in the 1780s and 1790s, but also to its popularity with antiquarians and collectors ever since. Three of Winterthur's examples, all of them red, are wholecloth quilts, while others take the form of bed curtains and valances—the very types of hangings described by both Shippen and Southey.

Contemporary observers would be able to identify not only the portraits of Washington and Franklin, but also the allegorical figures representing Liberty, Fame,

and America. What Robert Southey meant when he described the allegory as "coarse" had nothing to do with the fabric itself, but implied that the iconography was too obvious, almost trite. Allegory had long been the hallmark of the educated, wealthy elite, and the interpretation of elaborate emblematic figures, used by artists and designers since the sixteenth century was purposefully obscure, discernable only to the intellectual and learned. The attributes of the allegorical figures were often taken from a number of classical and biblical sources; some were even taken from Egyptian hieroglyphics (which were not understood by anyone at the time). The devices or objects held by these figures served as visual clues to be deciphered with much thought, and often had multiple meanings. The use of emblems and allegory was falling out of fashion in Britain by the late eighteenth century, when the practice was taken up so enthusiastically by the leaders of the new republic of the United States.[7] Their purpose in America was not obscurity but the celebration of a new republic, with visual representations that would delineate the high standing of the new country and which would be understood by all.

The same imagery was used time and time again. One of the first instances was a painting done by Robert Pine in London in 1778, at a time when an American victory was not at all assured. Pine later moved to Philadelphia where he sadly did not find a lucrative market for the paintings of historical subjects for which he was known in London. A dedication, "TO THOSE, who wish to SHEATHE the DESOLATING SWORD of WAR. And, to RESTORE the BLESSINGS of PEACE and AMITY, to a divided PEOPLE," was added by Joseph Strutt, who etched the printed version published on October 6, 1781, just as the British General Cornwallis was besieged in Yorktown, but before the British surrendered. To help decipher the iconography, an "Explanation" was provided, intended to be pasted to the back of the print when framed. Stating that "England and America were

flattered with the pleasing hope of an immediate Reconciliation," it went on to give the following exegesis:

"AMERICA, after having suffered the several Evils of War, bewail'd it's unhappy Cause, and lamented o'er the Victims of its Fury.—her ruin'd Towns-destroy'd Commerce, &c., &c., on the Appearance of PEACE, is represented in an Extacy of gratitude to the Almighty—HEROIC VIRTUE, presents LIBERTY, attended by CONCORD-INDUSTRY, followed by PLENTY AND HER train [to] FORM A Group expressive of POPULATION, & SHIPS, [and] denote the happy return of peaceful COMMERCE."[8]

The war had been going a lot better for the Americans throughout 1781 than it had in 1778, and the interpretation of the subject matter of this print had shifted slightly from that of the original painting. Amos Doolittle, an American engraver and printmaker, created a copy of this print, by which time it clearly had become a celebration of America's victory.

A fragment of a quilt in Winterthur's collection is made from a plate-printed fabric of the same image but in reverse. Reversing an image is not uncommon, and occurs because the engraver of the plate copied the original print exactly as he saw it but the image comes out in reverse because it is laid facedown to print the fabric. A silkwork embroidery in Winterthur's collection, also copied from the print, retains the original orientation. Sadly the provenance of the needlework is not known, but a label on the back of the original frame was provided by the firm of Campbell and Crieg of New York City.[9] The survival of a print, a needlework picture, and a quilt fragment would seem to imply that the image was widely disseminated in both Britain and America, but this plate-printed fabric is relatively rare. The design of the second compartment of the fabric is taken from another patriotic print, known as "America Presenting at the Altar of Liberty Medallions of Her Illustrious Sons."

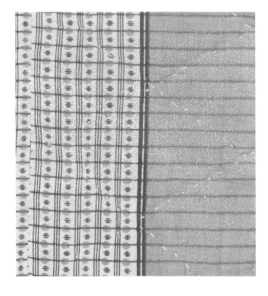

Left **Design Repeat, Wholecloth Quilt**
After the success of the American Revolution, leaders such as George Washington and Benjamin Franklin were hailed as heroes. They were depicted on commemorative furnishings and other decorative objects, which were in great demand in both Europe and the United States.

Above **Backing, Wholecloth Quilt**
Some of the rarest and most interesting, albeit inexpensive, fabrics are found as backings on quilts. This example imitates a woven fabric in two shades of madder.

Opposite **Wholecloth Quilt and Bedhangings**
Rarely have complete sets of eighteenth-century bedhangings survived. This partial set at Winterthur includes the tapes and rings that were originally used to draw up the curtains.

Opposite, above left **America**

The subject of this 1781 print was intended to encourage peace between the revolting Americans and the English. It was later interpreted as celebrating America's independence.

Opposite, below left **Silkwork**

The various silk threads used to embroider this picture have almost all faded to gold. Silks that were dyed subtle shades of red, pink, and lavender are notorious for their fading, giving viewers today a false impression of what they looked like when new.

Opposite, right **Fragment, Wholecloth Quilt**

Despite its poor condition, the plate-printed fabric from which this quilt was made is extremely rare. Although now brown in color, it may have been printed in purple. The degradation over time of the iron-based mordant used to fix the dye to the fiber can result in both a color shift and deterioration of the fabric.

The same image was also used as a printed cotton in a larger format on its own. Winterthur has an example of this fabric that was made up into a tied comforter at a much later date. This version seems to have been more popular, as more examples survive in museum collections. The medallions, drawn by the Swiss artist Pierre Eugène Du Simitière in Philadelphia but sent to France to be engraved, were copied by British engravers and used to decorate transfer-printed ceramics as well as cloak hooks or mirror knobs.[10]

Artists of the eighteenth century aspired to history painting, considered to have higher status than portraiture. Benjamin West, an American artist who studied in Italy, moved to London where he eventually became "History Painter to the King" for George III before, during, and—amazingly—even after the American Revolution. Originally from Pennsylvania, West created the enormous painting entitled *William Penn's Treaty with the Indians when he Founded the Province of Pennsylvania in North America in 1772*. West took great pains to ensure the historical accuracy of his painting, but relied on his own memory and that of his father for many of the details, with the result that the Quakers are depicted wearing eighteenth-century dress and the buildings in the background did not exist until at least a century after 1772. The garments worn by the native Americans are thought to be based on genuine examples of clothing of Lenape, Iroquois, and Northern Algonquin origin, which West had borrowed for the purpose. A smaller version of the painting was offered by West to the Pennsylvania Academy of Fine Arts in 1809, but was never finished. The printed version, engraved by John Hall and published in 1775 by John Boydell, was a huge commercial success on both sides of the Atlantic.[11] It is said to be "the only picture hung in most Quaker homes in both England and America." Over the next two centuries, *Penn's Treaty* was reproduced in every conceivable and some inconceivable ways: on china platters, gravy boats, vegetable dishes, tin trays, bed quilts, window

curtains, lamp shades, candle screens, letterheads, hand-blown glass, tavern signs, banknotes, cast-iron stove plates, medals, and Christmas cards.[12]

William Penn's grandson, John Penn Jr., himself owned the textile version. Listed in the sale of his goods in Philadelphia in May of 1788, it is described as "One set of hair color furniture cotton bed curtains, pattern William Penn's treaty with the Indians. Three window curtains to match ditto, with cord, tassels, and screws."[13] To complete the furnishing of a room, this fabric also survives in the form of case covers for side chairs made from the same fabric.

A common form of printed fabric commemorating historic events is the handkerchief, some of which were used as the centers of medallion quilts in the late eighteenth and early nineteenth centuries. On November 14, 1941, H. F. du Pont visited the showroom of Elinor Merrell on East 57th Street in New York City, where, as a collector of historical handkerchiefs, he was intrigued with a quilt whose central medallion was a handkerchief depicting George Washington on horseback. He immediately purchased it, but with an additional request. According to his wishes, Merrell's staff "removed" the handkerchief from the center of the quilt and delivered it to du Pont's Park Avenue apartment the following day, stating on the delivery note: "We are substituting red and white flowered cotton for this handkerchief and will deliver the spread as soon as work is completed." The substitution was also documented on a tag attached to the quilt.[14] The handkerchief was subsequently framed for display, but the quilt itself was put into storage.

Fifty-six years later, handkerchief and quilt were reunited in Winterthur's Textile Conservation Laboratory.[15] In good condition, and apparently little used, the quilt's original colors were discovered when protected areas in the seam allowance were exposed during treatment.

The handkerchief so coveted by du Pont was made in England, a copy with minor changes from one printed

by the London printing firm of Talwin & Foster of Bromley Hall, in Middlesex. One of the largest textile printing
firms near London, the name Talwin & Foster was in use
between 1783 and 1790, when it became known as
Foster & Co.[16] Surrounding the central figure of George
Washington are profile medallions of other important
leaders during the American Revolution. The pieced
work is made from various light and dark ground small-
pattern block-printed dress fabrics and a plate-printed
furnishing fabric with a chinoiserie design. These fabrics, fashionable from the late eighteenth through the
first years of the nineteenth century, were pieced in a
pattern sometimes known as "Yankee Puzzle."[17]

Described by Tommy Shippen as the "Hero of Heroes,"
Washington was a popular figure on commemorative
handkerchiefs.[18] It might be expected that women of
the period would lionize the heroes of the Revolution,
but they also quilted handkerchiefs commemorating
events perceived as significant at the time but which
are not as well known today. A handkerchief entitled
"The Dismemberment of Poland" has evidence of quilting lines, but the remainder of the quilt has not been
discovered. Full of political invective, the text above and
below the central medallion explains the subject and
also why portraits of Washington and Lafayette are jux-
taposed with those of the King of Poland and General
Kosciusko. What was known at the time as the Polish
Revolution occurred on May 3, 1791, when the
Polish King, "having secretly cherished the flame of
Liberty in the bosom of the Poles," presented the country with a constitution "Modelled after those of England
and America." The Polish Revolution was considered
particularly important because it was nonviolent, the
natural result of the influence of the Enlightenment on
an educated ruler, but it did not last long.

Catherine the Great, Empress of Russia, combined
with "some treacherous Polish Nobles, Villanous Prussia,
and ambitious Austria" to defeat and divide the country
in 1794. Americans followed events in Poland closely as

they were conscious of being a revolutionary model for
others. General Kosciusko was a hero of both the American and the Polish revolutions.[19] In America, he had
contributed greatly to the American victory in the battle
of Saratoga, and later he served under General Nathaniel Greene in the South and helped found The Society of
the Cincinnati in 1783. He returned to Poland the following year where he reformed the army and, in 1794,
assumed military and political leadership for Polish
independence. Later that year, "the valiant Poles were
forced to surrender to the armies of their rapacious
Invaders" after a battle in which Kosciusko was severely
wounded. Poland ceased to exist after it was partitioned
in 1795. Kosciusko came to the United States in 1797,
where he was greeted with a hero's welcome and given
pay for his war services in the form of both money and
land in Ohio.[20] Almost certainly printed in England,
the handkerchief was probably produced about the
time of Kosciusko's stay in Britain, just before his return
to America.

How many other commemorative handkerchiefs,
so popular with collectors of Americana, once formed
the centers of quilts? Judging from surviving examples,
the practice clearly correlates to the fashion for quilts
framing central medallions, a style that seems to date
from the 1790s through the 1840s.[21] The production
of commemorative handkerchiefs, however, spans a
much longer period of time, from the mid-seventeenth
century to today.[22] While the subject matter found on
printed handkerchiefs can range from maps, distances
and rates for toll roads, exotic fashions, children's
games, and education, the majority found in quilts tend
to be political in nature or depict national heroes.

Printed yardage, as well as commemorative
handkerchiefs, benefited from the technological developments associated with roller printing. A much faded
but fascinating example was used as the backing of
a later pieced quilt. The two central images relate to
Commander Stephen Decatur's resolution of the long-

Above **Partial Design Repeat, Wholecloth Quilt**

Opposite **Wholecloth Quilt**
Fashionable furnishing fabrics in
the late eighteenth century were
designed to match when seamed
in side-by-side or half-drop repeats.
The maker of this quilt, which depicts
Penn's Treaty, did not match the patterns, resulting in a visual effect that
is jarring to modern eyes.

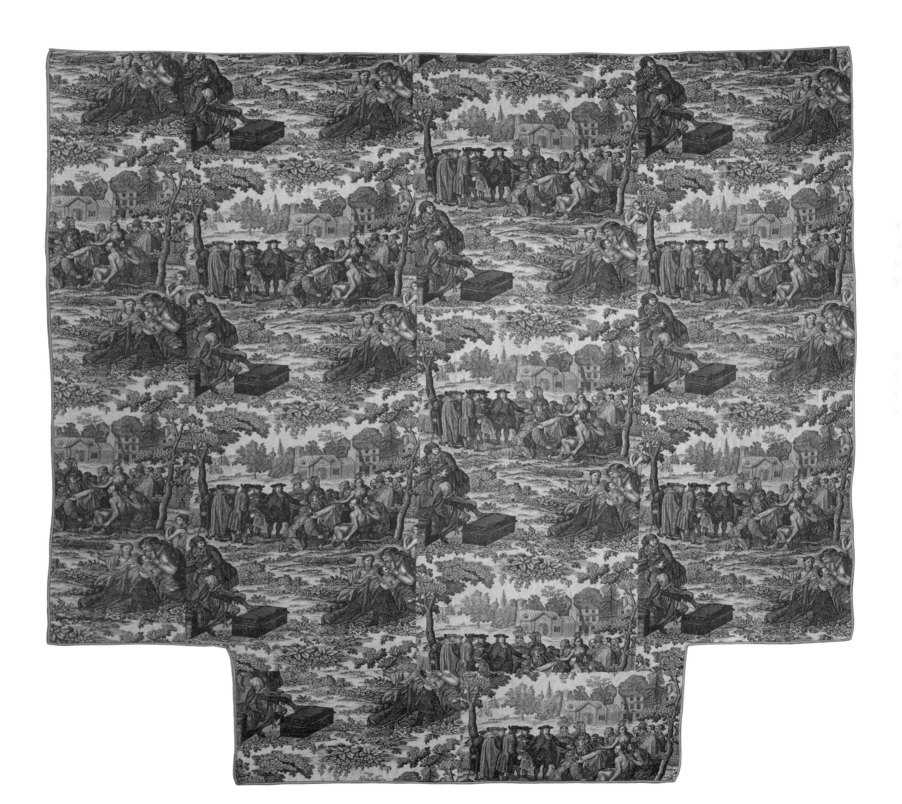

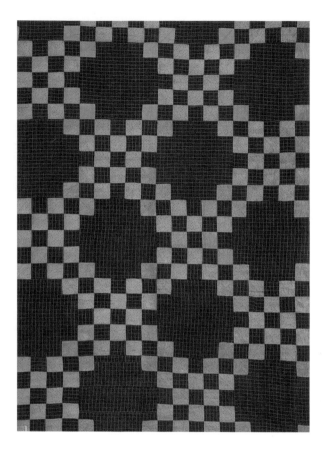

Above **Pieced Quilt**
The face of the quilt lined with fabric commemorating Stephen Decatur's role in the war with the Barbary Pirates is made of a common checked cloth, pieced in the design sometimes known as a "Double Irish Chain."

Right **Backing, Pieced Quilt**
The two scenes featured on this faded backing fabric are labeled "The Gallant Decatur and His Brave Tars Capturing the Algerine Admiral" and "The Brave Tars of America Granting Peace to the Barbary States."

standing problem of pirates capturing American sailors off the Barbary Coast of North Africa—one of the primary motivations for the creation of the United States Navy. Peace treaties had been signed in 1795 and again in 1805. One country's pirates are another country's privateers, and it seems that the so-called Barbary Pirates, featured in a number of romanticized melodramas of the time, were often encouraged to capture American ships by the British, French, and Dutch governments. Once the British had been defeated in the War of 1812, commemorated on this fabric by the depiction of the Battle of New Orleans as one of the secondary motifs along the right-hand side, Stephen Decatur sailed to North Africa in May 1815 where "he threatened and successfully intimidated the leaders of Algiers, Tunis, and Tripoli into signing treaties with the United States."[23] Mary Remington was enthralled by Decatur's heroism, and describes seeing his fleet blockaded by the British in Long Island Sound. But she never mentions the Barbary Pirates, perhaps Peleg Congdon was no longer at risk of being captured. The firm of Minturn & Champlin, for whom he worked, was out of business.

The fabric of political iconography changed, as did the style of politics, with the advent of what is known as "Jacksonian democracy" during the 1828 presidential election. One historian of material culture ascribes its cause "to a monumental temper tantrum." Andrew Jackson had actually won the highest percentage of the popular vote in 1824, but as no candidate had been the outright winner, the House of Representatives, influenced by Henry Clay, appointed John Quincy Adams as president. "The result was a generation of raucous, vitriolic political warfare that essentially created the modern American system of campaigning for public office. One key characteristic of this new political style was the introduction of manufactured and handmade objects of all sorts—visual items to capture the attention of voters."[24] Jackson won the popular vote in 1828 and again in 1832.

His election marked a turning point in American politics. Promoting himself as a "self-made man," he was the first president not to have taken part in the politics of the American Revolution. And while electioneering had certainly been quite vicious before his successful bid for the presidency, Jackson and his followers are generally credited with developing an effective propaganda machine to influence the populace by playing on Jackson's popularity as a beloved hero of the War of 1812. His opponents objected not only to aspects of his personal life (whether he committed bigamy, having married a woman who was not yet legally divorced, is still a matter of debate), but also to his actions against the Creek and Seminole Indians, and to the Indian Removal Act of 1830—a political debate with moral dimensions in which many women were active.[25] It was at this time that fabrics depicting the various American presidents were first produced in great numbers.

There was little doubt that Jackson's vice president, Martin Van Buren, would succeed him, so the real explosion in the use of printed textiles as tools for political propaganda was during the election that brought William Henry Harrison to the White House in 1841. Said to have once been part of a quilt, a handkerchief in Winterthur's collection has cut edges on all four sides, but no evidence of quilting stitches; however, another version of the same handkerchief has survived in a quilt that is believed to have been made in New Jersey.[26] The handkerchief depicts Harrison as a war hero. During the War of 1812, he won fame by defeating the Shawnee Indians at the Battle of Tippecanoe, but the figure of a hero on a horse is clearly reminiscent of the commemorative fabrics of previous campaigns.

The irony of Harrison's campaign is that, despite being the son of a wealthy Virginian, he became associated with log cabins and hard cider, a connection commemorated in cotton yardage. What could such cheap, coarse fabrics be used for? A few of these fabrics survive in the form of quilts, and an example of the Har-

rison campaign fabric in Winterthur's collection used to be a tied comforter before it was unpicked (it was acquired solely for the cloth from which it was made).[27]

Women were actively involved in the election campaign of 1840 in both the North and the South.[28] Written sources document their participation in parades and political rallies, and these cheap fabrics could have been used as a form of bunting to decorate floats or platforms. Women's groups are known to have taken up collections to purchase presentation gifts to war heroes, including silver swords or covered urns, and such activities continued in a similar vein in political campaigns, as when Mrs. Ruffner of Kanawha, West Virginia, presented a flag with a note attesting that she was "warmly attached to the principles of the American Party, and ardently desirous of their success at the approaching election."[29] Many examples of textiles printed with political iconography are found in quilts.

Henry Clay's presidential campaigns, five in total, were resplendent with commemorative textiles, and his image is found on many quilts, as well as needlework pictures, Staffordshire pottery, and other promotional objects.[30] Now nearly forgotten, Clay's popularity once approached and, according to some sources, actually exceeded that of George Washington (that "Hero of Heroes"). A quilt featuring Clay was once in Henry Francis du Pont's collection, displayed on a wall in his Long Island home. It remained there when the house was sold after du Pont's death in 1969.

Zachary Taylor, selected to run for the office of president because of his fame as a military hero, was the last to be portrayed using the almost generic emblem of a hero on a horse. He was also the last of the Whig politicians to hold office for any length of time (William Henry Harrison died within days of taking office). Both bandannas and printed yardage commemorated his victories during the Mexican-American War of 1847 to 1849. In the early years of the American republic, citizens and politicians worried about the stability of the

Opposite, left Pieced Quilt
Many quilts using commemorative handkerchiefs as their central medallion must have been destroyed in the early twentieth century, when collectors of Americana valued the handkerchiefs more highly than the quilts.

Opposite, top right Conservator with Pieced Quilt
The flowered fabric that replaced the original central handkerchief on this quilt was removed in the Winterthur conservation lab.

Opposite, center right Detail, Pieced Quilt
Fabric protected within the seams of the quilt provides evidence of the original color. The wool batting, linen backing, and two-ply linen quilting thread can be clearly seen.

Opposite, bottom right Requilting
A pattern was taken of the original stitching holes, which could be clearly seen with the assistance of a light table. The pattern was used to quilt the handkerchief onto new polyester batting before it was reintegrated into its original position on the quilt.

Right Handkerchief
The presence of stitching holes indicated that this commemorative handkerchief dating from around 1794–1810 had once been the center of a quilt. The remainder of the quilt has not survived.

Opposite, above left **Handkerchief**
Well-printed on high-quality cotton, this handkerchief is said to have been cut from the center of a quilt. There is no evidence of the remainder of the quilt in Winterthur's collection.

Opposite, below left **Colorways**
These printed cottons show a design created to support the presidential campaign of William Henry Harrison.

Opposite, right **Quilt at Chestertown House**
Many quilts and other furnishings were left at Chestertown House, Henry Francis du Pont's summer home on Long Island, and were sold by subsequent owners. The quilt seen here, in a design known as the "Whig's Defeat," is now in a private collection. It includes portraits of Henry Clay and George Washington.

Right **Printed Fabric**
Rainbow prints, stripes of different colors that were blurred at the edges, were fashionable in the 1840s. This inexpensive fabric depicts Zachary Taylor.

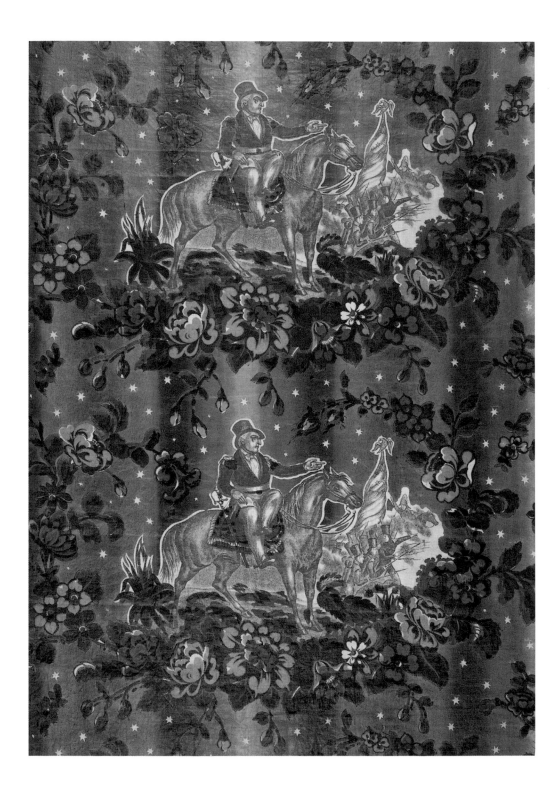

new nation, forging compromises that only put off difficult decisions. After Taylor, political debate became more focused on issues like slavery and states' rights. Quilts that essentially listed the presidents, first seen during Andrew Jackson's time, became a thing of the past, as the Civil War threatened the very existence of the country.

Side by side with the political partisanship of the first half of the nineteenth century, which effectively created the two-party system still in operation today, was a deeply felt sense of patriotism for the new republic, catered to by the calico printers of Britain who were in desperate competition with the calico printers of America in the 1830s. Roller-printing technology was speeding up the process and enabling manufacturers to easily provide consumers with a variety of colorways to tempt every taste. Difficult to date precisely, many of the imported examples of patriotic yardage seem to date to just after the Jubilee of 1826, when the United States celebrated fifty years of independence.

Much of this patriotic imagery featured the Great Seal of the United States. Adopted in 1782, this emblem is effectively the coat of arms of the government of the United States, intended to be used to officiate treaties and other documents of state. The eagle was already a symbol of power and authority. It had been used in ancient Egypt and was also found on standards of the Roman legions. It is this classical association that attracted the leaders of the early American republic, despite the use of a double-headed form by the Hapsburgs, hereditary rulers of the Holy Roman Empire. Napoleon also adopted the symbol of the eagle, but what distinguished the American version is that it is a distinct species, the bald eagle, that is indigenous to the United States.[31] Benjamin Franklin famously wrote to his daughter in 1784, complaining about the new symbol. "For my part, I wish the bald eagle had not been chosen as the representative of our country; he is a bird of bad moral character; he does not get his living honestly; you

may have seen him perched on some dead tree, where, too lazy to fish for himself, he watches the labor of the fishing-hawk; and, when that diligent bird has at length taken a fish, and is bearing it to his nest for the support of his mate and young ones, the bald eagle pursues him, and takes it from him. . . . I am, on this account, not displeased that the figure is not known as a bald eagle, but looks more like a turkey. For in truth, the turkey is in comparison a much more respectable bird, and a true native of America. Eagles have been found in all countries, but the turkey was peculiar to ours; the first of the species seen in Europe, being brought to France by the Jesuits from Canada, and served up at the wedding table of Charles the Ninth. He is, besides (though a little vain and silly, it is true, but not the worse emblem for that), a bird of courage, and would not hesitate to attack a grenadier of the British guards, who should presume to invade his farmyard with a red coat on."[32] Franklin's complaint notwithstanding, within ten years of its adoption, the bald eagle with a shield over its breast had become the most ubiquitous symbol in America, found on every conceivable object in every possible form, including fabric for quilts.

Many whitework quilts depict the great seal. The text that accompanied the official description of the seal provides an explanation of the symbolism behind the colors of red, white, and blue, and the reason that white quilts were often made in celebration of a marriage. "White signifies purity and innocence, Red, hardiness and valour, and Blue, vigilance, perseverance and justice."[33] Highly popular, whitework quilts are underrepresented in the published literature because of the difficulty of photographing them. A whitework quilt depicting the great seal under the motto "Liberty," made by N. Siler, was used by Henry Francis du Pont on his own bed in the Cottage, his residence on the estate after Winterthur Museum opened in 1951.[34]

Another example in Winterthur's collection was made by Helen Mar Ferguson and dated March 20,

Above **Design Repeat, Wholecloth Quilt**
A number of wholecloth quilts made from this elegant fabric have survived. The fabrics were printed in Mulhouse, France, using the latest technological developments.

Opposite **Wholecloth Quilt**
Henry Francis du Pont used this quilt featuring American presidents at Chestertown House, his summer residence on Long Island. It was later placed on a bed in Winterthur's South Room, which was decorated in yellow and lilac.

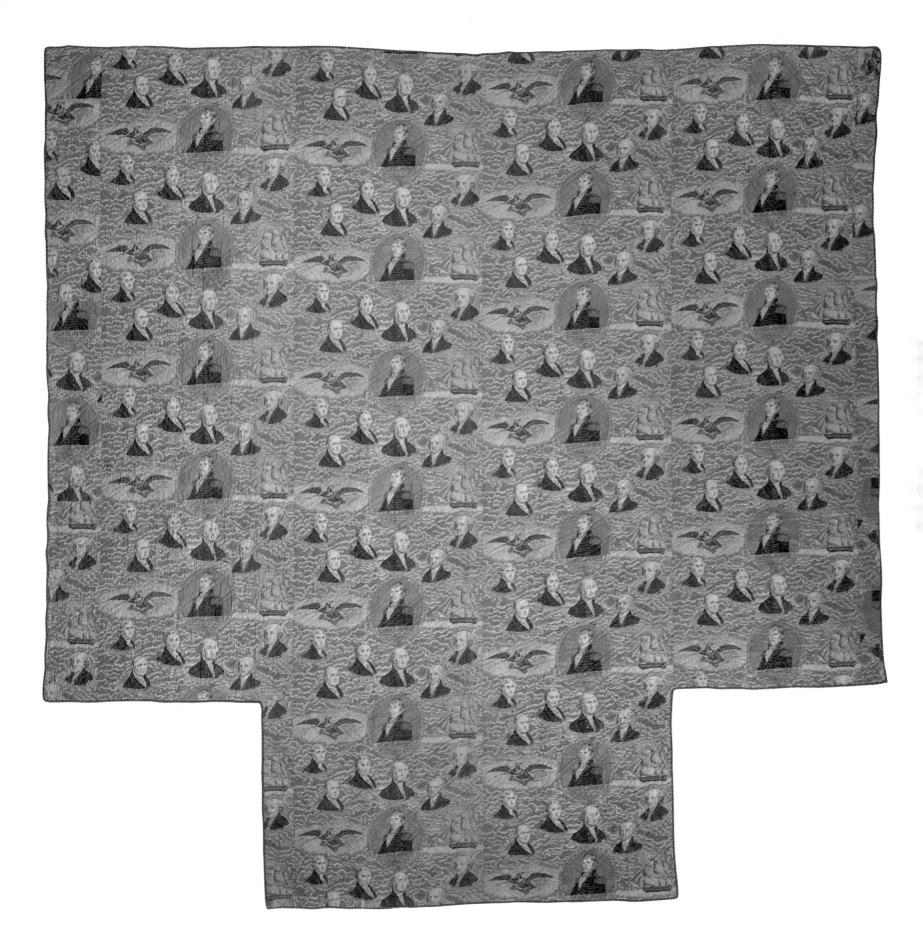

1852. Born in Albany in 1834, Helen made her quilt around the time of her marriage to George Passage Pratt. The actual date of their marriage is not known, but it was most likely to have been before the birth of their first child in July of 1856. Formal in format, the placement of the eagle and shield in the center is reflective of the placement of Mary Remington's family armorial device. Helen Mar was named for a character in *The Scottish Chiefs*, a historical romance novel written by the successful British author Jane Porter. Originally published in London in 1810, there were numerous American editions available throughout the nineteenth century, including two in 1831.[35] Perhaps her mother read it while she was pregnant with Helen. The novel tells the story of the Scottish hero William Wallace, who fought to liberate Scotland from the tyranny of England—a story that for obvious reasons resonated with Americans. Helen Mar, whose wicked stepmother betrays Wallace to the English, marries the virtuous Wallace just before his execution. In the 1830s, Porter claimed that she invented the genre of historical romance, and that her work had influenced Sir Walter Scott, but the accuracy of her statement has been disputed by scholars who feel that, unlike Scott's, Porter's historical research was, at best, sketchy. Porter's first literary success was her novel *Thaddeus of Warsaw*, said to be "inspired by [her] hero-worship of the Polish patriot Kosciusko," who has already been identified on a commemorative handkerchief made into a quilt.[36]

An as yet unidentified member of the Westervelt family quilted a whitework dressing-table cover celebrating peace and depicting the great seal. Between 1810 and 1840, it was fashionable, at least in parts of New England and the Mid-Atlantic states, to make bedroom suites of stuffed-work quilts, valances, and dressing-table covers, like those worked by Mary Remington. The most common motifs depicted are central baskets and urns, and there seems to have been some standardization of design, as three examples

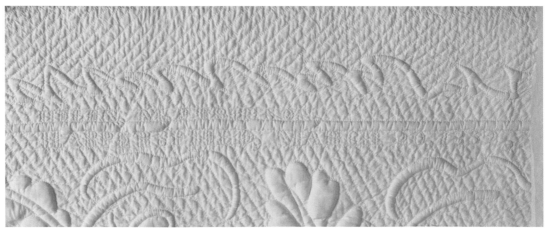

Left **Detail, Helen Mar Ferguson Quilt**
The banner in the beak of the eagle reads "American Eagle," just in case there was any doubt. This was one of the most common motifs found on quilts and other objects in the early 1800s.

Below **Detail, Helen Mar Ferguson Quilt**
The quilted inscription here reads "Helen Mar Ferguson/Harpersfield, March 20, 1852."

Opposite **Quilted Dressing-table Cover**
The edges of this stuffed-work dressing-table cover were never finished. The cover would have been placed on a pine demi-lune table, which would have been hidden by the skirt pinned or stitched to this cover. The cover was probably made in New York City.

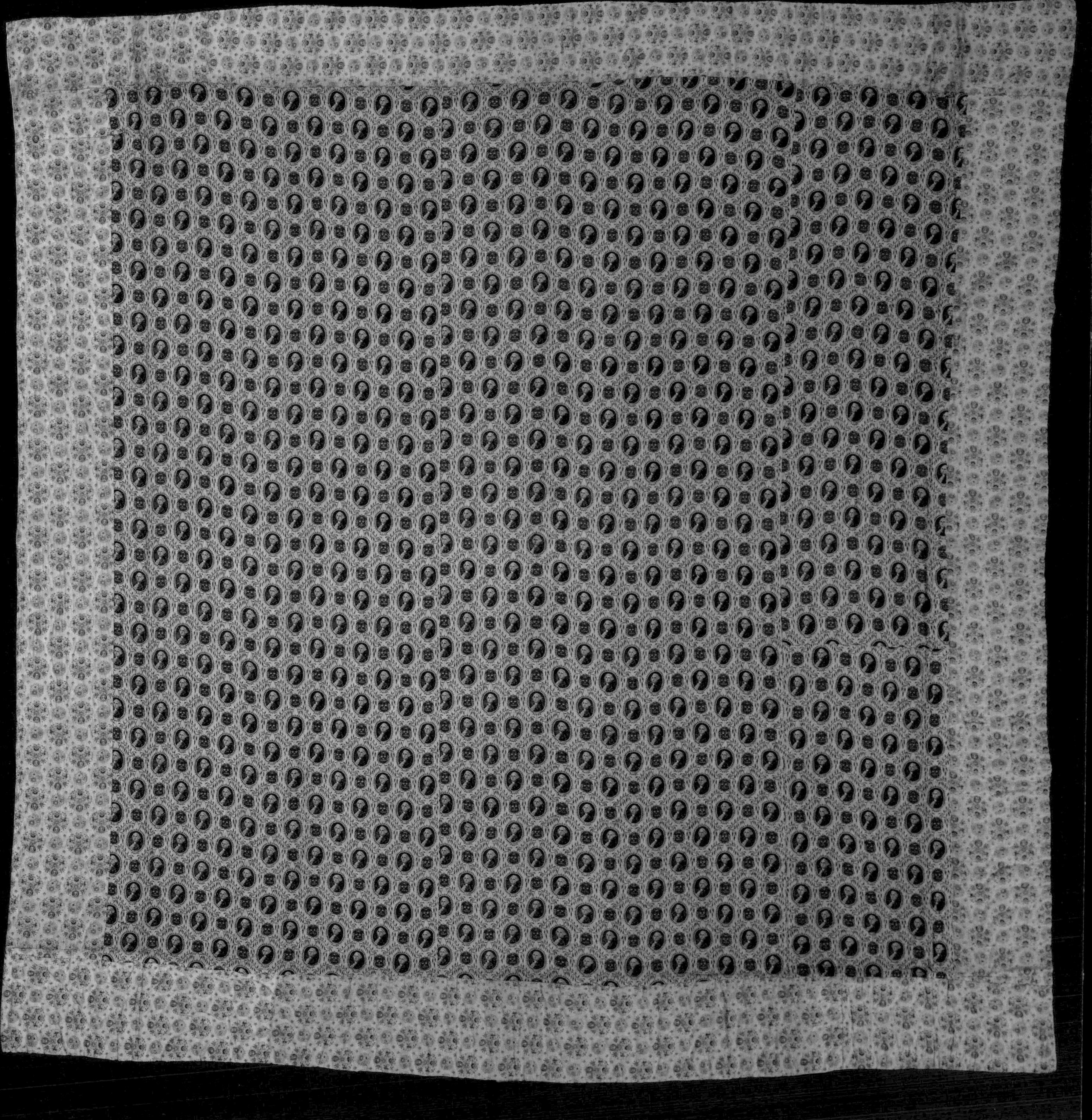

survive that were worked from the same pattern, one made in New Jersey and now in Winterthur's collection, one from Haverhill, Massachusetts, and another dated 1812 in the collection of the Metropolitan Museum of Art.[37] A typical pattern for a demi-lune-shaped dressing-table cover survives in Winterthur's library. The Westervelt dressing-table cover, marked with the initials "M.A.W.," is unusual for having baskets, cocks, and an animal that resembles a cat in mirror image on either side of the central eagle and shield. Difficult to date precisely without knowledge of its maker, this dressing-table cover could commemorate the end of the War of 1812, but stylistic evidence suggests that it could have been made to celebrate the end of the Mexican-American War in 1848.

Patriotic quilts depicting national heroes once again became widely fashionable around the time of the Centennial celebrations in 1876. Two fabrics commemorating Washington and Lafayette were produced by the American Print Works in Fall River, Massachusetts, that are commonly found in quilts and comforters from this time.[38] Snippets of the same inexpensive fabrics have been discovered having been carefully framed—evidence of the patriotic furor aroused during the Centennial.

After examining this selection of quilts with patriotic imagery in Winterthur's collection, the question remains: Why would women choose to make quilts with political imagery? One possible answer to these questions concerns the social nature of sewing. Letters written by Eleuthera du Pont describe the different types of needlework projects undertaken at different times of day and in different social situations. Although she does not mention quilting, it is clear that in the privacy of her home, in the company of her family or possibly a few very close female friends, Eleuthera would work on mundane projects, such as shirts, while in company she would create more decorative embroidery. On at least one occasion, "Eleuthera got caught.

She and Joanna Smith were sewing in the parlor when someone came calling. Eleuthera dashed to the back parlor to hide her work, a shirt, for it was not appropriate for the parlor."[39] The stories about quilting "bees" in the popular literature of the mid-nineteenth century have been shown to reflect romantic nostalgia rather than reality.[40]

Unlike more mundane sewing projects, such as shirts or underclothing, piecing quilts was an acceptable project while socializing with visitors at home or visiting others. The quilts depicted in this chapter clearly do show one type of needlework that women sewed in their parlors. As conversations turned to important political issues, women's hands were stitching quilts that provided physical evidence of their own opinions as well as their patriotism. An appliqué quilt featuring nine of the first ten presidents (William Henry Harrison was excluded, possibly because he died shortly after his inauguration) has an embroidered date of 1853, yet the last president depicted, John Tyler, left office in 1845. Neither the appliquéd figures nor the quilting pattern are particularly elaborate, so why did it take so long to complete? I would argue that this quilt was stitched as a social activity that was taken up only now and again. Quilts made with political iconography, therefore, are primary evidence of the participation of women in the political discourse of their time.

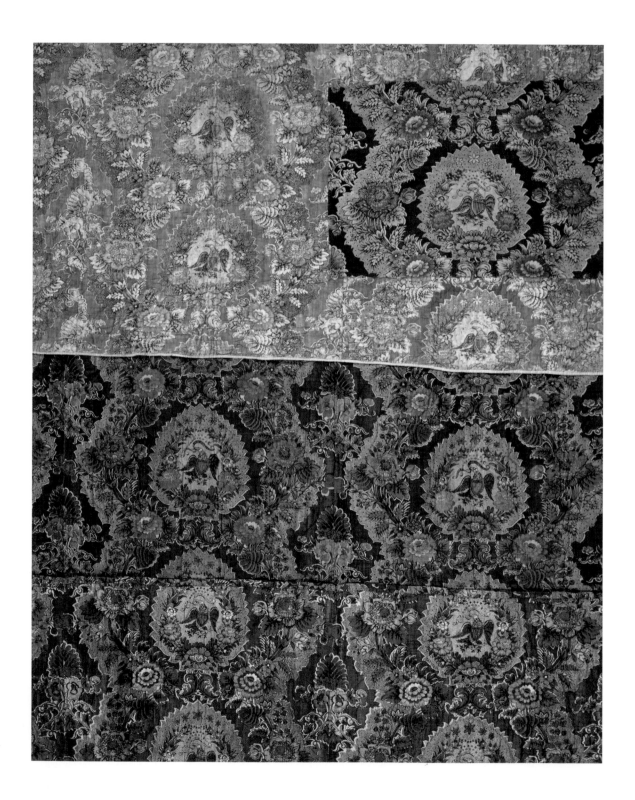

Colorways

Fabrics with patriotic imagery were produced in both the United States and Europe in different colorways. The red print seen here at the bottom was once a wholecloth quilt that was cut up to make curtains for the Essex Room at Winterthur.

Above **Detail, Wholecloth Quilt**
This wholecloth quilt from the early
1800s survives intact in the Winterthur collection.

Right **Wholecloth Quilt**
This example of a patriotic print has
survived in various colorways. The
red and brown fabrics are wholecloth
quilts.

7. *in themselves a textile museum:* decorating with quilts in the early twentieth century

Previous pages **H. F. du Pont's Bedroom at Chestertown House**

Henry Francis du Pont collected many examples of nineteenth-century pieced quilts, but relatively few are found today in the collection at Winterthur. Many of these remained at Chestertown House after du Pont's death and were sold along with the house to model, actress, and Warhol protégé "Baby" Jane Holzer and her husband, Leonard.

Right **Bedroom at Chestertown House**

The late-nineteenth-century quilt in this bedroom at Chestertown House was highly fashionable in the 1920s. Similar quilts were often featured in magazine articles giving hints on the decoration of bedrooms at the time.

Today, as in the past, people collect quilts for a variety of reasons. Some value quilts as colorful examples of folk art. Others find visual connections between historic quilts and stylistic movements in fine art, while a growing group of contemporary artists are building a rich body of work known collectively as art quilts. Some collectors may see quilts as important documents of women's history or as a means of visual or social expression within a particular region or cultural group. But perhaps the majority of collectors use quilts as decorative accessories in their home, to cover beds or to hang on walls.

Winterthur's founder, Henry Francis du Pont, used quilts in the carefully designed interiors he created in two of his houses during the first half of the twentieth century, and he was not alone. Other wealthy collectors of folk art and Americana, including Electra Havemeyer Webb, Ima Hogg, Bert and Nina Little, Henry and Helen Flynt, Henry Ford, and John D. and Abby Aldrich Rockefeller also began their collections for the purpose of decorating their own country homes.[1] Their impulse to collect, however, did not abate once their homes were complete. Often working with the same dealers and bidding at the same auctions, these individuals amassed collections that now form the basis of important museum holdings at Shelburne, Bayou Bend, Historic New England, Historic Deerfield, Greenfield Village, Colonial Williamsburg, and Winterthur. Using the rich resources of Winterthur's archives, where seemingly every letter, receipt, or scrap of paper associated with Henry Francis du Pont has been saved, this chapter looks at the way du Pont used quilts to furnish Chestertown, his summer residence on Long Island, as well as Winterthur, his Delaware estate. The interiors he created were regarded as among the most beautiful in the country, used for inspiration by professional decorators, personal friends, and, later, by many of the visitors to Winterthur Museum. Du Pont was elected to Honorary Membership of the American Institute of Decorators

in 1941 for "assembling and preserving important collections of American Furnishings," and his "generosity in opening these collections to the public and making them available to students of American design and decoration."[2]

H. F. du Pont collected during a time that is now known as the American colonial revival period. Closely allied to the Arts and Crafts movement, both looked back to a golden age before the advent of mechanization and mass production, when individual artisans created objects of simple, honest beauty.[3] The first phase of the colonial revival movement is associated with the celebrations surrounding America's Centennial celebration. At the many exhibitions and events held around the country, quilts were among the objects that were displayed because of their association with important historic figures or events. A good example is the quilt "made of pieces from the dresses which Mrs. General Washington wore at State receptions" displayed at a children's tea party organized in 1874 to commemorate the famous Boston Tea Party of a century before.[4] The second phase of the colonial revival, from about 1890 to 1920, was a period when domestic objects, later termed the "decorative arts," began to be seen in an aesthetic context as works of art in and of themselves. Marie Webster published her pioneering book on the history and design of quilts in 1915, and quilts were featured frequently in women's magazines.[5] Quilts really came into their own during the third phase of the movement, in the 1920s and 1930s, when they became highly desirable and were featured in magazines for collectors, such as *The Magazine Antiques,* as well as those on interior design, such as *Arts & Decoration.* Both antique and contemporary quilts are illustrated in these publications. While du Pont was not above using contemporary fabrics in his interiors, he always preferred the softer colors of antiques. Photographs of the bedrooms at Chestertown show fairly standard examples of nineteenth-century pieced and appliqué quilts.

Pansies

The combination of fabric, flowers, and wood in this Matisse painting entitled *Pansies* reflects the aesthetic that Henry Francis du Pont achieved when decorating at Winterthur. Du Pont collected examples of the same indigo resist fabric seen in the painting.

Du Pont evidently did not consider these quilts to be important historic examples; only a few were later donated to the museum collection at Winterthur.

Quilts were considered to be icons of early American domesticity, but their colors and patterns were also recognized as being appropriate for use with modernist furniture.[6] In the foreword to *Old Patchwork Quilts and the Women Who Made Them*, Ruth Finley wrote, "While the present-day vogue for patchwork is due primarily to a deeply stimulated interest in all things historically expressive of our national background and growth, the wide and varied use of old quilts undoubtedly has been greatly furthered by the modernistic trend in every branch of decoration toward brilliance of color and boldness of line. Today's taste is not shocked by such antique combinations as purple and cerise nor by composition so stark as to be geometrical."[7]

During the first years of the twentieth century, Henry Francis du Pont's collecting interests were not focused exclusively on American decorative arts. Like many of his contemporaries, he was fascinated by the colorfully embroidered peasant costumes he first saw while traveling through the Balkans in 1907, and later in Scandinavia, Russia, Poland, and Turkey. Interest in European folk art was strong at the time, influencing artists as well as historians and collectors.[8] Some of the examples du Pont acquired were displayed on mannequins in the Golf Room at Winterthur, and he wore others to parties. Although he later concentrated strictly on American furniture, glass, paintings, prints, and metalwork, du Pont continued to collect European textiles and ceramics throughout his life, often for their color and pattern. But his peasant costumes fell out of favor, and while a few pieces remain at Winterthur, du Pont donated the bulk to the Brooklyn Museum in 1932 and the Wilmington Fine Arts Society in 1939.[9]

Henry Francis du Pont had grown up surrounded by French and English antiques, and he continued to live with them in his New York apartment and later in the Cottage, the smaller house on the Winterthur estate to which he moved after the opening of the museum in 1951. In 1962, du Pont related the famous story about the beginning of his interest in American decorative arts. In 1922, while du Pont was visiting the home of W. Seward Webb in Shelburne, Vermont, Mrs. Webb offered to show him her daughter-in-law's old farmhouse known as the Brick House. According to du Pont, "I went upstairs and saw this dresser—this pine dresser, and I thought it was charming, quite lovely. It just took my breath away. . . . Then we went to see the house of Harry Sleeper in Gloucester which was very attractively arranged, so I said to my wife, 'Why don't we build an American house?'"[10] This was the impetus for Chestertown House in Southampton, New York, where the couple had rented a summer cottage for many years. It was also the start of his obsession with collecting American antiques.

James Watson and Electra Havemeyer Webb's house in Vermont influenced du Pont's choice of an architect. Chestertown House was designed by the New York firm of Cross and Cross, who had recently extended the Brick House for the Webbs in Shelburne. Working with Henry Davis Sleeper, an architect and interior designer in great demand among wealthy collectors of this period, du Pont created beautiful interiors that influenced many other collectors and decorators.[11] Fellow collector Nina Fletcher Little later wrote, "In the 1920s, most young antiquarians felt that their homes were not complete without a warming pan beside the hearth, a spinning wheel in the parlor, a patchwork quilt on the bed, hooked rugs on the floor, and a ship in a bottle on the windowsill."[12] These decorative accessories were certainly prevalent at Chestertown, but they do not tell the whole story.

The early twentieth century was a period of intense interest in interior design. In 1897, Edith Wharton and Ogden Codman Jr. published their influential book *The Decoration of Houses*, and a plethora of magazine articles expounded the principles of interior design for large and small homes, country houses, and city apartments.[13] Wharton was a childhood friend of du Pont's mother, Pauline Foster du Pont. His sister, Louise du Pont Crowninshield, called Codman "Uncle Ogden," after her marriage into the Crowninshield family.[14] By 1913, when interior decorator Elsie de Wolfe published *The House in Good Taste*, advocating the use of bright chintzes for curtains and upholstery and emphasizing subtle color harmonies, the field of interior design was booming. De Wolfe's most famous interior was that of the Colony Club in New York, where Henry Francis du Pont's wife, Ruth Wales du Pont, was a member.[15] That same year, Nancy McClelland, who later had her own successful decorating firm in New York, founded the first department of antiques and interior decoration at Wanamaker's, a department store where H. F. du Pont was a valued client.[16] Interior decoration was increasingly recognized as a profession. Parsons School of Design (then known as the Chase School, named for the American impressionist painter William Merritt Chase) was the first to teach interior design in the early years of the twentieth century, and in 1916, the New York School of Interior Design was founded to train the growing number of people going into the field.[17] Magazines such as *House and Garden*, *Arts & Decoration*, and *The Antiquarian* featured illustrations of interiors from homes in both Europe and America.

Words and phrases used to describe interior design at the time were closely related to those used in discussions about the new developments in fine art, where concepts of color and form, and balance and harmony were used in connection with the work of artists such as Picasso and Matisse. Such abstract associations were part of the philosophy developed by Dr. Albert C. Barnes, whose collection purposely displayed objects from disparate cultures, periods, and media together to illustrate his scientific method of looking at art. Albert and Laura Barnes were close friends with H. F.

and Ruth du Pont, speaking French at the dinner parties they gave for each other and exchanging advice about plants and furniture varnish.[18] The Barneses' Chester County country home was full of Pennsylvania German redware and late nineteenth-century Pennsylvania appliqué quilts. Today, few comparisons are made between a rococo high chest and a painting by Cézanne, but Dr. Barnes could clearly see a connection between his collection and du Pont's when he wrote, "I spent a whole afternoon with them [trustees of the University of Pennsylvania] in our gallery, pointing out furniture, iron and paintings how the creative artists of each era had used the contributions of their predecessors as points of departure for individual work of their own. It was then that I told them that your collection was in this respect the most important in the world because it had so many fine pieces of each era that showed the continuity of traditions most clearly."[19]

Perhaps interior design should not be considered on the same metaphysical plane as fine art, but the aesthetic connections were obvious. Artists, architects, and interior decorators were all influenced by the continuing debate about pattern and abstraction that took place after the Armory Show held in New York in 1913—the first large exhibition of modern art in America.[20] These ongoing discussions focused not only on contemporary painting and sculpture, but also on the artistic value of domestic objects, Navajo rugs, and folk art.[21] Du Pont never commented on the collection put together by Albert Barnes and there is no evidence that du Pont saw the Armory Show, but Frank Crowninshield, the art critic, editor of the magazine *Vanity Fair*, and a major supporter of the exhibition, was a frequent house guest at Winterthur. He gave du Pont prints of works by Chagall and Renoir as Christmas gifts in 1943 and 1946.[22] Du Pont may well have seen examples of modern art displayed in department stores—the Belmaison department at Wanamaker's, where he was a customer, displayed modern art in 1922, and Gimbel's toured exhibitions around

the country. Du Pont must have appreciated the modernist style because he ordered Wiener Werkstätte linens in the 1920s.[23] The influence of modern art on the design of interiors was widespread.[24]

The same aesthetic that du Pont later created in his interiors can be seen in a painting by Matisse. In *Pansies*, painted after the Armory Show, around 1918, Matisse placed a small glass vase of flowers at the edge of a wooden table in front of a draped piece of indigo resist-patterned cotton, a textile also owned by du Pont.[25] The juxtaposition of flowers, fabric, and furniture in du Pont's New York Room, or the Queen Anne Parlor at Winterthur, are exactly the same as in the painting, although the floral arrangements favored by du Pont were somewhat more elaborate. It is not coincidental that artists like Matisse were being criticized for being merely decorative.[26] Believing that his achievements at Winterthur, as well as his earlier interiors at Chestertown House, should be seen as art, du Pont wrote in 1952, "Each individual who collects anything of a serious nature thinks in increasingly creative terms, almost as if his collection were a kind of artistic medium."[27] Du Pont carefully placed his furniture within each room, striving for symmetry and balance, but his textiles were the primary means of bringing in color and pattern, as he carefully coordinated his rugs, curtains, upholstery, and bedcovers with the views of the changing garden seen through the windows. Although du Pont was systematically collecting American furniture to acquire various period and regional styles, his primary concern in creating interiors was aesthetic and not scholarly, and his use of quilts reflects this overarching sense.

Du Pont used quilts for more than bedcovers and wall hangings. Today it seems shocking to learn that quilts were considered a source of fabric to be cut up and used to upholster furniture (see page 9). This was once a common practice for collectors and was supported by many dealers, including Mary Allis, an important Connecticut collector and dealer in

Americana. She wrote to H. F. du Pont to offer him "a beautifully quilted camlet petticoat—a medium blue—soft and dull—not faded. It has been cut in half and joined to make a flat piece apparently used as a coverlet, but there is ample to upholster a chair. It would be particularly good for that purpose as the quilting is not too 'stuffed' but nice and flat."[28] Quilted petticoats were not valued as pieces of historic clothing and contained just enough yardage to cover an easy chair. It seems that only quilts considered to be common or of lesser quality, or ones that had suffered localized damage, were used in this way. These were often, but not always, wool or printed-cotton wholecloth quilts, selected for their color and texture.[29] This widespread practice somewhat skews our understanding of the number of wholecloth quilts compared to pieced or appliqué examples made and used in the nineteenth century. Such estimates should not be based solely on surviving examples because so many of the former have been cut to pieces. Sadly, du Pont was a major destroyer of quilts. In 1925, he wrote to the New Jersey dealer Wilmer Moore, "In regards to the chintz quilt, I am afraid that inasmuch as the chintz top is broken in a few small places it will not be strong enough for me to upholster on a chair, and that is what I am doing with all my quilts."[30] Evidence of this destruction survives because du Pont kept the many scraps that resulted from this practice. He stored them in bins and used them to repair damaged upholstery covers.

Although du Pont and his fellow collectors of Americana were eager to prove that American fine and decorative arts could hold their own with more sophisticated European styles, not all of their quilts were American. A Mrs. Tysen, who took over the antiques department of Wanamaker's, Au Quatrième, from Nancy McClelland, wrote to du Pont in 1924 to explain the high prices for a French quilt and quilted petticoats. "While they are all old, still they are not over one hundred years so that we are forced to pay duty on them.

Chestertown House

The first-floor hall at Chestertown House contains an eclectic mix of furnishings that range in date from the seventeenth to the early twentieth century. The political iconography so prominent in the homes of early collectors of Americana is seen here in the eagles above the window draperies, the eagle sculpture on a table, and the quilt on the wall that depicts the Battle of Resaca de la Palma during the Mexican-American War.

Our man who collects these quilted things for us in Paris tells us that they are probably sixty to seventy-five years old. We get them in rather deplorable condition and have them cleaned in Paris before they are sent on to us." The following year another letter from Wanamaker's mentioned the use of an antique quilted petticoat to cover a wing chair that du Pont had ordered.[31] This use of European quilts also seems to have been a fairly common and highly fashionable practice. The influential magazine *Arts & Decoration* featured many images of quilted furniture covers, including a walnut bench covered with "green blue Spanish quilting," and an "old-time Breton armchair" covered "with a Britanny quilted figured chintz," which they placed near a colonial buffet.[32]

Covering chairs with quilted chintz was all the rage, a fashion not limited to collectors of Americana. Elsa Schiaparelli, the famous designer closely associated with surrealist artists such as Salvador Dalí and Jean Cocteau, used quilted chair covers in her London and Paris apartments.[33] Emily Post, who is better known for her books on etiquette, illustrated a quilt-covered easy chair in *The Personality of a House*, her book on decorating published in 1930.[34] A historic example was used by Nancy McClelland in her own book, *Furnishing the Colonial and Federal House*, where she writes about "A conventional tulip design in a patchwork quilt . . . with exceptionally fine quilting. Many old bits of this sort can be used on beds, or made into wall hangings, or even employed as upholstery materials for comfortable chairs."[35]

Nancy McClelland knew du Pont well. She visited Winterthur on a number of occasions and brought clients to see the interiors he created. It was in 1941, when McClelland served as president of the American

Institute of Decorators, that du Pont was "unanimously elected to Honorary Membership" for his "distinguished achievement in assembling and preserving important collections of American Furnishings" and for "making them available to students of American design and decoration."[36] Other honorary members at that time were Elsie de Wolfe and both John D. Rockefeller Jr. and Henry Ford, whose period rooms at Williamsburg and Greenfield Village, respectively, also influenced the burgeoning fashion for traditional interiors.

Quilted chair-covers were so fashionable that printed imitations were manufactured by high-end fabric houses like F. Schumacher & Co., whose line of Perriwigg Prints included a faux pieced-work quilt pattern, a type of design that has been called "cheater's cloth." In 1927, the Novelty Selling Company promoted their "Patchwork printed by the yard instead of toilsomely sewn. We have seen nothing quainter for spreads, quilts, and for upholstering old-style furniture. Will harmonize with any old-style color scheme." This fabric could be purchased as plain fabric or already lined and quilted. Even the English firm of Warner & Sons produced a design simply called "Patchwork" for the American market in 1935.[37] Although he preferred historic examples, du Pont used modern printed-patchwork cloth to cover at least two easy chairs in his parlor at Chestertown. These trompe l'oeil fabrics had first become popular during the 1840s, with the fashion being revived in the 1920s.[38] A late-nineteenth-century example, imitating a quilt design sometimes known as "tumbling blocks," was used by du Pont at Chestertown House and was given to Winterthur after his death by his daughter Pauline Harrison.

H. F. du Pont furnished both of his American homes with many examples of quilts, ceramics, furniture, and sculpture that depicted patriotic and political imagery.[39] The 1920s and 1930s were years when "American intellectuals, historians, artists, museum curators, art dealers, and politicians became intensely preoccupied with

issues of cultural nationalism, with determining the links between American national identity and American art and material culture."[40] Eagles, whether carved in wood by Wilhelm Schimmel, depicted on transfer-printed Staffordshire jugs, or appliquéd on quilts, were a favorite motif among collectors of the period, with antiques dealers scrambling to satisfy the huge demand in what was becoming a very competitive market. Not everyone was equally obsessed with this patriotic iconography. Despite his intense commitment to the value and beauty of American decorative arts, R. T. H. Halsey, the scholar and collector who is credited with making the American Wing at the Metropolitan Museum of Art a reality, used what he described as "a term of admiring reproach," to name this syndrome "spread eagleism."[41]

Like his friends and fellow collectors, du Pont was insatiable in his quest for fabric, commemorative handkerchiefs, and quilts with patriotic images and political imagery, which he used on beds, for wall hangings, and for window curtains. A quilt he used as a wall hanging in the first floor hall at Chestertown depicts Zachary Taylor's victory at the Battle of Resaca de la Palma during the war with Mexico, made from fabric printed in 1848 in support of Taylor's bid for the American presidency (see page 173). Though he prized its political imagery, H. F. du Pont also valued this quilt for its color—its browns, blues, and greens were fashionable in both the 1840s and the 1920s. Although du Pont's interest was primarily the eighteenth century (he considered Chestertown to be illustrative of the 1780s),[42] he would often use fabrics from later periods to achieve the color harmonies he loved so dearly. Aesthetics always trumped historical accuracy; du Pont was notorious for wanting to display portraits of only good-looking people.[43]

Inheriting the Winterthur estate after his father's death in 1926, Henry Francis du Pont immediately began planning renovations and new construction. These changes transformed the house, designed and decorated in an eclectic French historical style popular

with wealthy Americans during in the Gilded Age, into a twentieth-century version of an early American home. Many of the early furnishing schemes at Winterthur, photographed in the 1930s, resembled those at Chestertown. These interiors changed throughout the 1930s and 1940s, as du Pont continued to add to and rearrange his collection.

Du Pont cared as much, if not more, about the arrangement of groups of objects as he did about individual pieces in his collection. Lending many valued items to the famous Girl Scouts Loan Exhibition at the Anderson Galleries in New York in 1929, he "got so involved with the right look of the display that at one point he threw off his hat and coat and simultaneously directed the workmen and fiddled with the exact positioning of pieces himself."[44] He was also notorious for rearranging furniture when visiting the homes of friends and relations, admitting that he knew that they would put it right back, but at least it had been correct for a short time.[45] Displays in museums, particularly in the American Wing of the Metropolitan Museum of Art, Henry Ford's Greenfield Village, and at Colonial Williamsburg, heavily influenced interior designers. The great emphasis placed on the beauty of these arrangements was of equal importance to museum curators. Fiske Kimball, an architect who restored Jefferson's Monticello before serving as director of the Philadelphia Museum of Art for more than thirty years, wrote of the "unity of spirit, expressed in line and color" that was "not mere historical pedantry. Conditions have not so changed here but that the simplicity of living which marked the Colonial still gives the characteristic American note."[46]

Each room at Winterthur was designed around a specific period, style, theme, or geographic region. In the early 1930s, as the new mansion was being completed and the room installations finalized, Charles O. Cornelius was commissioned to write descriptions of each room, including background information about the historical context as well as catalogue information

Henry Francis du Pont and His Grandson
Du Pont is seen here in a chair covered in 1920s "cheater's cloth", a printed imitation of patchwork.

Right **Detail, Wholecloth Quilt**
An example of a trompe l'oeil–printed patchwork from the 1880s, this printed wholecloth quilt was used at Chestertown House.

about individual objects. Cornelius was an architect who had worked as a curator at the Metropolitan Museum of Art, where, with R. T. H. Halsey, he wrote the first handbook describing the American Wing, published for its opening in 1924. The room settings in the American Wing greatly influenced the burgeoning interest in traditional interiors. Not everyone catalogues the furnishings in their new home, but du Pont was already thinking that Winterthur might someday become a museum. He had investigated the possibility of turning Chestertown into a museum in 1928, having requested information from Henry Davis Sleeper about instructions concerning plans for Isabella Stewart Gardner's own museum as spelled out in her will.[47] Du Pont must originally have commissioned a catalogue of the collection at Chestertown from Charles O. Cornelius, because he later wrote, "You have always been so delightfully vague in the past and I have had such poor results with the Southampton cataloguing that I am really a bit leery about all you charmingly artistic people."[48]

In 1930, du Pont planned to use an 1853 quilt depicting various American presidents (cut up and made into a bed valance and window curtains) in the Albany Dressing Room at Winterthur.[49] Cornelius wrote that the Albany Dressing Room reflected the "stridency" of patriotic fervor in America during the second quarter of the nineteenth century, which he saw reflected "in the sharp contrasts of color in this small room," seen in the curtains, valance, hooked rug, and painted woodwork.[50] Du Pont had purchased the quilt at the Pennypacker auction rooms in Reading, Pennsylvania, where it had been described as a "rare specimen."[51] This did not prevent him from cutting up the original quilt. The borders of appliqué soldiers were made into a bed valance. Eight of the quilt blocks were made into window curtains. The squares labeled "J. Q. Adams, J. Tyler, J. Monroe, and J. Adams were used on the left, and General Jackson, T. Jefferson, General Washington, and

M Van Buren" were used on the right. The remaining block, depicting Madison, covered a chair cushion.

Although he considered Winterthur to be a country estate, Henry Francis du Pont designed his Delaware home with a more sophisticated style than Chestertown. Pieced and appliqué quilts, traditionally associated with informal country houses, did not have a place in the furnishings on display during private tours of Winterthur, but could be used to provide comfort for guests. The Nemours Room was designed to display du Pont family memorabilia and the French influence on American home furnishings in the early 1800s. "The statement made by the Nemours Room is that America was created of and by men, ideas and influences coming from foreign countries, but that these men and these ideas created in the United States a culture which developed its own distinctive personality."[52] Because du Pont liked to change the textile furnishings in his rooms to coordinate with the changing colors in his beloved garden, many of the rooms have two or more sets of window curtains, bedcovers and hangings, rugs, slipcovers for furniture, and even slipseats for chairs. The winter hangings for the bedstead in the Nemours Room were made from silk believed to have been brought from France by Eleuthère Irenée du Pont in 1800. The summer change features a wholecloth counterpane made up in the early twentieth century from antique fabric that was originally fashionable in the 1810s. Du Pont purchased a bedspread and valance made from this fabric from Nancy McClelland, who told him that they had come from a house in Bethel, Connecticut, where they were said to have been used on a bed since 1800. "I thought you would be terribly interested in the design of the chintz because it shows such lovely curtains—almost as lovely as those in your house and the price of the two pieces is only $100.00."[53] Du Pont copied the drapery depicted on the cloth for the window in the Nemours Room.

Winterthur was considered to be a show house,

Wholecloth Quilt
Created from roller-printed fabric in 1848, in support of Zachary Taylor's bid for the American presidency, this wholecloth quilt is one of many political quilts collected by Henry Francis du Pont.

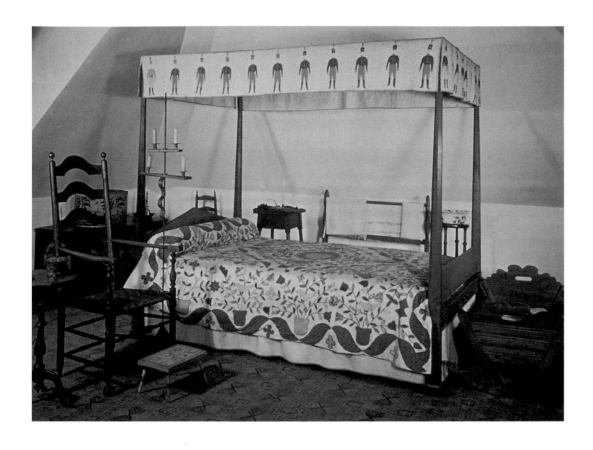

Opposite **Pieced and Appliqué Quilt**
Digitally reconstructed here, this
1853 quilt survives in the Winterthur
collection in the form of a valance
(seen at left) and window curtains.

Left **Lebanon Room**
The valance seen here, made from
the border of an 1853 quilt, was used
in the Albany Dressing Room during
the 1930s. Du Pont and other collectors of Americana frequently made
quilts into window curtains, bedhangings, and upholstery covers.

with regular tours of the rooms, including bedrooms,
for visiting guests. In addition to the seasonal changes
of furnishing textiles used "for show," H. F. du Pont also
kept distinct bedcovers for guests. These were often
patchwork or appliqué quilts. One such quilt, which like
all his collection was carefully labeled to document its
use in a particular room for a specific season, was put in
the Nemours Room during the months of July, August,
and September "for guests." A list of bedspreads compiled
for the Maple Room down the hall included seasonal
changes for show and for use, but also two white bedspreads "for careless guests."[54] Although these quilts
were not part of his formal decorating scheme, du Pont
valued them as important objects in their own right,
instructing his executors that "Besides the bedspreads

(quilts) that go on the beds at the different seasons,
there are the guest bedspreads and quite a few that I
have not been able to use. These are to be shown in the
Bedspread Room with the ones not in use on the beds,
and, some of the least interesting can be disposed of."[55]

Staying at Winterthur could be quite stressful for
guests who may not have been accustomed to din-
ing with a footman behind every chair or sleeping in a
museum setting. Because du Pont had carefully placed
every object, from major pieces of furniture down to
needlework pocketbooks or other small decorative
accessories, family and visitors alike knew they had to
be careful of the priceless antiques that surrounded
them. Mrs. Reginald Rose, the daughter of du Pont's
close friend Bertha Benkard and a frequent guest at

Winterthur, described the experience: "Before dinner you would get dressed. You would obviously mess up your room a bit. In fact, I'm not at all sure the bed didn't have the bedspread off . . . if you wanted to lie down and take a nap. And your clothes were around and your things were there. You would go down and have dinner, and then there would be the house tour . . . if he had important people naturally he conducted it himself. You would trail along and as you got towards your room you would think 'God, I wonder if my stockings are hanging over something.' And you would go into the room and you might have died. Absolutely no sign that you were staying in that room at all."[56] One of the worst offenses was to sit or lie down on the beds before the bedcover, on which du Pont lavished such care and attention, had been removed. An anonymous guest, clearly a frequent visitor, speaks for many others in a poem entitled "A Good Girl's Soliloquy":

I never break or mar antiques
Or drop the birds with china beaks:
An ash or spark I never let
Drop from my lighted cigarette
As others do.

I never touch or use the cards
When both my hands are stuck with lards
Or ever on a table set
A tumbler when it's damp or wet
As others do.

My husband, too, is always neat
And walks about in stocking-feet
In order not to mar or bruise
The parquet floors in hob-nailed shoes
As others do.

When playing golf and when I pivot
I right away replace the divot:—

Opposite, above **Nemours Room**
The Nemours Room at Winterthur
is seen here in a 1935 stereopticon
with the printed cotton bedhangings
and wholecloth counterpane used
in the summer months "for show."
This fabric, fashionable in the 1810s,
survives in at least three colorways.
The bedstead is attributed to French
cabinetmaker Charles-Honoré Lan-
nuier, who was working in New York
City between 1803 and 1819.

Opposite, below **Nemours Room**
A pieced quilt with a border of the
same fabric, depicting a draped
window, was used in the Nemours
Room for guests during the summer
months. Henry Francis du Pont felt
that pieced quilts were inappropriate for Winterthur's formal interiors,
which is why the collection contains
so many wholecloth examples.

Right **Pieced Quilt**
The central part of this quilt is made
from 577 pieces. Although the border
fabric was fashionable in the 1810s,
the designs and dyestuffs in some of
the pieces date this quilt to the mid-
1820s. Its origin is unknown, but a
label sewn to one corner records that
it was used in the Nemours Room
"for guests."

In fact I always try to do
Just what my parents taught me to.

So when I visit Winterthur
Most strange discomfort I endure
For ne'er I lie upon the bed
Or put my shoes on the Franklin spread
As others do.[57]

Henry Francis du Pont's sophisticated sense of
color harmonies resulted in some unusual uses of quilts.
One example with a very bold design of strongly contrasting colors is very different from his usual aesthetic
preferences. Labeled for use in the Patuxent Room, this
quilt was installed upside down on the bed, displaying
the backing, a tightly woven, light brown glazed cotton,
which blends beautifully with the chintz curtains and
bedhangings. The quilt can be recognized in the black-
and-white photograph here by the pattern of quilting
stitches seen clearly around the edges.[58] This was
not a mistake, but was intentional. In a letter to his
executors, du Pont acknowledges that "There are
some nineteenth-century materials in the house, of
which I am fully aware. There are also a few pieces
of new fringe here and there, and some materials are
wrong side out. This has been done deliberately, and
I am writing this simply to assure the Director and
members of the Board that I have not been hood-
winked but that it was the best thing to be done
under the circumstances."[59]

Du Pont worked with many people to create his
interiors, although he made all the detailed decisions
himself. The house was designed by Albert Ely Ives,
but another architect and historian, Thomas T. Waterman, worked to ensure that the interiors fit the historic
architectural features that du Pont had been purchasing
through various dealers for many years, storing them,
until needed, in various barns around the Winterthur
estate. Du Pont's good friend Marian Cruger Coffin

Opposite, above **Patuxent Room**
Quilts could be used in unusual ways at Winterthur. The quilt on the bed in the Patuxent Room is the 1880s mosaic quilt shown on pages 180–81, but displayed wrong-side out. It can be identified by the pattern of quilting stitches. Du Pont valued the glazed-cotton backing for the way its color harmonized with other fabrics in the room.

Opposite, below **Benkard Parlor**
Bertha Benkard, a close friend of Henry Francis du Pont, was renowned for her scholarship and her good taste. Du Pont once wrote to tell her how much a group of visitors from France had admired the beauty of the parlor in her home in Oyster Bay, seen here. The chairs are upholstered with a dark blue wool wholecloth quilt that dates to the late eighteenth or early nineteenth century.

Right **Wholecloth Quilt**
Henry Francis du Pont purchased this indigo-resist printed wholecloth quilt from Bertha Benkard's estate after her death in 1945. He also acquired bedcovers and other blue and white quilts and fabrics. Two different fabrics were used on either side of the quilt. The striped design of animals is unique; the decorative floral pattern an the other side is more conventional in style.

Opposite **Pieced Quilt**
This mosaic quilt from about 1880, made with a variety of colorful silks and wools, was used upside down in the Patuxent Room. The vivid colors and strong contrasts of tone were not valued by Henry Francis du Pont.

Right **Detail, Pieced Quilt and Bed-hangings, Patuxent Room**
The bedhangings in Patuxent Room were a perfect color match for the glazed-cotton backing on the quilt.

OLD CHINTZES and EMBROIDERIES
ELINOR MERRELL
18 E. 69th ST. & 833 Madison Ave. *(bet. 69th & 70th Sts.)* New York 21

Opposite **Wholecloth Quilts**
In the early 1930s, H. F. du Pont
cut up a printed wholecloth quilt,
made from an English pillar print
from about 1830, to cover chairs
and cushions in the Albany Room
at Winterthur. In 2000, Winterthur
acquired a quilt made of the same
fabric, shown here in an arranged
studio setting.

Above **Elinor Merrell's Shop**
Elinor Merrell's New York showroom
was a mecca for collectors of historic
furnishing fabrics and a regular meeting place for Henry Francis du Pont
and Bertha Benkard. Merrell sold so
many historic fabrics to du Pont that
she claims her business was scarcely
affected by the Great Depression.

worked closely with him to landscape the garden area
around the new construction. The many curtains, bedhangings, and furniture covers were executed by Ernest
Lo Nano, who worked at Winterthur from 1929 until his
death in 1958. Becoming known as an expert in the field
of historic interiors, Lo Nano eventually had showrooms
in both New York and Williamsburg, and worked for
virtually all of the important museums, historic houses,
and private collectors.[60]

The person who helped the most with du Pont's
interiors was Bertha Benkard (Mrs. Harry Horton Benkard), without whose "expert advice and absolutely
faultless taste and eye . . . the results never could have
been accomplished."[61] An important collector in her
own right, Mrs. Benkard was known as "an outstanding
authority on antique furniture," particularly pieces made
by Duncan Phyfe. She donated objects to the Metropolitan Museum of Art and furnished a room at the
Museum of the City of New York with Phyfe furniture
in memory of her husband, who died in 1928.[62] Mrs.
Benkard was renowned for her sense of color and was a
major textile collector. She was particularly fond of blue
and used a dark blue wholecloth quilt to upholster the
chairs in the parlor of her home in Oyster Bay on Long
Island, which was photographed just after her death
in 1945.[63] Du Pont purchased many textiles from her
estate, including an important bed rug made by Mary
Foot in 1778 and other blue and white quilts, bedhangings, and yardage.

According to her daughter, Mrs. Benkard spent
hours and hours on the telephone with du Pont avidly
discussing every detail of the fringes and tassels being
used to embellish the curtains and bedhangings for
Winterthur. This was in addition to a voluminous correspondence between the two that records yet more
discussions about decorative details, letters that can
range in length from one short sentence to pages of
suggestions, questions, and requests for help. Mrs.
Benkard would often visit textile dealers to select pieces

that might be of interest to du Pont, which would be
put aside for his approval. They also would frequently
meet at Ernest Lo Nano's or at textile scholar and dealer
Elinor Merrell's showroom to look at fabrics, always with
a specific project in mind. This was the height, or depth,
of the Great Depression, but Merrell remembered "I
didn't know anything about the Depression, really, for
quite a while because that was the time that Mr. du
Pont was buying stuff from me."[64] Benkard would frequently travel to Winterthur, sometimes while du Pont
was away, to oversee the installations and to help make
final decisions about decorative details once a room
had been completed. Merrell remembered that "Mrs.
Benkard had made her little touches around there, toss-
ing on a chaise lounge in some bedroom or other . . . an
old garment of some kind, something beautiful. Oh, the
colors were enough to kill you."[65]

"Green is one of the prettiest colors there is."[66]
Although he was discussing plants at the time, this
opinion is no doubt what attracted du Pont to a
wholecloth quilt made from a type of design known
as a pillar print, which he cut up to make slipcovers for
the chairs and daybed in the Albany Room. Du Pont
was renowned for his attention to myriad small details
within a room that created a pleasing ensemble, a
symphony of pattern and color. The strong green of the
background of this former quilt was repeated in the
Feraghan rug, and in the floral striped chintz used for
the bed- and window hangings. But it was more than
just the color that made this fabric work in the Albany
Room; it was the pillar motif itself, which was repeated
in the reeded high posts of the bedstead with their
overlapping leaves on flaring capitals. The bellflower
motif, also carved on these posts, was echoed in the
woodwork surrounding the windows and on other
decorative accessories in the room.

It was this attention to detail that was commented
upon by so many people who visited Winterthur both
before and after it became a museum. Elinor Merrell

remembered that du Pont, along with Henry Sleeper and the Chicago-based architects Sam Marx and David Adler, "would have an idea and then build everything around it in two seconds, you know. A color and design and everything. It was fascinating to see them operate."[67] The Albany Room is furnished with objects dating between 1800 and 1810, but this pillar print is from around 1830, when British textile printers were developing incredible expertise in both dye chemistry and roller-printing technology. Although it was not possible to establish a firm date for these pillar prints until the 1950s, du Pont was clearly using it for the color and design, not for its historical accuracy in the room. A popular design in America at the beginning of both the nineteenth and twentieth centuries, Winterthur has sixty examples of pillar prints in the collection, the majority collected by du Pont in the 1930s, although a few important examples were donated or purchased after the museum opened in 1951. In 2000, Winterthur was able to acquire a complete wholecloth quilt made from this same pillar print.

Henry Francis du Pont was exceedingly proud of a wholecloth quilt and bedhangings originally owned by the Ten Eyck family of Albany, New York.[68] Du Pont was related to the Ten Eycks through his mother's family. Pauline Foster du Pont's father was Herman Ten Eyck Foster, whose middle name celebrated the family heritage of his mother, Anna Ten Eyck.[69] The quilt and bedhangings had long been used in a bedroom at Winterthur, but had become quite tattered and discolored by 1911, when Henry Francis had the fabric copied in Paris by Tassinari & Chatel. Better known for their elaborate silks woven with gold and silver thread for the courts of Europe, Tassinari & Chatel continue to reproduce many historic fabrics from their own archives for museums and historic houses today. The firm had supplied many of the elaborately elegant furnishing fabrics used at Winterthur, so Henry Francis du Pont may have preferred to work with a firm he knew to make this

reproduction. He also may have selected a French firm thinking that the fabric in question had been printed in that country.[70]

At the time almost all of the eighteenth-century plate-printed cottons—which were highly valued, widely discussed, and often exhibited—were thought to have originated in France. Early textile scholarship was focused on what were known then, and continue to be known today, as toiles de Jouy, whatever their country of origin. The 1911 reproduction is quite faithful to the original, but was printed on linen cloth, unlike the original, which was printed on cotton. This may have been an attempt to reproduce the texture of the ground cloth, but may also have been a misidentification of the fiber, an assumption based on the indiscriminate use of the word "linen" associated with historic textiles at that time. This design is still being reproduced by the firm Brunschwig & Fils, from this example in Winterthur's collection.

It was not until the 1950s, when textile scholar Peter Floud discovered sample books in England and France documenting 335 different designs, that the extent of British copperplate printing from the eighteenth century was recognized.[71] His research was conducted in preparation for an exhibition of printed cottons assembled by the Victoria and Albert Museum and exhibited at the Cotton Board's Colour, Design and Style Center in Manchester, England. Winterthur's first curator of textiles, Florence Montgomery, was so impressed with Floud's research that she and her husband, Charles, who was Winterthur's director at the time, invited Floud to visit America in 1958 (funded by du Pont) to help identify the collection of printed textiles at Winterthur and take the opportunity to visit other collections.

After his visit, Floud wrote to du Pont, "I should like you to know how amazed I was at the wealth of English printed textiles in the Museum. There is no doubt whatever that it is the largest such collection in the world, and contains substantially more important eighteenth

century examples than any other collection. I personally find it particularly interesting that your instinct as a collector led you so unerringly to choose such a high proportion of what we now know are English rather than French textiles at a time when no one could have been very sure of their nationality. I could not have hoped for any clearer conformation [sic] of my belief that there is a basic difference in the general style and appearance of English chintzes as against French."[72] A second, larger exhibition containing many textiles from Winterthur and other American collections took place in London in 1960, just after Floud's untimely death. Du Pont preferred not to lend objects to exhibitions but, because of his high regard for Floud, he agreed, and in fact delivered some of the textiles himself.[73] Some of these loans became gifts, as Floud convinced the Montgomerys to exchange sixty examples of Winterthur's eighteenth-century printed cottons for the same number of samples from the 1820s and 1830s that had been removed from sample books donated to the Victoria and Albert Museum by the Calico Printers' Association. Like du Pont, Florence Montgomery preferred the eighteenth-century designs and was not pleased with this exchange. She later became reconciled to the nineteenth-century samples when she realized their historic value. Many of these pieces documented the work of important designers, engravers, and printworks.[74]

Almost half of the quilts in Winterthur's collection are wholecloth, some made from silk or wool, but mostly made from eighteenth- and early nineteenth-century printed cottons. Some pieced quilts that date to the 1830s and 1840s were, in fact, collected for the eighteenth-century English plate-prints used as backings. Florence Montgomery sometimes catalogued these for the fabrics alone, never mentioning that they formed part of a quilt. Du Pont was always interested in the English plate-prints, probably due to his fondness for the Ten Eyck family quilt and bedhangings. He added other examples of this same design to his

Detail, Wholecloth Quilt

This copperplate design of ducks was first printed at the London print-works of Bromley Hall between 1785 and 1790, but furniture prints like this could stay in production for as long as twenty years. Du Pont avidly collected other examples of this design, including two wholecloth quilts printed in red and various bed curtains and yardage printed in blue.

growing collection of printed cottons, which included not only extensive yardage to be used in his interiors but also smaller samples of design repeats. In the 1940s, many museums collected textiles as examples of design and would often only acquire enough fabric to show one design repeat. Du Pont's purchases of these shorter lengths indicate a change from collecting fabric to use in interiors to collecting historic examples of textile design for academic purposes.

Du Pont kept up to date with the textile scholarship of his time. Elinor Merrell, who wrote extensively on the history of French printed textiles and staged many exhibitions in her New York showroom, sent du Pont a copy of the 1955 Manchester exhibition catalogue, telling him that "The three pattern books," containing the impression that documented the Ten Eyck fabric to the important London textile printing firm Talwin & Foster, were "the most interesting part of the exhibition for me." Merrell shared information about du Pont's important collection with French textile scholar Paul Schwartz, and kept du Pont informed of the recent publications from Schwartz's research at the Musée de l'Impression sur Étoffes in Mulhouse, France. Du Pont wrote to Merrell in 1956, thanking her for the information she had sent, and telling her, "Were not my plans all made to go to Greece at the end of August and the Italian Hill Towns—Mulhouse would be my destination. . . . I am having my handkerchiefs photographed now and in due time Mr. Paul Schwartz will receive a list and quite a few photographs. . . . I feel you are in Christopher Columbus' class."[75]

Du Pont was taking an increasingly scholarly approach to his collection, writing to antiques dealer Winsor White, "I find that some museums know a good deal more about the histories of their things than I do about ours; therefore, I want to get family histories whenever possible."[76] He requested this information from his old friends Rockwell and Avis Gardiner, who offered him Mary Remington's quilt, valances, quilted

dressing-table cover, sampler, and Queen-stitch pocketbook on approval in 1957, asking $575.00 for the lot.[77]

After opening his museum in 1951 and moving into the smaller cottage nearby, du Pont no longer purchased objects for his personal collection but generously funded many acquisitions for the museum. Although the Remington quilt that underpins the central themes for this book carries the anonymous credit line "museum purchase," it was the sophisticated eye, scholarly taste, and generous funding of Winterthur's founder, Henry Francis du Pont, that ensured its addition to the museum's important collection of early American quilts.[78] A product of du Pont's voracious collecting during the first half of the twentieth century, Winterthur's collection has continued to grow after his death through bequests, purchases, and donations.

Opposite **Fabric Sample**
Henry Francis du Pont had this fabric reproduced by the French firm Tassinari & Chatel in 1911. The original design, on the left, is printed on a cotton ground; the reproduction is printed on linen.

Above **Albany Room**
Sally Ellis Nicolson, one of the many du Pont cousins, sits in front of the Ten Eyck family quilt and bedhangings, which had descended in the family of H. F. du Pont's mother, Pauline Foster du Pont.

notes

INTRODUCTION

1. Virginia Gunn, "From Myth to Maturity: The Evolution of Quilt Scholarship," *Uncoverings* (San Francisco: American Quilt Study Group, 1993), pp. 192–205. Patricia J. Keller, "Methodology and Meaning: Strategies for Quilt Study," *The Quilt Journal* 2, no. 2 (1993): 1–4.

CHAPTER 1. *MY SITUATION IN LIFE:* THE STORY OF MARY REMINGTON

1. The letters survive in the Congdon Family Papers, MSS 363, series 4, subseries 5, box 3, Rhode Island Historical Society Library, Providence. Quote is from a letter from Mary Remington to Peleg Congdon (hereafter MR to PC), April 10, 1815. The quilt is in the Winterthur collection, acc. no. 1957.67.4.

2. Rev. Thomas Cook, A. M., *The New and Complete Letter Writer. Containing a Course of Interesting Original Letters, On the Most Important, Instructive, and Entertaining Subjects* (Wilmington, Del.: Printed and sold by Robert Porter, 1820), preface.

3. John Krill, *English Artists' Paper: Renaissance to Regency* (New Castle, Del.: Oak Knoll Press, 2002), pp. 60–69.

4. See Andrew Burstein, "The Political Character of Sympathy," *Journal of the Early Republic* 21, no. 4 (Winter 2001): 601–32.

5. Oliver P. Fuller, *History of Warwick, Rhode Island, from Its Settlement in 1642 to the Present Time* (Providence: Angell, Burlingame & Co., 1875), p. 167.

6. MR to PC, March 28, 1813; Henry Remington's will is in the Warwick City Hall. Genealogical Society microfilm, *Warwick, Rhode Island Probate Records: Wills* (1973), reel 5, Rhode Island Historical Society Library. The will was made on June 8, 1840, and recorded August 10, 1841.

7. Letter, John Jenkes to Remington, Arnold & Arnold, December 27, 1805, Henry Arnold Papers, MSS 268, folder 2, Rhode Island Historical Society Library; Henry Remington's probate inventory recorded September 13, 1841, Genealogical Society microfilm.

8. Donald D'Amato, *Images of Warwick* (Mount Pleasant, S.C.: Arcadia Publishing, 2003), p. 13.

9. MR to PC, June 3, 1812.

10. Fuller, *History of Warwick,* p. 153.

11. A copy of John Congdon's will is recorded in the Exeter, Rhode Island, Town Clerk's Office, *Council & Probate Records, Town of Exeter,* vol. 4, 1776–86, pp. 170–71.

12. Noah Webster, *A Compendious Dictionary of the English Language: A Facsimile of the First (1806) Edition* (New York: Bounty Books, 1970), p. 355.

13. MR to PC, June 11, 1815.

14. MR to PC, January 16, 1813.

15. MR to PC, March 11, 1815.

16. MR to PC, July 31, 1815.

17. MR to PC, July 31, 1815.

18. MR to PC, April 2, 1816.

19. MR to PC, January 1, 1817.

20. Jane Lancaster, "By the Pens of Females: Girls' Diaries from Rhode Island, 1788–1821," *Rhode Island History* 57, nos. 3/4 (1999): 86–97.

21. MR to PC, April 14, 1816.

22. MR to PC, July 11, 1816.

23. Earl P. Crandall, *Great-Grandma Was a Congdon* (Salem: Higginson Book Co., 1995).

24. MR to PC, July 13, 1816.

25. MR to PC, July 24, 1816.

26. MR to PC, August 6, 1816.

27. MR to PC, October 20, 1816.

28. Sheldon S. Cohen, "The Broken Bond: Divorce in Providence County, 1749–1809," *Rhode Island History* 44, no. 3 (1985): 69–71.

29. MR to PC, January 1, 1817.

30. MR to PC, January 1, 1817.

31. Fuller, *History of Warwick,* p. 167.

32. S. E. Ahlstrom, *A Religious History of the American People* (New Haven: Yale University Press, 1972), pp. 170, 173. Fuller, *History of Warwick,* p. 297.

33. Fuller, *History of Warwick,* pp. 322–25, 304, 309, 335, 357.

34. For examples, see Martha Tomhave Blauvelt, "Making a Match in Nineteenth-Century New York: The Courtship Diary of Mary Guion," *New York History* 76, no. 2 (April 1995): 153–72; Martha Tomhave Blauvelt, "The Work of the Heart: Emotion in the 1805–35 Diary of Sarah Connell Ayer," *Journal of Social History* 35, no. 3 (2002): 577–92.

35. Blauvelt, "Work of the Heart," pp. 577–92; quote, n. 5, p. 587.

36. David Hume, *The History of England, from the Invasion of Julius Caesar to the Revolution in 1688* (Philadelphia: Levis and Weaver, 1810), p. 78.

37. Jacqueline Belanger et al., British Fiction 1800–1829: A Database of Production and Reception, Phase II: The Flowers of Literature, http://www.cf.ac.uk/encap/corvey/articles/printer/flowers.html.

38. Betty Ring, *Let Virtue Be a Guide to Thee: Needlework in the Education of Rhode Island Women, 1730–1830* (Providence: Rhode Island Historical Society, 1983), pp. 238–39. Ring also quotes from Mary Remington's letters.

39. http://222.amphilsoc.org/library/guides/stape/pt2_printed.htm.

40. *Oxford English Dictionary,* http://www.oed.com. Thanks to Lynne Z. Bassett for alerting me to the earlier probate inventories.

41. *Godey's Lady's Book* 69 (July 1864): 79.

42. George Richardson, *A Book of Ceilings, Composed in the Style of the Antique Grotesque* (London: Printed for the author, 1776), pl. 17. Thanks to Cate Cooney for introducing me to this source.

43. Eileen Harris, *The Genius of Robert Adam: His Interiors* (New Haven: Yale University Press, 2001), fig. 258, p. 175.

44. N. Wallis, *A Book of Ornaments in the Palmyrene Taste Containing Upwards of Sixty New Designs for Ceilings, Panels, Pateras & Mouldings, and with the Raffle Leaves at Large* (London: I. Taylor, 1771), pl. 40.

45. Two pertinent discussions are Wendy A. Cooper, *Classical Taste in America, 1800–1840* (New York: Abbeville Press, 1993); Sumpter T. Priddy, *American Fancy: Exuberance in the Arts, 1790–1840* (Milwaukee: Chipstone Foundation, 2004).

46. Charles Knowles Bolton, *Bolton's American Armory: A Record of Coats of Arms which Have Been in Use within the Present Bounds of the United States* (Baltimore: Clearfield Co., 1964).

47. Illustrated in Betty Ring, *Girlhood Embroidery: American Samplers & Pictorial Needlework* (New York: Alfred A. Knopf, 1993), fig. 212, p. 185; Betty Ring, *American Needlework Treasures* (New York: E. P. Dutton, 1987), fig. 142, p. 90. An undated example is published in Ethel Stanwood Bolton and Eva Johnston Coe, *American Samplers* (Boston: Massachusetts Society of the Colonial Dames of America, 1921), pl. 123. Ring has done extensive research on the use of coats of arms in America, much of which has yet to be published. I am grateful to her for sharing her research.

48. Ring, *Girlhood Embroidery,* fig. 139, p. 123.

49. Letter, Abigail Adams to John Adams, July 25, 1775, *Adams Family Papers: An Electronic Archive.* Massachusetts Historical Society, http://www.masshist.org/digitaladams.

50. Joanna Bowen Gillespie, *The Life and Times of Martha Laurens Ramsay, 1759–1811* (Columbia: University of South Carolina Press, 2001), unpaginated list, "Family Birth Order."

51. MR to PC, January 15, 1815.

52. MR to PC, January 15, 1815; April 2, 1816; August 6, 1816; January 1, 1817.

53. Gary Kulik and Julia C. Bonham, *Rhode Island: An Inventory of Historic Engineering and Industrial Sites* (Washington, D.C.: Historic American Engineering Record, 1978), pp. 262–69.

54. Tench Coxe, *A View of the United States of America in a Series of Papers Written at Various Times, in the Years between 1787 and 1794* (1794; reprint, New York: Augustus M. Kelley, 1965), p. 267.

55. MR to PC, December 4, 1812.

56. J. R. Cole, *History of Washington and Kent Counties, Rhode Island, Including Their Early Settlement and Progress to the Present Time* (New York: W. W. Preston & Co., 1889), p. 964; Kulik and Bonham, *Rhode Island: An Inventory,* pp. 262–63.

57. Fuller, *History of Warwick,* p. 168; Kulik and Bonham, *Rhode Island: An Inventory,* p. 265.

58. MR to PC, August 10, 1813.

59. The fabric currently measures approximately 43½ in. wide, so probably would be 45 in. The thread count is 84–96 ends per inch (warps) and 104–8 picks per inch (wefts). With hand weaving, the warp count is often higher than that of the weft, hence the assumption that this fabric was woven on a mechanized loom.

60. The thread count for the backing fabric is only 44 ends per inch (warps) and 36 picks per inch (wefts).

61. Gail Mohanty, "Handloom Outwork and Outwork Weaving in Rural Rhode Island, 1810–1821," *American Studies* 30, no. 2 (1989): 41–68.

62. Cole, *History of Washington and Kent Counties,* p. 965.

63. Historical Society of Rhode Island, finding aid for S. H. Green & Sons records.

64. Coxe, *View of the United States,* p. 267.

65. For more on *broderie de Marseilles,* see Kathryn Berenson, *Quilts of Provence: The Art and Craft of French Quiltmaking* (New York: Henry Holt & Co., 1996), pp. 48–67. I was fortunate to have a lesson in identifying and dating *broderie de Marseilles* when Kathryn was a Winterthur research fellow in 2004.

66. Sally Garoutte, "Marseilles Quilts and Their Woven Offspring," in *Quiltmaking in America: Beyond the Myths: Selected Writings from the American Quilt Study Group,* ed. Laurel Horton (Nashville: Rutledge Hill Press, 1994), pp. 70–79; Berenson, *Quilts of Provence*; and Clare Rose, "The Manufacture and Sale of 'Marseilles' Quilting in Eighteenth-Century London," *CIETA Bulletin* 76 (1999): 105–13.

67. MR to PC, September 1, 1813. On Rhode Island merchants, see Linda L. Leven, ed., *Federal Rhode Island: The Age of the China Trade, 1790–1820* (Providence: Rhode Island Historical Society, 1978).

68. MR to PC, March 6, 1812. A tippet is a type of scarf or shawl, often made of fur. For more on American trade with Russia, see David W. McFadden, "John Quincy Adams, American Commercial Diplomacy, and Russia, 1809–1825," *New England Quarterly* 66, no. 4 (December 1993): 613–29.

69. A. A. Rasch, "American Trade in the Baltic, 1783–1807," *Scandinavian Economic History Review* 13, no. 1 (1965): 31–64.

70. Alfred W. Crosby Jr., "Richard S. Smith: Baltic Paul Revere of 1812," *Pennsylvania Magazine of History and Biography* 86, no. 1 (1962): 42–48.

71. Crosby, "Richard S. Smith."

72. PC to MR, May 16, 1812.

73. PC to MR, May 16, 1812.

74. MSS 363, Congdon Family Papers, subseries 5, box 3, folder 32, memoranda book, ca. 1810–13.

75. Harvey Strum, "Rhode Island and the War of 1812," *Rhode Island History* 50, no. 1 (1992): 23–31; "Rhode Island and the Embargo of 1807," *Rhode Island History* 52, no. 2 (1994): 58–67.

76. PC to MR, May 16, 1812.

77. Catherine Allgor, *Parlor Politics: In Which the Ladies of Washington Help Build a City and a Government* (Charlottesville: University of Virginia Press, 2000); Ronald J. Zboray and Mary Saracina Zboray, "Whig Women, Politics, and Culture in the Campaign of 1840: Three Perspectives from Massachusetts," *Journal of the Early Republic* 17 (Summer 1997): 277–315; and Elizabeth R. Varon, "Tippecanoe and the Ladies, Too: White Women and Party Politics in Antebellum Virginia," *Journal of American History* 82, no. 2 (September 1995): 494–521.

78. MR to PC, July 13, 1813.

79. MR to PC, March 11, 1815.

80. MR to PC, March 11, 1815.

CHAPTER 2. *THE HURRY OF WORK:* THE ROLE OF QUILTS IN WOMEN'S LIVES

1. MR to PC, January 8, 1815.

2. See Sandi Fox, *For Purpose and Pleasure: Quilting Together in Nineteenth-Century America* (Nashville: Rutledge Hill Press, 1995); Ricky Clark, George W. Knepper, and Ellice Ronsheim, *Quilts in Community: Ohio's Traditions* (Nashville: Rutledge Hill Press, 1991); Candace Kintzer Perry, *Cotton in Pennsylvania German Life: Catalogue of the Exhibition* (Pennsburg, Pa.: Schwenkfelder Library and Heritage Center, 2005); and Patricia J. Keller, *Of the Best Sort but Plain: Quaker Quilts from the Delaware Valley, 1760–1890* (Chadds Ford, Pa.: Brandywine River Museum, 1996).

3. Lynne Z. Bassett, "The Romantic Era: Understanding Friendship Quilts," paper presented at the Litchfield Historical Society, November 12, 2004. See also Jessica F. Nicoll, *Quilted for Friends* (Winterthur, Del.: Henry Francis du Pont Winterthur Museum, 1986); Fox, *For Purpose and Pleasure*; and Lynne Z. Bassett, *Telltale Textiles: Quilts from the Historic Deerfield Collection* (Deerfield, Mass.: Historic Deerfield, 2004).

4. Lynne Z. Bassett, "A Dull Business Alone: Cooperative Quilting in New England, 1750–1850," in Dublin Seminar for New England Folklife, *Textiles in Early New England: Design, Production, and Consumption* (Boston: Boston University, 1999), pp. 27–42; Jeanette Lasansky, *A Good Start: The Aussteier or Dowry* (Lewisburg, Pa.: Oral Traditions Project of the Lewis County Historical Society, 1990).

5. See Emma Jones Lapansky and Anne A. Verplanck, eds., *Quaker Aesthetics: Reflections on a Quaker Ethic in American Design and Consumption* (Philadelphia: University of Pennsylvania Press, 2003).

6. Elaine Forman Crane, ed., *The Diary of Elizabeth Drinker: The Life Cycle of an Eighteenth-Century Woman* (Boston: Northeastern University Press, 1994); Catherine La Courreye Blecki and Karin A. Wulf, eds., *Milcah Martha Moore's Book: A Commonplace Book from Revolutionary America* (University Park: Pennsylvania State University Press, 1997); and Susan M. Stabile, *Memory's Daughter: The Material Culture of Remembrance in Eighteenth-Century America* (Ithaca: Cornell University Press, 2004).

7. Sarah Suzanne Woodman, "The Fabric of Their Lives: A Commemoration of Family, Friends, and Community by Three Women in Salem County, New Jersey" (Master's thesis, University of Delaware, 2003).

8. William Wade Hinshaw, *Encyclopedia of American Quaker Genealogy*, vol. 2 (Baltimore: Genealogical Publishing, 1994), p. 160.

9. Keller, *Of the Best Sort but Plain*, p. 20.

10. Winterthur acc. no. 1991.23a–o, gift of Ms. Ruth Young Buggy.

11. Woodman, "Fabric of Their Lives."

12. Catalogued as relic #17. Thanks to Patricia O'Donnell.

13. Located on the west coast of Africa just south of Sierra Leone, Liberia was a colony (later a republic) founded by the American Colonization Society (whose members were primarily white) in the early nineteenth century to provide a place to send freed African Americans. For more on Liberia, see P. J. Staudenraus, *The African Colonization Movement, 1816–1865* (New York: Columbia University Press, 1961); James Wesley Smith, *Sojourners in Search of Freedom: The Settlement of Liberia of Black Americans* (Lanham, Md.: University Press of America, 1987).

14. For other examples, see Linda Otto Lipsett, *Remember Me: Women & Their Friendship Quilts* (San Francisco: Quilt Digest Press, 1985).

15. Emily Constance Cline, "Fashioning Quaker Identity: Nineteenth-Century Women's Clothing in the Friends Historical Association Collection" (Master's thesis, University of Delaware, 2005).

16. For genealogy and background about this quilt and five others made by Rebecca Scattergood Savery, see Mimi Sherman, "A Fabric of One Family: A Saga of Discovery," *The Clarion* (Spring 1989): 55–62.

17. Hugh Barbour and J. William Frost, *The Quakers: Denominations in America* (New York: Greenwood Press, 1988), p. 173.

18. The Orthodox-Hicksite split was elegantly summarized in Erin Eisenbarth's thesis "Plain and Peculiar: A Case Study of Nineteenth-Century Quaker Clothing" (Master's thesis, University of Delaware, 2002), pp. 18–20. See also Bruce Dorsey, "Friends Becoming Enemies: Philadelphia Benevolence and the Neglected Era of American Quaker History," *Journal of the Early Republic* 18 (Fall 1998): 395–428.

19. Nicoll, *Quilted for Friends*.

20. See Lapansky and Verplanck, *Quaker Aesthetics*; Dorsey, "Friends Becoming Enemies," pp. 395–428.

21. Nancy Tomes, "The Quaker Connection: Visiting Patterns among Women in the Philadelphia Society of Friends, 1750–1800," in *Friends and Neighbors: Group Life in America's First Plural Society,* ed. Michael Zuckerman (Philadelphia: Temple University Press, 1982), pp. 174–95.

22. Katherine Hunt, "The Emlen-Williams Quilt, 1851," *Winterthur Portfolio* (forthcoming). I am grateful to Katherine for researching the background and family histories of a number of quilts in the collection.

23. Anne A. Verplanck, "Facing Philadelphia: Social Functions of Silhouettes, Miniatures, and Daguerreotypes, 1760–1860" (Ph.D. diss., College of William and Mary, 1996).

24. Eliza Cope Harrison, ed., *Philadelphia Merchant: The Diary of Thomas P. Cope, 1800–1851* (South Bend: Gateway Editions, Ltd., 1978), p. 400.

25. Hinshaw, *Encyclopedia of American Quaker Genealogy*; Salem Monthly Meeting; Green Street Monthly Meetings, Minutes 1815–1836, Friends Historical Library of Swarthmore College, MR-Ph 207; Green Street Monthly Meeting, Membership Records, 1862–1905, Friends Historical Library of Swarthmore College, Film MR-Ph 209. Hunt, "Emlen-Williams Quilt," p. 12.

26. Hunt, "Emlen-Williams Quilt," p. 12.

27. Barbara Brackman, "Signature Quilts: Nineteenth-Century Trends," *Uncoverings* (San Francisco: American Quilt Study Group, 1990), pp. 25–37; Jessica Fleming Nicoll, "A Mirror to Show Thy Friends to Thee: Delaware Valley Signature Quilts, 1840–1855" (Master's thesis, University of Delaware, 1989).

28. Frederick Barnes Tolles, *Meeting House and Counting House:*

The Quaker Merchants of Colonial Philadelphia (New York: W. W. Norton, 1963); Morisa A. Morra, "Daily Life under Duress: Richard Vaux, A Philadelphia Textile Merchant and His Business during and Just after the American Revolution," *Textiles in Daily Life: Proceedings of the Third Biennial Symposium of the Textile Society of America* (Seattle: By the society, 1992), pp. 119–27.

29. Lorri Glover, *All Our Relations: Blood Ties and Emotional Bonds among the Early South Carolina Gentry* (Baltimore: Johns Hopkins University Press, 2000).

30. Judith Wellman, "The Seneca Falls Women's Rights Convention: A Study of Social Networks," *Journal of Women's History* 3, no. 1 (1991): 9.

31. Brackman, "Signature Quilts," pp. 25–37; Nicoll, *Quilted for Friends.*

32. I am grateful to quilt maker and author Donna Thomas and to Jinny and Reed Clayton for sharing their extensive family genealogical research, for so generously donating the quilt to Winterthur, and for providing me with a copy of Henry F. Hepburn, *The Clayton Family* (Wilmington, Del.: Historical Society of Delaware, 1904). Thanks to Heather Hanson and Kathleen Kiefer for documenting the location of the names on this quilt and for providing conservation treatment.

33. Examples can be found in Jennifer Faulds Goldsborough and Barbara K. Weeks, *Lavish Legacies: Baltimore Album and Related Quilts in the Collection of the Maryland Historical Society* (Baltimore: Maryland Historical Society, 1994), pp. 60–61, 96–97, 110–111; Nancy E. Davis, *The Baltimore Album Quilt Tradition* (Tokyo: Kokusai Art, 1999), pp. 82–89, 122–23.

34. Thanks to Katherine Haas for research and the identification of names found on this quilt and to Lois Stoehr for assistance.

35. J. William Joynes, *A Collection of Footnotes to History* (Baltimore: Old Otterbein United Methodist Church, 1997); S. E. Ahlstrom, *A Religious History of the American People* (New Haven: Yale University Press, 1972), pp. 246–50, 439–41.

36. Joynes, *Collection of Footnotes to History*, p. 15.

37. Joseph Garonzik, "The Racial and Ethnic Make-up of Baltimore Neighborhoods, 1850–70," *Maryland Historical Magazine* 71, no. 3 (Fall 1976): 401.

38. *Reminiscences of Adeline L. Dorr, May 7, 1821 to April 4, 1915*, unpublished typescript, October 1, 1951. Thanks to Nancy Tatnall Fuller for making this extraordinary family history available. Unless otherwise indicated, all information about the life of Abigail Horton Van Nostrand comes from this source.

39. This and other family genealogy also supplied by Nancy Tatnall Fuller.

40. *Elliot & Crissy's New-York Directory, for the Year 1811* (New York: Elliot and Crissy, 1811).

41. Reported in *Ming's New-York Price-Current* 599, October 3, 1807, p. 3; 557, May 2, 1807, p. 3, http://infoweb.newsbank.com.

42. *The Evening Post*, July 5, 1809, p. 2, http://infoweb.newsbank.com.

43. *Reminiscences of Adeline Dorr*, p. 2.

44. *Reminiscences of Adeline Dorr*, p. 12.

45. *Reminiscences of Adeline Dorr*, p. 15. For thirty years, John van

Nostrand was president of the New York Guardian Insurance Company, incorporated on April 6, 1838, but liquidated in 1947; see *Longworth's American Almanac, New York Register and City Directory* (New York: T. Longworth & Son, 1842); *Doggett's New-York City Directory for 1846 and 1847* (New York: John Doggett Jr., 1847).

46. *Reminiscences of Adeline Dorr*, p. 5.

47. *Reminiscences of Adeline Dorr*, p. 24.

48. Myrtle Hardenbergh Miller, *The Hardenbergh Family: A Genealogical Compilation* (New York: American Historical Co., 1958).

49. Jane's burial place is noted in *The Hardenbergh Family Genealogy*. For more on Green-wood Cemetery, see *Green-Wood Cemetery* (Brooklyn: Fritschler & Selle, 1887).

50. Lee Virginia Chambers-Schiller, *Liberty, A Better Husband: Single Women in America: The Generations of 1780–1840* (New Haven: Yale University Press, 1984), p. 3.

51. Zsuzsa Berend, "The Best or None! Spinsterhood in Nineteenth-Century New England," *Journal of Social History* 33, no. 4 (2000): 935. For a more wide-ranging discussion of single women in late eighteenth- and early nineteenth-century New England, see Chambers-Schiller, *Liberty, a Better Husband.*

52. David W. Robson, "Hardenbergh, Jacob Rutsen," *American National Biography*, http://www.anb.org/articles/01/01-00370.html.

53. Betty Ring, *Let Virtue Be a Guide to Thee: Needlework in the Education of Rhode Island Women, 1730–1830* (Providence: Rhode Island Historical Society, 1983), pp. 238–39.

54. *Self-Controul* was originally published in Edinburgh in 1811, reissued at least twice in the nineteenth century, and reprinted by Pandora Press in 1986.

55. See Catherine Lynn, *Wallpaper in America from the Seventeenth Century to World War I* (New York: W. W. Norton, 1980); Florence M. Montgomery, *Printed Textiles: English and American Cottons and Linens, 1700–1850* (New York: Viking Press, 1970), pp. 272–78.

56. For a discussion on the genealogy and identification of Sarah Furman Warner Williams, see Amelia Peck, *American Quilts and Coverlets in the Metropolitan Museum of Art* (New York: Dutton Books, 1990), pp. 16–19. I am grateful to Amelia for sharing her unpublished research notes.

57. For an illustration of an early heraldic banner, see Ottfried Neubecker, *Heraldry: Sources, Symbols, and Meaning* (New York: McGraw-Hill, 1976), p. 108. An English example from about 1670 is illustrated in Lanto Synge, *Art of Embroidery: History of Style and Technique* (Woodbridge, Eng.: Antique Collectors' Club, 2001), p. 105. For examples of slips, see Margaret Swain, *Figures on Fabric: Embroidery Design Sources and Their Application* (London: Adam & Charles Black, 1980).

58. Illustrated in Synge, *Art of Embroidery*, p. 168.

59. Sandi Fox, *Wrapped in Glory: Figurative Quilts & Bedcovers, 1700–1900* (New York: Thames & Hudson, 1990), pp. 54–667. Fox also illustrates a similar example made in northern New Jersey, pp. 48–53.

60. John Irwin and Katharine B. Brett, *Origins of Chintz* (London: Her Majesty's Stationery Office, 1970), pp. 16–21.

61. Marriage Records of Trinity Church, www.trinitywallstreet.org/historia/content/registers. Thanks to Amelia Peck for sharing this information, which corrects the date she previously cited.

62. Catherine Hoover Voorsanger and John K. Howat, eds., *Art and the Empire City: New York, 1825–1861* (New Haven: Yale University Press, 2000), p. 351.

63. Kevin Hayes, *A Colonial Woman's Bookshelf* (Knoxville: University of Tennessee Press, 1996), pp. 62–63.

64. Hayes, *Colonial Woman's Bookshelf*, p. 10.

65. Lynn, *Wallpaper in America*, pp. 205, 218–19; Richard Nylander et al., *Wallpaper in New England: Selections from the Society for the Preservation of New England Antiquities* (Boston: By the society, 1986), pp. 123–24.

66. David S. Shields, "Happiness in Society: The Development of an Eighteenth-Century American Poetic Ideal," *American Literature* 55, no. 4 (December 1983): 541–59. Timothy Dwight was a writer, theologian, and president of Yale; see William C. Dowling, "Dwight, Timothy," *American National Biography*, http://www.anb.org/articles/09/09-00244.html.

67. Roger Daniels, *Coming to America: A History of Immigration and Ethnicity in American Life* (New York: Harper Perennial, 1990), p. 121; Maldwyn A. Jones, "The Background to Emigration from Great Britain in the Nineteenth Century," in *Perspectives in American History*, ed. Donald Fleming and Bernard Bailyn (Cambridge, Mass.: Harvard University Press, 1973), pp. 3–92. My thanks to Katherine Hunt for these sources.

68. Quilt illustrated in Henry Joyce, *Art of the Needle: 100 Masterpiece Quilts from the Shelburne Museum* (Shelburne, Vt.: By the museum, 2003), p. 14.

69. Letter in the Gratz Collection, Historical Society of Pennsylvania. Thanks to Zara Anishanslin Bernhardt.

70. Nathalie Rothstein, *The Victoria and Albert Museum's Textile Collection: Woven Textile Design in Britain from 1750 to 1850* (New York: Canopy Books, 1994), p. 43.

CHAPTER 3. *THE BEDSPREAD GETS ALONG FINELY: MAKING QUILTS IN EARLY AMERICA*

1. MR to PC, January 15, 1815.

2 Betty Ring, *Girlhood Embroidery: American Samplers & Pictorial Needlework* (New York: Alfred A. Knopf, 1993), p. 369; Susan B. Swan, "Delaware Samplers," *Delaware Antiques Show Catalogue* (Winterthur, Del.: Henry Francis du Pont Winterthur Museum, 1985), pp. 52–57.

3. David Jaffee, "The Village Enlightenment in New England, 1760–1820," *William and Mary Quarterly*, 3d ser., 47, no. 3 (July 1990): 327–46. Benjamin Rush, "Thoughts upon the Mode of Education Proper in a Republic," and "Thoughts on Female Education," in *Essays on Education in the Early Republic*, ed. Frederick Rudolph

(Cambridge, Mass.: Belknap Press/Harvard University Press, 1965), pp. 1–40.

4. Sarah Fatherly, "The Sweet Recourse of Reason: Elite Women's Education in Colonial Philadelphia," *Pennsylvania Magazine of History and Biography* 128, no. 3 (July 2004): 229–56. Much of the work on women's education in America concentrates on the Early Republic; see Linda K. Kerber, "Daughters of Columbia: Educating Women for the Republic, 1787–1805," in *The Hofstadter Aegis: A Memorial,* ed. Stanley Elkins and Eric McKitrick (New York: Alfred A. Knopf, 1974), pp. 36–59; Linda K. Kerber, *Women of the Republic: Intellect and Ideology in Revolutionary America* (Chapel Hill: University of North Carolina Press, 1980).

5. Thomas Woody, *A History of Women's Education in the United States* (New York: Octagon Books, 1974).

6. Lucia McMahon and Deborah Schriver, eds., *To Read My Heart: The Journal of Rachel Van Dyke, 1810–1811* (Philadelphia: University of Pennsylvania Press, 2000), pp. 340–42.

7. *A Manual of the System of Teaching Needlework in the Elementary Schools of the British and Foreign School Society* (London: By the society, 1821). Winterthur Library also owns a manual dated 1817. The society was formed in 1808 to promote the educational methods of Joseph Lancaster. Only plain sewing skills were taught in society schools, which educated the children of the poor. For more on the subject, see Carl F. Kaestle, *Pillars of the Republic: Common Schools and American Society, 1790–1860* (New York: Hill and Wang, 1983); Dell Upton, "Lancasterian Schools, Republican Citizenship, and the Spatial Imagination in Early Nineteenth-Century America," *Journal of the Society of Architectural Historians* 55, no. 3 (September 1996): 238–53.

8. Late nineteenth-century examples in Winterthur's Downs Collection include sewing workbooks by Stella P. Bayley dated 1897–1898 (Doc. 457). Surviving examples of plain sewing from the eighteenth and nineteenth centuries show little change in the teaching of those techniques over that time period.

9. Thanks to Janneken Smucker for documenting this quilt and identifying the original use of the fabric.

10. Lynne Z. Bassett, "Inspired Fantasy: Design Sources for New England's Whole-Cloth Wool Quilts," *The Magazine Antiques* 168, no. 3 (September 2005): 120–27.

11. Lynne Z. Bassett, "Design Influences of the Foote Bed Rug and New England's Wool Whole-Cloth Quilts," in *Textiles in New England II: Four Centuries of Material Life,* ed. Peter Benes (Boston: Boston University, 2001), pp. 15–23; Lynne Z. Bassett, "Spun Me Some Worsted to Quilt With: New England's Early Wool Quilts," in *What's New England about New England Quilts?* ed. Lynne Z. Bassett (Sturbridge: Old Sturbridge Village, 1999), pp. 2–18.

12. Janneken Smucker, "From Rug to Blanket: Early Nineteenth-Century Embroidered Bedcovers," unpublished paper, object file folder 1969.562, Registration Office, Winterthur.

13. Lucinda R. Cawley, "Ihr Teppich: Quilts and Fraktur," *Uncoverings* (San Francisco: American Quilt Study Group, 2004), pp. 11–40.

Thanks to Trish Herr for sharing her research and the similar example in her collection. For other examples of quilts made in the German community, see Patricia T. Herr, *Quilting Traditions: Pieces from the Past* (Atglen, Pa.: Schiffer Publishing, 2000); Sharon P. Angelo et al., *Quilts: The Fabric of Friendship* (Atglen, Pa.: Schiffer Publishing, 2000).

14. Other quilts with embroidered decoration have been published in Patsy Orlofsky and Myron Orlofsky, *Quilts in America* (New York: Abbeville Press, 1992), pp. 140–41. See also Aimee E. Newell, "Embroidered Quilts and Coverlets in Early Nineteenth-Century Rural New England," *Proceedings of the Textile History Forum 2002* (Lowell, Mass: American Textile History Museum, 2002), pp. 127–43.

15. Lynne Z. Bassett, "Stenciled Bedcovers," *The Magazine Antiques* 163, no. 2 (February 2003): 70–77. Until this research was published, the quilt was attributed to Reading, Pennsylvania, rather than Reading, New York. Winterthur's collection also includes a stenciled table cover and what was probably a bedcover that was made into curtains in the early twentieth century.

16. For further discussions of changes in beds and bedding in America, see Elisabeth Donaghy Garrett, *At Home: The American Family, 1750–1870* (New York: Harry N. Abrams, 1990); Jane C. Nylander, *Our Own Snug Fireside: Images of the New England Home, 1760–1860* (New Haven: Yale University Press, 1994).

17. Celia Oliver, "The Emergence and Development of Block Set Quilts in New England," in *What's New England about New England Quilts?* ed. Lynne Z. Bassett (Sturbridge: Old Sturbridge Village, 1999), pp. 63–80.

18. Jules David Prown, "Style as Evidence," *Winterthur Portfolio* 15, no. 3 (Autumn 1980): 197–210.

19. Bassett, "Inspired Fantasy," pp. 120–27.

20. The quilt is in the collection of Independence National Historic Park, Philadelphia, and is illustrated in Patricia J. Keller, *Of the Best Sort but Plain: Quaker Quilts from the Delaware Valley, 1760–1890* (Chadds Ford, Pa.: Brandywine River Museum, 1997), p. 11. A detail of the center is illustrated on the cover.

21. The Emlen family quilt is illustrated in Keller, *Of the Best Sort but Plain,* p. 10. The silk quilt attributed to Mary Norris Dickinson is in the collection at Stenton, in Philadelphia. Ann Marsh's petticoat is illustrated in Sharon Ann Burnston, *Fitting & Proper: Eighteenth-Century Clothing from the Collection of the Chester County Historical Society* (Texarkana: Scurlock Publishing Co., 1998), p. 29. Rebecca Mifflin's quilted petticoat is in the collection of the Philadelphia Museum of Art. The wool quilt attributed to Hannah Trotter is in the collection of the Elfreth's Alley Association, Philadelphia.

22. Florence M. Montgomery, *Textiles in America, 1650–1870* (New York: W. W. Norton, 1984), p. 318.

23. Such a reference prompted a question to me by Dean Lahikainen, which undermined my confidence in distinguishing between pieced and appliqué techniques in period documents.

24. For further information about the elaborate formal beds of Britain, see Geoffrey Beard, *Upholsterers & Interior Furnishing in England, 1530–1840* (New Haven: Yale University Press, 1997); Annabel Westman, "Spendours of State: The Textile Furnishings of the King's Apartments," *Apollo* 140 (August 1994): 39–45; Peter Thornton, *Authentic Decor: The Domestic Interior, 1620–1920* (New York: Viking Penguin, 1984); and John Fowler and John Cornforth, *English Decoration in the Eighteenth Century* (London: Barrie & Jenkins, 1974).

25. My thanks to Amy Henderson for sharing this information from the 1809 inventory of the house.

26. Bassett, "Inspired Fantasy," pp. 120–27.

27. Illustrated in Lanto Synge, *Art of Embroidery: History of Style and Technique* (Woodbridge, Eng.: Antique Collectors' Club, 2001), p. 101.

28. George Smith, *The Cabinet-maker and Upholsterer's Guide* (London: Jones & Co, 1826), p. 173. The social significance of this was overlaid with a moral message; Smith reported that the style of Louis XIV was being used in a "mansion . . . solely appropriated to nightly purposes of pleasure" and was contrasted with the home of James Wyatt, just across the street, which was decorated with "chaste Grecian taste."

29. *Recueil de planches sur les sciences, les arts libéraux, et les arts méchaniques: avec leur explication,* vol. 5 (Paris: Briasson, 1762–72), pl. 1. This is the illustrated companion volume to the larger *Encyclopédie* by Diderot and d'Alembert. The term "Yankee Puzzle," associated with this design, can be attributed to Ruth Finley; see Barbara Brackman, *Encyclopedia of Pieced Quilt Patterns* (Paducah, Ky.: American Quilter's Society, 1993), pp. 166–67, design 1195a. For more on the influence of the *Encyclopédie,* see Elisabeth Lavezzi, "The Encyclopédie and the Idea of the Decorative Arts," *Art History* 28, no. 2 (April 2005): 174–79.

30. The idea has been well documented; see Prown, "Style as Evidence"; Wendy A. Cooper, *Classical Taste in America, 1800–1840* (New York: Abbeville Press, 1993); and Oliver, "Emergence and Development of Block Set Quilts."

31. Lynne Z. Bassett, "The Romantic Era: Understanding Friendship Quilts," paper presented at the Litchfield Historical Society, November 12, 2004. One of the most notable Gothic Revival churches, Trinity Church, Wall Street, New York, was attended by Abigail Horton Van Nostrand (see chp. 2). See also, Katherine Howe and David Warren, *The Gothic Revival Style in America, 1830–1870* (Houston: Museum of Fine Arts, 1976).

32. Found in eastern Pennsylvania, this quilt is in the collection of Patricia Herr.

33. Woody, *History of Women's Education,* pp. 563–65. On the connection between quilt designs, geometry, and women's education, see Tandy Hersh, "1842 Primitive Hall Pieced Quilt Top: The Art of Transforming Printed Fabric Designs through Geometry," in *Uncoverings* (San Francisco: American Quilt Study Group, 1986), pp. 47–59.

34. Charles Hayter, *An Introduction to Perspective, Drawing, and Painting in a Series of Pleasing and Familiar Dialogues between the Author's Children* (London: Black, Perry & Co, 1815), pp. 7–8. The first edition had been published in 1807; see Ann Bermingham, *Learning to Draw: Studies in the Cultural History of a Polite and Useful Art* (New Haven: Yale University Press, 2000), p. 122.

35. Sumpter T. Priddy, *American Fancy: Exuberance in the Arts, 1790–1840* (Milwaukee: Chipstone Foundation, 2004), pp. 81–97.

36. *Oxford Dictionary of National Biography*, s.v. "Hay, David Ramsey," http://www.oxforddnb.com/view/article/12712.

37. David Ramsey Hay, *Original Geometrical Diaper Designs: Accompanied by an Attempt to Develop and Elucidate the True Principles of Ornamental Design, as Applied to the Decorative Arts* (London: D. Bogue, 1944), p. 1.

38. For early weaving patterns, see Patricia Hilts, "The Weaver's Art Revealed: Marx Ziegler's *Weber Kunst und Bild Buch (1677)*," *Ars Textrina* 14 (December 1990): 1–379. For early lace and embroidery patterns, see Margaret Abegg, *Apropos Patterns for Embroidery, Lace, and Woven Textiles* (Riggisberg, Switz.: Abegg-Stiftung, 1978).

39. Lynne Z. Bassett, "American Fancy Bedcovers," unpublished paper presented at Peabody Essex Museum, October 2, 2004.

40. John T. Scharf, *The History of Western Maryland,* vol. 2 (Philadelphia: L. H. Everts, 1882), pp. 830–901, http://www.accessible.com. For the regional attribution of design and fabrics as well as genealogical information, see Gloria Seaman Allen and Nancy Gibson Tuckhorn, *A Maryland Album: Quiltmaking Traditions, 1634–1934* (Nashville: Rutledge Hill Press, 1995), pp. 52–53. This quilt was first published in William Rush Dunton, *Old Quilts* (Catonsville: By the author, 1947), pp. 244–46.

41. Anne C. Allnutt, *William Allnutt Family Registry Report* (Silver Spring, Md: By the author, 1996), cited in an unpublished paper by Caroline M. Riley, "Textiles Project: Montgomery County Appliquéd Quilt," object file folder 1971.140, Registration Office, Winterthur.

CHAPTER 4. *FABRICS OF THE SIMPLE, BUT MOST IMPORTANT AND NECESSARY KINDS:* QUILTS AND AMERICAN TEXTILE PRODUCTION

1. MR to PC, August 10, 1813.

2. For discussions about weaving in two different parts of the country, see Laurel Thatcher Ulrich, "Martha Ballard and Her Girls: Women's Work in Eighteenth-Century Maine," in *Work and Labor in Early America,* ed. Stephen Innes (Chapel Hill: University of North Carolina Press, 1988), pp. 70–105; Adrienne D. Hood, *The Weaver's Craft: Cloth, Commerce, and Industry in Early Pennsylvania* (Philadelphia: University of Pennsylvania Press, 2003).

3. Tench Coxe, *A View of the United States of America in a Series of Papers Written at Various Times, in the Years between 1787 and 1794* (1794; reprint, New York: Augustus M. Kelley, 1965), p. 168.

4. For information about early cotton spinning, see Victor S. Clark, *History of Manufactures in the United States* (New York: McGraw-Hill, 1929); William R. Bagnall, *Samuel Slater and the Early Development of the Cotton Manufactures in the United States* (Middletown, Conn., 1890); William Bagnall, *Sketches of Manufacturing Establishments in New York City, and of Textile Establishments in the Eastern United States* (Washington, D.C.: Carnegie Institution, 1908); and Gary Kulik and Julia C. Bonham, *Rhode Island: An Inventory of Historic Engineering and Industrial Sites* (Washington, D.C.: Historic American Engineering Record, 1978).

5. On the New England textile industry, see Paul E. Rivard, *A New Order of Things: How the Textile Industry Transformed New England* (Hanover, N.H.: University Press of New England, 2002); David J. Jeremy, *Transatlantic Industrial Revolution: The Diffusion of Textile Technologies between Britain and America, 1790–1830* (Cambridge, Mass.: M.I.T. Press, 1981); and Clark, *History of Manufactures.*

6. J. Leander Bishop, *A History of American Manufactures from 1608 to 1860* (Philadelphia: E. Young & Co., 1866), p. 197.

7. *New Paltz Times*, May 10, 1861, Esopus (Town of), II Rifton, Haviland-Heidgerd Historical Collection, Elting Library, New Paltz, New York.

8. "An Act to Incorporate the Dashville Falls Manufacturing Company. Passed April 24, 1832," newspaper clipping, Wallkill River I, Haviland-Heidgerd Historical Collection, Elting Library, New Paltz, New York.

9. Louise Hasbrouck Zimm et al., comp. and ed., *Southeastern New York: A History of the Counties of Ulster, Dutchess, Orange, Rockland, and Putnam* (New York, 1946), pp. 541–42.

10. The yellow-dyed backings for New England quilts were first identified by Lynne Z. Bassett; see her article "Spun Me Some Worsted to Quilt With: New England's Early Wool Quilts," in *What's New England about New England Quilts?* ed. Lynne Z. Bassett (Sturbridge: Old Sturbridge Village, 1999), p. 6.

11. Thanks to Alan Keyser and Bill and Doris Hoag for sharing the unpublished results of their research and experiments.

12. Thomas Cooper, *A Practical Treatise on Dyeing and Callicoe Printing* (Philadelphia: T. Dobson, 1815), p. 335.

13. *Dictionary of National Biography* (1938), s.v. "Thomas Cooper."

14. Stanley D. Chapman and S. Chassagne, *European Textile Printers in the Eighteenth Century: A Study of Peel and Oberkampf* (London: Heinemann Educational Books, 1981), pp. 26–27.

15. Florence M. Montgomery, *Printed Textiles: English and American Cottons and Linens, 1700–1850* (New York: Viking Press, 1970), pp. 88–89.

16. Montgomery documents the varied business ventures of both Walters and Bedwell in *Printed Textiles*, pp. 89–91. That Walters was the artistic part of the partnership is indicated by his subsequent attempt to earn a living by painting portrait miniatures.

17. *Pennsylvania Evening Post*, June 5, 1777, Alfred Coxe Prime File, Decorative Arts Photographic Collection (hereafter Prime File, DAPC), Winterthur Library. Montgomery gives a more complete history of the various endeavors attempted by these two Philadelphia artisans in *Printed Textiles,* pp. 88–91.

18. *Pennsylvania Evening Post*, May 30, 1775, p. 220, http://infoweb.newsbank.com.

19. Values taken from table in Appendix A, Chapman and Chassagne, *European Textile Printers*, pp. 216–17.

20. For comments on job printers earlier in the eighteenth century, see Geoffrey Turnbull, *A History of the Calico Printing Industry of Great Britain* (Altrincham, Eng.: John Sherratt and Son, 1951), p. 21. There are few surviving records of this part of the industry.

21. Winterthur acc. no. 1958.605.

22. *Pennsylvania Packet,* September 18, 1784, Prime File, DAPC, Winterthur Library.

23. Montgomery, *Printed Textiles*, p. 94.

24. Wansey is quoted in Montgomery, *Printed Textiles*, pp. 85, 87.

25. "Stephen Addington," Prime File, DAPC, Winterthur Library.

26. Montgomery, *Printed Textiles*, p. 100. For more on Rowan, see W. Drummond, ed., *The Autobiography of Archibald Hamilton Rowan* (Shannon, Ire.: Irish University Press, 1972); Kathleen Kiefer, "Archibald Hamilton Rowan's Pattern Book: A Preliminary Technical and Stylistic Analysis," unpublished typescript, 1994, Winterthur Library.

27. Montgomery, *Printed Textiles*, p. 102.

28. Stanley D. Chapman, "Financial Restraints on the Growth of Firms in the Cotton Industry, 1790–1850," *Economic History Review*, n.s., 32, no 1 (February 1979): 50–59. Chapman addresses the issue in Britain, and although the experience of the industry in America may differ somewhat, I believe the overall issues relating to credit and capital were perhaps even more pronounced in what was a much smaller market.

29. Alfred P. Wadsworth and Julia de Lacy Mann, *The Cotton Trade and Industrial Lancashire, 1600–1780* (New York: Augustus M. Kelley, 1968), p. 307.

30. For an overview of these economic fluctuations, see David Hackett Fischer, *The Great Wave: Price Revolutions and the Rhythm of History* (New York: Oxford University Press, 1996). For the Philadelphia textile industry, see Philip Scranton, *Proprietary Capitalism: The Textile Manufacture at Philadelphia, 1800–1885* (Cambridge: Cambridge University Press, 1983). On the failures of Philadelphia merchants, see Toby L. Ditz, "Shipwrecked; or, Masculinity Imperiled: Mercantile Representations of Failure and the Gendered Self in Eighteenth-Century Philadelphia," *Journal of American History* 81, no. 1 (June 1994): 51–80. The best overview of the trials, tribulations, and successes of the calico printing business in Britain and France is Chapman and Chassagne, *European Textile Printers*. For a shorter summary of the situation in France, see A. Juvet-Michel, "The Great Textile Printing Factories in France," *Ciba Review* 31 (March 1940): 1098–1106.

31. Florence Montgomery, "John Hewson: Calico Printer of

Philadelphia," unpublished typescript, Col. 107, Joseph Downs Collection of Manuscripts and Printed Ephemera, Winterthur Library; see also Charles S. Olton, "Philadelphia's Mechanics in the First Decade of Revolution, 1765–1775," *Journal of American History* 59, no. 2 (September 1972): 311–26.

32. Chapman and Chassagne, *European Textile Printers,* p. 8.

33. *Pennsylvania Evening Post,* June 28, 1777, p. 344, http://infoweb. newsbank.com. John Douglass had also fled from John Walters, who advertised for his return in the *Pennsylvania Evening Post,* February 22, 1777. Because of gout, Walters had difficulties in the printing business, but he was back in Philadelphia boasting of his skill in miniature painting in the *Independent Gazette,* August 16, 1763. Douglass and Walters went off after Walters announced the closure of his printing business. If Hewson's identification is correct, Walters (aka Groase) was Bedwell's partner in his failed calico printing business in England.

34. "Four Dollars Reward," *Pennsylvania Evening Post*, June 21, 1783, p. 84, http://infoweb.newsbank.com.

35. Advertisement, *Pennsylvania Packet*, October 15, 1778, http:// infoweb.newsbank.com.

36. Letter, Benjamin Franklin to Richard Bache, July 25, 1773, in William B Willcox, ed., *The Papers of Benjamin Franklin,* vol. 20 (New Haven: Yale University Press, 1976), pp. 320–21.

37. William Lang's name appears in the advertisement concerning their apprentice John Douglass, *Pennsylvania Evening Post,* June 28, 1777, p. 344. Lang's role is described in the account of the Grand Federal Procession, *Pennsylvania Gazette*, July 9, 1788, quoted in Montgomery, *Printed Textiles,* p. 96. Other ads at this time identify the firm as "John Hewson and Co."; see *Pennsylvania Evening Post,* July 3, 1777, p. 352, http://infoweb. newsbank.com.

38. Advertisement, *Pennsylvania Evening Herald and the American Monitor,* July 16, 1785, p. 1, http://infoweb.newsbank.com.

39. For Taylor's ad, see Prime File, DAPC, Winterthur Library; for the society's opinion, see Montgomery, *Printed Textiles,* p. 94.

40. *Federal (Philadelphia) Gazette,* February 9, 1795, Prime File, DAPC, Winterthur Library.

41. Advertisement, *Pennsylvania Evening Post,* July 3, 1777, p. 352, http://infoweb.newsbank.com.

42. *Pennsylvania Gazette,* July 20, 1774, item 55770, http://www. accessible.com.

43. Minutes of the society, February 18, 1789, quoted in Montgomery, *Printed Textiles,* p. 94.

44. Montgomery, *Printed Textiles,* p. 94.

45. Both quotes from *Pennsylvania Packet*, November 9, 1779, Prime File, DAPC, Winterthur Library. For an excellent description of the styles of calico printing, see Martin Bide, "Secrets of the Printer's Palette: Colors and Dyes in Rhode Island Quilts," in *Down by the Old Mill Stream: Quilts in Rhode Island,* ed. Linda Welters and Margaret T. Ordonez (Kent, Ohio: Kent State University Press, 2000), pp. 83–121.

46. Reported in *The Pennsylvania Journal*, April 15, 1789, Prime File, DAPC, Winterthur Library.

47. *Pennsylvania Packet*, March 24, 1790, Prime File, DAPC, Winterthur Library.

48. Notice in *The Pennsylvania Journal,* March 7, 1792, Prime File, DAPC, Winterthur Library.

49. For a full description, see Chapman and Chassagne, *European Textile Printers*.

50. Advertisement, *Poulson's American Daily Advertiser*, November 10, 1808, p. 1; July 24, 1817, p. 3, http://infoweb.newsbank.com.

51. Prime File, DAPC, Winterthur Library.

52. Receipts dated July 15, 1818; July 28, 1815; August 10, 1815; and August 14, 1815, Ashhurst Family Papers, Col. 290, Joseph Downs Collection of Manuscripts and Printed Ephemera, Winterthur Library.

53. Receipt dated July 28, 1815, Joseph Downs Collection of Manuscripts and Printed Ephemera, Winterthur Library.

54. Information about provenanced examples can be found in Patsy Orlofsky and Myron Orlofsky, *Quilts in America* (New York: Abbeville Press, 1992), p. 63; Jeannette Lasansky and Celia Oliver, *On the Cutting Edge: Textile Collectors, Collections, and Traditions* (Lewisburg, Pa.: Oral Tradition Project of the Union County Historical Society, 1994), p. 24; Shelley Zegart, *American Quilt Collections: Antique Quilt Masterpieces* (Tokyo: Nihon Vogue, 1996), p. 41. A quilt described as being from Virginia is published in Stella Rubin, *How to Compare and Value American Quilts* (London: Octopus Publishing Group, 2001), p. 20, but no provenance is given.

55. Tench Coxe, *A Statement of the Arts & Manufactures of the United States of America for the Year 1810* (Philadelphia: A. Cornman, 1814). A later source claims that three calico printers (Hewson, Stewart at Germantown, and Thorburn at Darby) were expected to produce 300,000 yards of goods between them in 1803; Bishop, *History of American Manufactures*.

56. Chapman and Chassagne, *European Textile Printers,* pp. 14–15, 213.

57. Peel figures from Chapman and Chassagne, *European Textile Printers,* p. 53. Hewson's will is in the Hewson Family Papers, Col. 203, Joseph Downs Collection of Manuscripts and Printed Ephemera, Winterthur Library.

58. Chapman and Chassagne, *European Textile Printers*, pp. 179, 53.

59. Edward Baines, *History of the Cotton Manufacture in Great Britain* (London: H. Fisher, R. Risher, and P. Jackson, 1835), p. 266.

60. Chapman, "Financial Restraints," p. 55. There is no evidence that the Hewsons ever used cylinder technology to print cloth, although John Jr. did advertise a new hot calender machine in *Poulson's American Daily Advertiser,* May 19, 1813.

61. *Philadelphia Directories*, 1822, 1835, 1847. For a discussion of the Hewsons, see Philip Scranton, *Proprietary Capitalism: The Textile Manufacture at Philadelphia, 1800–1885* (Cambridge: Cambridge University Press, 1983), pp. 69–71. Hewson Jr. died in Philadelphia in 1860. He had no children. Although his brothers James and Robert are listed as calico printers in the 1807 and

1814 directories, there is no evidence that they continued to work in the firm. Each was left $30 in their father's will, with Robert's share to go to his dependents should he not reappear within two years of his father's death. John Jr. may have become a merchant; there are two mentions of a firm known as Hewson & West at 101 South Front Street in 1845 and at 37 South Wharfs in 1846, but it has not been confirmed whether the Hewson involved was John Jr.

62. *Pennsylvania Gazette,* July 20, 1774; for more on Bromley Hall, see Wendy Hefford, *The Victoria and Albert's Textile Collection: Design for Printed Textiles in England from 1750 to 1850* (London: V&A Publications, 1992); Muriel Clayton and Alma Oakes, "Early Calico Printers around London," *Burlington Magazine* 96, no. 614 (May 1954): 135–38. For Richard Vaux's imports, see Morisa Morra, "Daily Life under Duress: Richard Vaux, A Philadelphia Textile Merchant and His Business during and Just after the American Revolution," *Textiles in Daily Life: Proceedings of the Third Biennial Symposium of the Textile Society of America* (Seattle: Textile Society of America, 1992).

63. Letter from John Hewson, February 27, 1793, Library of Congress. My thanks to Todd Fielding for sharing the letter and his unpublished manuscript, "The Life and Times of John Hewson: December 1744–October 1821."

64. See Cooper, *Practical Treatise on Dyeing,* preface.

65. *L'Art de Peindre et d'Imprimer les Toiles en Grand et Petit Teint* (Paris: Goeury, 1800), pp. 139–40.

66. Joy Gardiner et al., "That Fabric Seems Extremely Bright: Non-Destructive Characterization of Nineteenth-Century Mineral Dyes via XRF Analysis," *Conservation Combinations: Preprints of the North American Textile Conservation Conference 2000* (Asheville, N.C.: NATCC, 2000), pp. 100–115.

67. Martin Bide, "Technology Reflected: Printed Textiles in Rhode Island Quilts," in *Down by the Old Mill Stream: Quilts in Rhode Island,* ed. Linda Welters and Margaret T. Ordonez (Kent, Ohio: Kent State University Press, 2000), pp. 88, 111.

68. For images and information about these fabrics, see Dominique Cardon, "A La Découverte d'un Métier Médiéval: La Teinture, L'Impression, et la Peinture des Teintures et des Tissus D'Ameublement dans L'Arte della Lana," *Mélanges de L'École Française de Rome: Moyen Age* (Rome: MEFRM, 1999), pp. 323–56; Donald King, "Textiles and the Origins of Printing In Europe," *Pantheon* 20 (1962): 23–30; David Mitchell and Milton Sonday, "Printed Fustians, 1490–1600," *CIETA Bulletin* 77 (2000): 99–118; and Walter C. McCrone, *Judgment Day for the Shroud of Turin* (Chicago: Microscope Publications, 1997).

69. Winsor White to H. F. du Pont, May 28, 1949, dealer files, Registration Office, Winterthur.

70. *Historical Homesteads of Norwell*, typescript, Norwell Historical Society, p. 54. Thanks to Barbara Barker.

71. L. Vernon Briggs, "North River and Shipbuilding on Its Banks," in *Old Scituate* (1921; reprint, Scituate, Mass.: DAR, 2000), p. 148.

72. Jedediah Dwelley and John F. Simmons, *History of the Town of Hanover* (Hanover, Mass.: By the town, 1910), p. 204.

73. Published in Lynne Z. Bassett and Jack Larkin, *Northern Comfort: New England's Early Quilts, 1780–1850* (Nashville: Rutledge Hill Press, 1998), p. 35.

74. Janice Carlson, Scientific Research and Analysis Laboratory (hereafter SRAL) Analytical Report No. 4637, October 20, 2004, Winterthur.

75. Quote from Elisabeth West Fitzhugh, ed., *Artist's Pigments: A Handbook of Their History and Characteristics*, vol. 3 (Washington, D.C: National Gallery of Art, 1975), p. 192; see also Rosamond Harley, *Artists Pigments 1600–1835: A Study in English Documentary Sources* (New York: American Elsevier, 1970), p. 56; and Leslie Carlyle, *The Artist's Assistant* (London: Archetype Publications, 2001), p. 476.

76. Addendum, SRAL Report No. 4637, January 2, 2006. Thanks to Catherine Matsen, Chris Petersen, Jennifer Mass, and Janice Carlson for their analysis of and discussions about this mystery pigment.

77. Janice Carlson, SRAL Report No. 4638, October 20, 2004, Winterthur.

78. Carlson, SRAL Report No. 4638.

79. Smithsonian Catalogue sheet T. 15294, acc. no. 292230. My thanks to Doris Bowman.

80. Smithsonian Institution, "Facts about the American Flag," http://www.si.edu/resource/faq/nmah/flag.htm.

81. George Davidson Todd, "The First Cotton Factory in the West," *Cotton History Review* 1, no. 4 (1960): 195–221.

82. Carlson, SRAL Report No. 4638. File, DAPC, Winterthur Library.

CHAPTER 5. *YOU MAY CIRCUMNAVIGATE THE GLOBE:* QUILTS AND INTERNATIONAL TRADE

1. For just a few of the many examples, see advertisements in the *Pennsylvania Gazette* for Ebenezer Currie, February 2, 1744; Robert and Amos Strettell, April 21, 1748; Charles Batho, August 4, 1748; Samuel Hazard, October 25, 1750; John Ackeroyd, March 8, 1775; Kugn & Risberg, July 28, 1784; and William and John Sitgreaves, October 3, 1792.

2. Oliver Fuller, *History of Warwick, Rhode Island, from Its Settlement in 1642 to the Present Time* (Providence: Angell, Burlingame & Co., 1875), p. 151.

3. For a discussion of the lives of common sailors, see Paul A. Gilje, *Liberty on the Waterfront: American Maritime Culture in the Age of Revolution* (Philadelphia: University of Pennsylvania Press, 2004).

4. Congdon Family Papers, box 2, folder 19, Rhode Island Historical Society Library.

5. Illustrated in Patsy Orlofsky and Myron Orlofsky, *Quilts in America* (New York: Abbeville Press, 1992), p. 19.

6. List of objects sent by Elinor Merrell on approval, January 22, 1943, stock number 12945 "Yellow taffeta quilt about 7 ft sq" at a price of $110, dealer files, Registration Office, Winterthur. The low cost probably was due to its relatively poor condition.

7. Margaret Renner Lidz, "The Mystery of Seventeenth-Century Quilts," *The Magazine Antiques* 154, no. 6 (December 1998): 834.

8. Letter and analytical results from Dr. Jan Wouters, March 24, 1999. The analysis of the dyes was by Marie-Christine Maquoi and the fibers by Ina Vanden Berghe. My thanks to Dr. Wouters.

9. Judith H. Hofenk de Graaff, *The Colourful Past: Origins, Chemistry, and Identification of Natural Dyestuffs* (London: Archetype Publications, 2004), p. 214; Jan Wouters, "The Dyes of Early Woven Indian Silks," in *Samit & Lampas: Indian Motifs*, ed. Krishna Riboud (Paris: AEDTA/Calico Museum, 1998), pp. 145–52.

10. B. C. Mohanty, K. V. Chandramouli, and H. D. Naik, *Natural Dyeing Processes in India* (Ahmedabad: Sarabhai Foundation, 1987), cited in Wouters letter, March 24, 1999.

11. Philip P. Argenti, *The Costumes of Chios* (London: B. T. Batsford, 1953), pp. 36, 53; cited in Lidz, "Mystery of Seventeenth-Century Quilts." Silk of this width was also woven in China, but the selvages do not conform to any Chinese examples.

12. Janet Rae et al., *Quilt Treasures of Great Britain: The Heritage Search of the Quilters' Guild* (Nashville: Rutledge Hill Press, 1995), pp. 65–67. The quilt, in a private collection, was seen at Truro, in Cornwall.

13. Lidz, "Mystery of Seventeenth-Century Quilts," p. 838.

14. Images of this ship are illustrated in Michael Snodin and John Styles, *Design & the Decorative Arts: Britain, 1500–1900* (London: V&A Publications, 2001), pp. 150, 153.

15. Lidz, "Mystery of Seventeenth-Century Quilts," pp. 841–42.

16. Sara Desvernine, "Thomas Hart and His House, 1670: A Furnishing Plan," unpublished paper, Hart Room file, Registration Office, Winterthur. Other primary and secondary source material has been published in *Essex Antiquarian*, vol. 1 (May 1859), and *Winterthur Newsletter,* November 28, 1958, pp. 4–6. Thanks to Lynne Z. Bassett for sharing her work on the Puritans and the quality of their textiles.

17. Rosemary Crill, "Textile for the Trade with Europe," in *Trade, Temple & Court: Indian Textiles from the Tapi Collection*, ed. Ruth Barnes, Steven Cohen, and Rosemary Crill (Mumbai: India Book House, 2002), p. 94. According to Crill, this type of bedcover is so uncommon that they are not discussed in any secondary source on the early Indo-Portuguese trade. Two additional examples appear in the catalogue for an auction of Indian and Islamic art and textiles, October 14, 2005, South Kensington, London, lots 483, 487.

18. Note in object file 1968.46, Registration Office, Winterthur. Thanks to Rosemary Crill for confirming the date and attribution of this bedcover.

19. For a more complete description of the house and some of its contents, see Christopher Hussey, "Ashburnham of Ashburnham: The Origins and End of a Great Sussex House," *Country Life* (April 16, 1953): 1158–60; "Ashburnham Place, Sussex–II," *Country Life* (April 23, 1953): 1246–50; and "Ashburnham Place, Sussex–III," *Country Life* (April 30, 1953): 1334–38. For information about specific objects and prices realized, see T. P. Greig, "In the Auction Rooms," *The Connoisseur* (June and November 1953). This quilt is not mentioned by Greig.

20. Sean Kelsey, "Ashburnham, John (1602/3–1671)," *Oxford Dictionary of National Biography* (2004), http://www.oxforddnb.com/view/aritcle/738; Administrative History, Ashburnham Family Papers, East Sussex Record Office.

21. http://members.tripod.com/-India_Resource/Europetrade.html. For further information about the history of Bengal, see Biplab Dasgupta, *European Trade and Colonial Conquest* (London: Anthem, 2005); Narenda Krishna Sinha, *The Economic History of Bengal* (Calcutta: Firma K. L. Mukhopadhyay, 1961).

22. Rosemary Crill et al., *Arts of India, 1550–1900* (London: V&A Publications, 1990), p. 47.

23. William Foster, *The English Factories in India, 1618–1621* (Oxford: Clarendon Press, 1906), p. 206. Descriptions of these early quilts are rare and imprecise; Hughes could also be describing cotton quilts embroidered in yellow silk in this reference.

24. Henry Yule and A. C. Burnell, *Hobson-Jobson: A Glossary of Colloquial Anglo-Indian Words and Phrases,* ed. William Crooke (1886; reprint, London: Routledge and Kegan Paul, 1985), p. 662.

25. "The Burial of an Eccentric Woman," *Every Evening–Wilmington Delaware*, December 18, 1884, p. 1. Jean Rumsey, *Charles Rumsey of Cecil County, Maryland: A Tentative Genealogy of His Descendants,* typescript, 1997, CS71 R938, Historical Society of Delaware. My thanks to Katherine Hunt for researching the family genealogy.

26. Natalie Rothstein, "The Calico Campaign of 1719–1721," *East London Papers* 7, no. 1 (July 1964): 5.

27. *The Female Manufacturers Complain . . . Being the Humble Petition of Dorothy Distaff* (Goldsmith's Library Broadsides), quoted in Rothstein, "Calico Campaign," p. 6.

28. *A Brief State of the Question between the Printed and Painted Calicoes and the Woollen and Silk Manufactures, 1719,* quoted in Rothstein," Calico Campaign," p. 6. A Merry-Andrew is defined by the *Oxford English Dictionary* as a clown or buffoon. Bartholomew Fair was held each August in Smithfield and featured sideshows, acrobats, freaks, and wild animals.

29. Rothstein, "Calico Campaign," pp. 11–12.

30. Illustrated in Dorothy Osler, *Traditional British Quilts* (London: B. T. Batsford, 1987), p. 88.

31. Angharad Rixon, "A Fault in the Thread? Examining Fibers Taken from Laces of the Sixteenth and Seventeenth Centuries," *Strengthening the Bond: Science & Textiles*, comp. Virginia Whelan (Philadelphia: PMA, 2002), pp. 101–9; Mary Gale, "Indigo-Resist Prints from Eighteenth-Century America: Production and Provenance" (Master's thesis, University of Rhode Island, 2001).

32. John Irwin and Katharine B. Brett, *Origins of Chintz* (London: Her Majesty's Stationery Office, 1970), p. 12.

33. Irwin and Brett, *Origins of Chintz,* p. 5.

34. Kathryn Berenson, *Quilts of Provence: The Art and Craft of French Quiltmaking* (New York: Henry Holt & Co., 1996), p. 43. Josette

Brédif, *Printed French Fabrics: Toiles de Jouy* (New York: Rizzoli, 1989), pp. 17–21.

35. Doris M. Bowman, *The Smithsonian Treasury: American Quilts* (Washington, D.C.: Smithsonian Institution Press, 1991), pp. 14–15.

36. Irwin and Brett, *Origins of Chintz*, p. 6.

37. Irwin and Brett, *Origins of Chintz*, p. 21.

38. Advertisement, *Pennsylvania Gazette*, October 12, 1785.

39. David G. Dickason, "The Nineteenth-Century Indo-American Ice Trade: An Hyperborean Epic," *Modern Asian Studies* 25, no. 1 (1991): 53–89, quote on p. 71.

40. Administrative History, Ashburnham Family Papers, East Sussex Record Office.

41. For a design for a bed with a similar quilt or counterpane and matching cushion cover from the 1720s, see Peter Thornton, *Authentic Decor: The Domestic Interior, 1620–1920* (New York: Viking Press, 1984), p. 114.

42. W. C. Peterson, Scientific Research and Analysis Laboratory Report No. 4738, May 25, 2005, Winterthur.

43. Charles Germain de Saint-Aubin, *Art of the Embroiderer,* trans. Nikki Scheuer (Los Angeles: Los Angeles County Museum of Art, 1983), pp. 20–21.

44. Lucy Trench, ed., *Materials & Techniques in the Decorative Arts: An Illustrated Dictionary* (Chicago: University of Chicago Press, 2000), p. 36.

45. Peter Floud of the Victoria & Albert Museum and Paul Schwartz of the Textile Museum in Mulhouse identified and published this evidence.

46. Morisa Morra, "Daily Life under Duress: Richard Vaux, A Philadelphia Textile Merchant and His Business during and Just after the American Revolution," *Textiles in Daily Life: Proceedings of the Third Biennial Symposium of the Textile Society of America* (Seattle: By the society, 1992), pp. 119–27.

47. Wendy Hefford, *The Victoria and Albert Museum's Textile Collection: Design for Printed Textiles in England from 1750 to 1850* (London: V&A Publications, 1992), p. 156.

48. Florence M. Montgomery, *Printed Textiles: English and American Cottons and Linens, 1700–1850* (New York, Viking Press, 1970), p. 235.

49. Stanley D. Chapman, "Financial Restraints on the Growth of Firms in the Cotton Industry," *Economic History Review*, n.s., 32, no. 1 (February 1979): 50–69.

50. Melanie Riffel and Sophie Rouart, *Toile de Jouy: Printed Textiles in the Classic French Style,* trans. Barbara Mellor (London: Thames & Hudson, 2003), p. 28.

51. Joy Gardiner et al., "That Fabric Seems Extremely Bright: Non-Destructive Characterization of Nineteenth-Century Mineral Dyes via XRF Analysis," *Conservation Combinations: Preprints of the North American Textile Conservation Conference 2000* (Asheville, N.C.: NATCC, 2000), pp. 101–15.

52. Discussions of these techniques and terms can be found in Sally Garoutte, "Marseilles Quilts and Their Woven Offspring," *Quiltmaking in America: Beyond the Myths: Selected Writings from the American Quilt Study* Group, ed. Laurel Horton (Nashville: Rutledge Hill Press, 1994), pp. 70–79; Kathryn Berenson, *Quilts of Provence: The Art and Craft of French Quiltmaking* (New York: Henry Holt & Co, 1996), pp. 17–22; Janine Janniere, "The Hand Quilting of Marseilles," *Quilt Journal* 2, no. 1 (1993): 5–9; and Jean Taylor Federico, "White Work Classification System," *Uncoverings* (Mill Valley, Calif.: American Quilt Study Group, 1980), pp. 68–71. Corded and stuffed quilting is also described in Saint-Aubin, *Art of the Embroiderer*, pp. 56–57.

53. Clare Rose, "The Manufacture and Sale of Marseilles Quilting in Eighteenth-Century London," *CIETA Bulletin* 76 (1999): 107.

54. Alfred P Wadsworth and Julia de Lacy Mann, *The Cotton Trade and Industrial Lancashire, 1600–1780* (1931; reprint, Bristol: Thoemmes Press, 1999), p. 23; see also Berenson, *Quilts of Provence;* and Janniere, "Hand Quilting of Marseilles."

55. Clare Rose, "A Group of Embroidered Eighteenth-Century Bedgowns," *Costume* 30 (1996): 70–85; Rose, "Manufacture and Sale of Marseilles Quilting," pp. 105–13.

56. Rose, "Group of Embroidered Eighteenth-Century Bedgowns," p. 106.

57. Illustrated in Peter B. Brown, *In Praise of Hot Liquors: The Study of Chocolate, Coffee, and Tea-Drinking, 1600–1850* (York, Eng.: York Civic Trust, 1995), p. 81.

58. Thanks to Alan Carswell, Principal Curator of Military History, National War Museum of Scotland, for identifying this figure as a grenadier.

59. Avril Hart and Susan North, *Fashion in Detail from the Seventeenth and Eighteenth Centuries* (New York: Rizzoli, 1998), pp. 200–201. Linda Baumgarten, *What Clothes Reveal: The Language of Clothing in Colonial and Federal America* (Williamsburg, Va.: Colonial Williamsburg Foundation, 2002), p. 191.

60. Mildred Lanier, "Marseilles Quiltings of the Eighteenth and Nineteenth Centuries," *CIETA Bulletin* 47/48 (1978): 77.

61. Illustrated in Rose, "Manufacture and Sale of Marseilles Quilting," p. 104.

62. Hart and North, *Fashion in Detail*, pp. 30–31.

63. Deborah Kraak, "Early American Silk Patchwork Quilts," *Textiles in Early New England: Design, Production, and Consumption,* ed. Peter Benes (Boston: Boston University, 1999), pp. 7–28.

64. Although Elizabeth Bennis was named as the maker by Robert H. Palmiter, the dealer who sold the bedcover to H. F. du Pont, her name had not been included in the museum catalogue records. I am grateful to Barbara Parshley, a descendant of Eliza Bennis, who enquired about this bedcover, thus initiating a search that enabled us to make this connection. A second quilt by Bennis is in the collection of the National Museum of American History.

65. John F. Crosfield, *A History of the Cadbury Family* (London: By the author, 1978), pp. 36–41.

66. Crosfield, *History of the Cadbury Family,* pp. 83–91. The bills are illustrated on pp. 84 and 87.

CHAPTER 6. *THE NEWS OF THE PEACE:* QUILTS AND POLITICS

1. PC to MR, May 16, 1812.

2. Judith Apter Klinghoffer and Lois Elkis, "The Petticoat Electors: Women's Suffrage in New Jersey, 1776–1807," *Journal of the Early Republic* 12, no. 2 (1992): 159–93.

3. For discussions about women's involvement in politics, see Catherine Allgor, *Parlor Politics: In Which the Ladies of Washington Help Build a City and a Government* (Charlottesville: University of Virginia Press, 2000); Linda K. Kerber, *Women of the Republic: Intellect & Ideology in Revolutionary America* (New York: W. W. Norton, 1986); and Mary Beth Norton, *Founding Mothers and Fathers: Gendered Power and the Forming of American Society* (New York: Alfred A. Knopf, 1996). For more on politically active women, see Ronald J. Zboray and Mary Saracina Zboray, "Whig Women, Politics, and Culture in the Campaign of 1840: Three Perspectives from Massachusetts," *Journal of the Early Republic* 17 (Summer 1997): 277–315; Elizabeth R. Varon, "Tippecanoe and the Ladies, Too: White Women and Party Politics in Antebellum Virginia," *Journal of American History* 82, no. 2 (September 1995): 494–521. On other examples of quilts with political iconography, see G. Julie Powell, *The Fabric of Persuasion: Two Hundred Years of Political Quilts* (Chadds Ford, Pa.: Brandywine River Museum, 2000); Robert Bishop and Carter Houck, *All Flags Flying: American Patriotic Quilts as Expressions of Liberty* (New York: E. P. Dutton, 1986).

4. Thomas Shippen to Nancy Shippen, quoted in Florence M. Montgomery, *Printed Textiles: English and American Cottons and Linens, 1700–1850* (New York: Viking Press, 1970), p. 281.

5. Quoted in Edith Standen, "English Washing Furnitures," *Metropolitan Museum of Art Bulletin* (November 1964): 122.

6. William Ayres, "At Home with George: Commercialization of the Washington Image, 1776–1876," in *George Washington: American Symbol*, ed. Barbara J. Mitnick (New York: Hudson Hills Press, 1999), p. 92.

7. Frank H. Sommer, "Emblem and Device: The Origin of the Great Seal of the United States," *Art Quarterly* 14, no. 1 (Spring 1961): 56–76; Cesare Ripa, *Baroque and Rococo Pictorial Imagery: The 1758–60 Hertel Edition of Ripa's Iconologia* (reprint; New York: Dover Publications, 1971).

8. E. McSherry Fowble, *Two Centuries of Prints in America, 1680–1880: A Selective Catalogue of the Winterthur Museum Collection* (Charlottesville: University of Virginia Press, 1987), pp. 213–14.

9. A similar needlework picture has been attributed to Charleston; see letter from Paula Locklair, March 8, 1999, object file 1959.663, Registration Office, Winterthur. For more on print sources being used as needlework designs, see Jane C. Nylander, "Some Print Sources of New England Schoolgirl Art," *The Magazine Antiques* 110, no. 2 (August 1976): 292–301; Davida Tenenbaum Deutsch, "Washington Memorial Prints," *The Magazine Antiques* 111, no. 2 (February 1977): 324–31;

and Davida Tenenbaum Deutsch and Betty Ring, "Homage to Washington in Needlework and Prints," *The Magazine Antiques* 119, no. 2 (February 1981): 402–19.

10. Edna Donnell, "Portraits of Eminent Americans after Drawings by Du Simitière," *The Magazine Antiques* 24, no. 1 (July 1933): 17–21. Winterthur has a number of these in the collection.

11. Helmut von Erffa and Allen Staley, *The Paintings of Benjamin West* (New Haven: Yale University Press, 1986), pp. 206–8.

12. Robert C. Alberts, *Benjamin West: A Biography* (Boston: Houghton Mifflin Company, 1978), p. 111.

13. Victoria & Albert Museum, *Loan Exhibition of English Chintz* (London: Her Majesty's Stationery Office, 1960), no. 177, p. 34.

14. Deborah Kraak, when curator of textiles at Winterthur, matched the framed handkerchief with the original quilt; bill of sale dated November 14, 1941, and delivery memo dated November 15, 1941, Elinor Merrell folder, du Pont correspondence files, Registration Office, Winterthur.

15. Virginia Whelan, "Condition Report and Treatment Proposal," February 2, 1997; "Treatment Proposal Addendum," February 25, 1997; and "Treatment Report," June 11, 1997, object folder 1969.655, Conservation Files, Winterthur. All technical details have been taken from these reports.

16. Wendy Hefford, *The Victoria and Albert Museum's Textile Collection: Design for Printed Textiles in England from 1750 to 1850* (New York: Canopy Books, 1992), p. 156.

17. This quilt has been published and described in Powell, *Fabric of Persuasion*.

18. A quilt with a central medallion handkerchief entitled "The Death of General Washington" is published in Bishop and Houck, *All Flags Flying*, p. 13.

19. Grzegorz Leopold Seidler and Maria Smolka, "Poland as Seen by Americans, 1785–1795," *Annales Universitatis Mariae Curie-Sklodowsk. Sectio G: Ius* 26 (1979): 13–36.

20. Quotes are taken from the inscriptions on the handkerchief. Other historical information from Harry M. Ward, "Kosciuszko, Tadeusz Andrzej Bonawentura," *American National Biography*, http://www.anb.org/articles/03/03-00134.html.

21. Barbara Brackman, *Clues in the Calico: A Guide to Identifying and Dating Antique Quilts* (McLean, Va.: EPM Publications, 1989), pp. 123–24. Examples are posted on the Quilt Index, http://www.quiltindex.org, conceived and developed by the Alliance for American Quilts in partnership with Michigan State University's MATRIX: The Center for Humane Arts, Letters, and Social Sciences Online and the MSU Museum.

22. Mary Schoeser, *Printed Handkerchiefs* (London: Museum of London, 1988); Mary Schoeser, "The Mystery of the Printed Handkerchief," in *Disentangling Textiles: Techniques for the Study of Designed Objects,* ed. Mary Schoeser and Christine Boydell (London: Middlesex University Press, 2002), pp. 13–22.

23. Samuel Willard Crompton, Decatur, Stephen," *American National Biography,* http://www.anb.org/articles/03/03-00134.html. For

more on Barbary pirates, see also Robert J. Allison, "Sailing to Algiers: American Sailors Encounter the Muslim World," *American Neptune* 57, no. 1 (1997): 5–17.

24. Roger A. Fischer, *Tippecanoe and Trinkets Too: The Material Culture of American Presidential Campaigns, 1828–1984* (Urbana: University of Illinois Press, 1988), p. 1.

25. Robert V. Remini, "Jackson, Andrew," *American National Biography*, http://www.anb.org/aticles/03/03-00238.html. Norma Basch, "Marriage, Morals, and Politics in the Election of 1828," *Journal of American History* 80, no. 3 (1993): 890–918; Norma Basch, "Mobilizing Women, Anticipating Abolition: The Struggle against Indian Removal in the 1830s," *Journal of American History* 86, no. 1 (1999): 15–40.

26. Illustrated in Powell, *Fabric of Persuasion*, p. 16.

27. For a discussion on how Henry Francis du Pont used fabrics, see Chapter 7.

28. Zboray and Zboray, "Whig Women, Politics, and Culture," pp. 277–315; Varon, "Tippecanoe and the Ladies, Too," pp. 494–521.

29. Varon, "Tippecanoe and the Ladies, Too," pp. 515–16.

30. Examples can be found in Powell, *Fabric of Persuasion*, pp. 18–20; Bishop and Houck, *All Flags Flying,* p. 22 (the quilt owned by du Pont is illustrated on p. 24).

31. Ottfried Neubecker, *Heraldry: Sources, Symbols, and Meaning* (New York: McGraw-Hill, 1976), pp. 124–29.

32. Quoted in *The History of the Seal of the United States* (Washington, D.C.: Department of State, 1909), pp. 65–66.

33. http://www.heraldic.org/topics/usa/usheroff.htm.

34. The acc. no. for this quilt is 1969.1705. It is illustrated in Susan Burrows Swan, *A Winterthur Guide to American Needlework* (New York: Crown Publishers, 1976), p. 127.

35. At least two American editions were published in 1831, one in New York and the other in Philadelphia.

36. Dorothy McMillan, "Porter, Jane (bap. 1776, d. 1850)," *Oxford Dictionary of National Biography,* http://www.oxforddnb.com/view/article/22571. Thanks to Lynne Bassett for making this connection.

37. Amanda Isaac, "A Collection Survey: Dressing Table Covers," unpublished paper, December 10, 2003, object file 1969.1131, Registration Office, Winterthur. Elisabeth Donaghy Garrett, *At Home: The American Family, 1750–1870* (New York: Harry N. Abrams, 1989), pp. 127–33. I am grateful to Amanda Isaac for her research on the twenty-five dressing table and bureau covers in Winterthur's collection, twenty of which are white stuffed work.

38. Montgomery, *Printed Textiles*, pp. 346–47.

39. Amy Boyce Osaki, "The Needle's Web: Sewing in One Early Nineteenth-Century American Home" (Master's thesis, University of Delaware, 1988), p. 34.

40. Lynne Z. Bassett, "A Dull Business Alone: Cooperative Quilting in New England," in *Textiles in New England II: Four Centuries of Material Life*, ed. Peter Benes (Boston: Boston University, 1999), pp. 27–42.

CHAPTER 7. *IN THEMSELVES A TEXTILE MUSEUM: DECORATING WITH QUILTS IN THE EARLY TWENTIETH CENTURY*

1. For information about these collectors and their homes, see Julie Eldridge Edwards, "The Brick House: The Vermont Country House of Electra Havemeyer Webb," *The Magazine Antiques* 163, no. 1 (January 2003): 192–201; David B. Warren, *Bayou Bend: The Interiors and the Gardens* (Houston: Museum of Fine Arts, 1988); Nina Fletcher Little, *Little by Little: Six Decades of Collecting American Decorative Arts* (New York: E. P. Dutton, 1984); Elizabeth Stillinger, *Historic Deerfield: A Portrait of Early America* (New York: Dutton Studio Books, 1992); Elizabeth Stillinger, *The Antiquers* (New York: Alfred A. Knopf, 1980); and Bland Blackford, Burke Davis, and Patricia Hurdle, *Bassett Hall: The Williamsburg Home of Mr. and Mrs. John D. Rockefeller Jr.* (Williamsburg, Va.: Colonial Williamsburg Foundation, 1984).

2. Many thank-you notes sent by guests to du Pont comment on the beauty of his interiors. Quotation is from a letter from interior designer Nancy McClelland, writing as president of the American Institute of Decorators to H. F. du Pont, October 23, 1941, box 580N, Winterthur Archives. McClelland brought important clients to Winterthur to show them du Pont's outstanding rooms. Interior designers Ruby Ross Wood and Billy Baldwin also visited Winterthur; Wood to du Pont, November 16, 1937; August 18, 1938, box HF 444, Winterthur Archives. Elissa Cullman describes the influence of Henry Francis du Pont on her own work in Susan Gray, ed., *Designers on Designers: The Inspiration Behind Great Interiors* (New York: McGraw-Hill, 2004).

3. For discussions of the Colonial Revival period, see Alan Axelrod, ed., *The Colonial Revival in America* (New York: W. W. Norton, 1985); Stillinger, *Antiquers*.

4. "Centennial Tea Party," *Godey's Lady's Book* 88 (February 1874): 189.

5. Marie Webster, *Quilts: Their Story and How to Make Them* (Garden City, N.Y.: Doubleday, 1926). Mr. du Pont owned this reprint of the 1915 original. Webster's quilts were first published in *Lady's Home Journal* in 1911. Many quilts were illustrated in *The Modern Priscilla* through the 1910s.

6. "Dressing the Modern Bed," *Arts & Decoration* 35, no. 5 (September 1931): 56–58, 89.

7. Ruth Finley, *Old Patchwork Quilts and the Women Who Made Them* (Philadelphia: J. B. Lippincott, 1929), p. iv. Mr. du Pont owned a copy of Finley's book.

8. There is little written on collecting peasant costumes in America. For collecting in Europe and Britain, see Lou Taylor, *Establishing Dress History* (Manchester, Eng.: Manchester University Press, 2004). The Peasant Art Society was founded in Britain in 1897. Charles Home edited an influential series of books on peasant art in Sweden, Lapland, Iceland, Austria, Hungary, Russia, and Italy between 1911 and 1913, all published by The Studio Ltd. John Lane, London. Collections of peasant embroidery were

donated to many American museums in the 1910s and 1920s, including the Indianapolis Museum of Art; the Phoebe Hearst Museum of Anthropology; the Philadelphia Museum of Art; the Museum of Fine Arts, Boston; and the Brooklyn Museum. For an important article about an early collector of European folk art in America, see Elizabeth Stillinger, "Elie and Viola Nadelman's Unprecedented Museum of Folk Arts," *The Magazine Antiques* 146, no. 1 (October 1994): 516–25.

9. Maggie Lidz, "Notes on H. F. du Pont's First Decorative Arts Collection: Peasant Costumes and Embroideries from Eastern Europe," unpublished typescript, March 24, 2005, Winterthur. My thanks to Maggie for sharing her research and for many discussions about Mr. du Pont's collecting and furnishing practices.

10. "The Reminiscences of Henry F. du Pont as Recorded in Talks with Dr. Harlan B. Phillips," Archive of American Art, Brandeis University, 1962, p. 13, box WC 39, Winterthur Archives.

11. Joshua Ruff and William Ayres, "H. F. du Pont's Chestertown House, Southampton, New York," *The Magazine Antiques* 160, no. 1 (July 2001): 98–107; Edwards, "Brick House," pp. 192–201. Chestertown House was sold after Mr. du Pont's death in 1969. After having been substantially altered by a series of owners, it was purchased in 2003 by Calvin Klein.

12. Little, *Little by Little,* p. 6.

13. Magazines with regular articles on interior decoration at this time included *Arts & Decoration, Good Furniture,* and *House & Garden.*

14. Edith Wharton and Ogden Codman, Jr., *The Decoration of Houses* (New York: Charles Scribner's Sons, 1897). Thanks to Maggie Lidz for the information about the personal connection between Wharton, Codman, and du Pont.

15. Jane S. Smith, *Elsie de Wolfe: A Life in the High Style* (New York: Atheneum, 1982), pp. 102–12; Allen Tate and C. Ray Smith, *Interior Design in the Twentieth Century* (New York: Harper & Row, 1986), pp. 243–45; bills from the Colony Club, box RW16, Winterthur Archives.

16. Du Pont's correspondence with Wanamaker's, box AD196, HF218N, HF483, HF615, Winterthur Archives. Although Wanamaker's originated in Philadelphia, du Pont dealt exclusively with the store in New York.

17. Elsie de Wolfe, *The House in Good Taste* (New York: The Century Co., 1913); "Miss M'Clelland, Antiquary, Here," *New York Times,* October 2, 1959, http://www.parsons.edu/about/history.aspx, http://www.nysid.edu/why.htm.

18. Barnes correspondence, box 937N, box 524N, Winterthur Archives.

19. Letter, Alfred Barnes to H. F. du Pont, May 31, 1946, box HF524N, Winterthur Archives.

20. For a description of the show, see Milton Wolf Brown, *The Story of the Armory Show* (New York: Joseph Hirshhorn Foundation, 1988). The text of some contemporary reactions can be found in *1913 Armory Show: 50th Anniversary Exhibition 1963* (Utica, N.Y.:

Munson-Williams-Proctor Institute, 1963). For a discussion of the continuing debate about the Armory Show, see J. A. Mancini, "One Term is as Fatuous as Another: Responses to the Armory Show Reconsidered," *American Quarterly* 51, no. 4 (December 1999): 833–70.

21. For a discussion about the connection between contemporary artists and folk art, see Stillinger, "Elie and Viola Nadelman"; Virginia Tuttle et al., *Drawing on America's Past: Folk Art, Modernism, and the Index of American Design* (Chapel Hill: University of North Carolina Press, 2002). For a concise history of interior design and its relation to the art and architecture of its time, see Tate and Smith, *Interior Design in the Twentieth Century.* On the international context of American interior design, see Stephen Calloway, *Twentieth-Century Interior Decoration, 1900–1980* (New York: Rizzoli, 1988). Thanks to Cynthia Fowler, whose research on Marguerite Zorach's hooked rugs led to some interesting discussions on relationships between modernist art and traditional design.

22. Michael J. Bugeja, "Crowninshield, Frank," *American National Biography*, http://www.anb.org/articles/16/16-02599.html. Crowninshield visited Winterthur fifteen times between 1909 and 1946, box HF396–397, Winterthur Archives. Frank Crowninshield (Francis W.) should not be confused with Frank Crowninshield (Francis B.), who was married to du Pont's sister, Louise. Gifts documented in box HF982, Winterthur Archives.

23. Boxes HF218, HF436, Winterthur Archives. Thanks to Maggie Lidz.

24. Shelley Staples, "Marketing Modern Art in America: From the Armory Show to the Department Store," http://xroads.virginia.edu/~MUSEUM/Armory/marketing.html; Marilyn F. Friedman, *Selling Good Design: Promoting the Early Modern Interior* (New York: Rizzoli, 2003).

25. Catalogued by Florence Montgomery as T20 and illustrated in Florence M. Montgomery, *Printed Textiles: English and American Cottons and Linens, 1700–1800* (New York: Viking Press, 1970), fig. 189, p. 202. Dr. Albert Barnes and Frank Crowninshield both collected works by Matisse.

26. Hilary Spurling et al., *Matisse, His Art and His Textiles: The Fabric of Dreams* (London: Royal Academy of Arts, 2004). *Pansies* is illustrated as cat. no. 16, and is featured on the back cover.

27. Joseph Downs, *American Furniture: Queen Anne and Chippendale Periods* (New York: McMillan, 1952), p. vi. Seven Winterthur interiors are shown at the beginning of this catalogue.

28. Mary Allis to H. F. du Pont, June 30, 1945, box AD7, Winterthur Archives. By this time, Mr. du Pont was no longer using quilts for upholstery at Winterthur, and he did not buy the petticoat she offered.

29. An example of a late nineteenth-century charm quilt used to upholster an armchair survives in Electra Hayemeyer Webb's bedroom at the Brick House in Shelburne. Surviving examples of pieced or appliqué quilt blocks used to cover sofa cushions can be found at any flea market or antiques shop.

30. H. F. du Pont to Wilmer Moore, May 27, 1925, box AD44, Winterthur Archives.

31. Mrs. Tysen to H. F. du Pont, August 18, 1924, March 25 1925, box AD196, Winterthur Archives.

32. *Arts & Decoration* 25, no. 4 (August 1926):10. Thanks to Katherine Hunt for her research assistance.

33. Her apartments are illustrated in *Arts & Decoration* 41, no. 1 (May 1934): 38–39.

34. Emily Post, *The Personality of a House* (New York: Funk & Wagnalls, 1930).

35. Nancy McClelland, *Furnishing the Colonial and Federal House* (Philadelphia: J. B. Lippincott, 1947), p. 155.

36. Nancy McClelland to H. F. du Pont, October 23, 1941, box AD41, Winterthur Archives.

37. Perriwigg prints were advertised in *Arts & Decoration* 46, no. 6 (August 1937), inside front cover. For the Novelty Selling Company ad, see *The Magazine Antiques* 11, no. 5 (May 1927): 333. The Warner's fabric is illustrated in Frank Lewis, *English Chintz* (Benfleet, Eng.: F. Lewis Ltd., 1935), pl. 147.

38. For more on cheater's cloth, see Deborah Kraak, "Nineteenth-Century American Printed Patchwork and Japonisme," *CIETA Bulletin* 80 (2003): 84–92; and Diane Fagan Affleck, *Just New from the Mills: Printed Cottons in America* (North Andover, Mass: Museum of American Textile History, 1987). Faux patchwork goes back to the late eighteenth century; thanks to Lynne Bassett for information about these early examples.

39. His Park Avenue apartment was decorated with English and French antiques, while his home in Boca Grande, Florida, was decorated with modern furniture and du Pont's extensive shell collection, box P56, P66, Winterthur Archives.

40. Erika Doss, "American Folk Art's Distinctive Character: The Index and American Design and New Deal Notions of Cultural Nationalism," in *Drawing on America's Past: Folk Art, Modernism, and the Index of American Design,* ed. Virginia Tuttle Clayton, Elizabeth Stillinger, and Erika Doss (Washington, D.C.: National Gallery of Art, 2002), p. 61.

41. "Seen in New York," *Good Furniture* 23. no. 5 (November 1924): 242.

42. "Reminiscences of Henry F. du Pont."

43. H. F. du Pont to Hannah Mae Horner, December 27,1929, box AD28, Winterthur Archives. Thanks to Anne Verplanck for sharing this reference.

44. Jay E. Cantor, *Winterthur: The Foremost Museum of American Furniture and Decorative Arts* (New York: Harry N. Abrams, 1997), p. 141.

45. H. F. du Pont to Harlan Phillips, March 25, 1962, box WC39, Winterthur Archives.

46. Fiske Kimball, "Interior Design: An Introductory Chapter," *House Beautiful Furnishing Annual* (Boston: Atlantic Monthly Company, 1925), p. 11. Kimball illustrates this chapter with examples of rooms in the American Wing of The Metropolitan Museum of Art as well as private interiors created by designers such as Ogden Codman and architects David Adler and Delano & Aldrich.

47. H. F. du Pont to Sleeper, June 21, 1927, box AD54, Winterthur Archives.

48. Quoted in Cantor, *Winterthur*, p. 155. The catalogue was eventually written by Ruth Ralston from The Metropolitan Museum of Art.

49. House Notes and Proposed Location of Furniture, January 8, 1930, typescript, box WC43, Winterthur Archives. This room, whose furnishings have been changed, has been renamed the Sheraton Room.

50. Room descriptions written by Charles Cornelius, box WC44, Winterthur Archives.

51. The original auction catalogue has not yet been located; a photocopy of the relevant page is in object file 1963.0505, Registration Office, Winterthur.

52. Anonymous typescript (probably written by Charles Cornelius), Nemours Room file, Registration Office, Winterthur.

53. Nancy McClelland to H. F. du Pont, November 7, 1934, box AD2, Winterthur Archives. Du Pont also purchased considerable yardage of this fabric from Elinor Merrell.

54. Cited in Pam Smith's undated research notes, Winterthur. Ruth Lord describes her chagrin after discovering that her father would refurnish her own bedroom with lesser-quality materials when she stayed at Winterthur; see Ruth Lord, *Henry F. du Pont and Winterthur: A Daughter's Portrait* (New Haven: Yale University Press, 1999), p. 150.

55. Letter to the Executors, p. 66, box HF619, Winterthur Archives. A number of quilts were sold at auction in 1975.

56. Oral History, Mrs. Reginald Rose, Winterthur Archives.

57. Box HF496, Winterthur Archives.

58. Identified by Justina Barrett, unpublished report, "A Patchwork of Silk and Color," object file 1957.1283, Registration Office, Winterthur.

59. Letter to the Executors, p. 50, box 619, Winterthur Archives.

60. Jeni Sandberg, "Re-covering the Past: Ernest Lo Nano and Upholstery for Historic Interiors," paper presented at Winterthur, October 17, 1996, author's copy.

61. Letters to the Executors, p. 60, box HF619, Winterthur Archives.

62. Obituary, HF449, Winterthur Archives.

63. Bertha King Benkard, Portfolio of Photographs of Her Home in Oyster Bay, Long Island, F. W. Lincoln, photographer, 1945, Winterthur Library.

64. Oral history, Elinor Merrell, Winterthur Archives.

65. Oral history, Elinor Merrell, Winterthur Archives.

66. "Reminiscences of Henry F. du Pont."

67. Oral history, Elinor Merrell, Winterthur Archives.

68. Oral history with antiques dealer Benjamin Ginsburg, Winterthur Archives.

69. Once again I am indebted to Maggie Lidz, who shared the family genealogy with me.

70. Correspondence and invoices, box AD482N, Winterthur Archives.

71. The publication was produced in conjunction with the first of two important exhibitions of printed textiles; see Peter Floud, *English Chintz: Two Centuries of Changing* Taste (London: Her Majesty's Stationery Office, 1955), p. 2.

72. Peter Floud to H. F. du Pont, May 18, 1957, box HF427, Winterthur Archives.

73. "Mr. du Pont will bring them with him on the boat when he comes to England in mid-May," Charles Montgomery to Peter Floud, April 20, 1959, box ARC14, Winterthur Archives.

74. This exchange was documented in an unpublished paper given by Kim Ahara, April 12, 2005, Registration Office, Winterthur. This report includes a table listing all of the textiles sent to the V&A and copies of the correspondence.

75. H. F. du Pont to Elinor Merrell, February 22, 1956, box AD43, Winterthur Archives.

76. H. F. du Pont to Winsor White, September 23, 1954, box AD63, Winterthur Archives.

77. List of objects sent on approval to Mr. du Pont by Avis & Rockwell Gardiner, August 14, 1957, box AD22, Winterthur Archives.

78. The accession files in the Registration Office list this quilt as being purchased with H. F. du Pont funds.

selected bibliography

Ahlstrom, Sydney E. *A Religious History of the American People.* New Haven: Yale University Press, 1972.

Allen, Gloria Seaman. *First Flowerings: Early Virginia Quilts.* Washington, D.C.: DAR Museum, 1987.

Allen, Gloria Seaman, and Nancy Gibson Tuckhorn. *A Maryland Album: Quiltmaking Traditions, 1634–1934.* Nashville, Tenn.: Rutledge Hill Press, 1995.

Allgor, Catherine. *Parlor Politics: In Which the Ladies of Washington Help Build a City and a Government.* Charlottesville: University of Virginia Press, 2000.

Ames, Kenneth L. *Beyond Necessity: Art in the Folk Tradition.* Winterthur, Del.: Henry Francis du Pont Winterthur Museum, 1977.

Bassett, Lynne Zacek. "A Dull Business Alone: Cooperative Quilting in New England, 1750–1850." In *Textiles in Early New England: Design, Production, and Consumption.* Boston: Boston University, 1999.

Baumgarten, Linda. *What Clothes Reveal: The Language of Clothing in Colonial and Federal America: The Colonial Williamsburg Collection.* Williamsburg, Va.: Colonial Williamsburg Foundation, 2002.

Beard, Geoffrey. *Upholsterers & Interior Furnishing in England, 1530–1840.* New Haven: Yale University Press, 1997.

Berenson, Kathryn. *Quilts of Provence: The Art and Craft of French Quiltmaking.* New York: Henry Holt & Co., 1996.

Bishop, Robert, and Jacqueline M. Atkins. *Folk Art in American Life.* New York: Viking Studio Books, 1995.

Bishop, Robert, and Carter Houck. *All Flags Flying: American Patriotic Quilts as Expressions of Liberty.* New York: E. P. Dutton, 1986.

Bowman, Doris M. *The Smithsonian Treasury: American Quilts.* Washington, D.C.: Smithsonian Institution Press, 1991.

Cantor, Jay E. *Winterthur.* New York: Harry N. Abrams, 1985.

Chapman, S. D., and S. Chassagne. *European Textile Printers in the Eighteenth Century: A Study of Peel and Oberkampf.* London: Heinemann Educational Books, 1981.

Chapman, S. D. "Financial Restraints on the Growth of Firms in the Cotton Industry, 1790–1850." *Economic History Review,* n.s., 32, no. 1 (February 1979): 50–69.

Clayton, Virginia Tuttle. *Drawing on America's Past: Folk Art, Modernism, and the Index of American Design.* Chapel Hill: University of North Carolina Press, 2002.

Cochran, Rachel, et al. *New Jersey Quilts, 1777 to 1950.* Paducah, Ky.: American Quilter's Society, 1992.

Colby, Averil. *Patchwork.* London: B. T. Batsford Ltd., 1958.

_____. *Quilting.* New York: Charles Scribner's Sons, 1971.

Collins, Herbert Ridgeway. *Threads of History: Americana Recorded on Cloth, 1775 to the Present.* Washington, D.C.: Smithsonian Institution Press, 1979.

Cunningham, Noble E. Jr. "Political Dimensions of Everyday Life in the Early Republic." In *Everyday Life in the Early Republic,* ed.

Catherine E. Hutchins. Winterthur, Del.: Henry Francis du Pont Winterthur Museum, 1994.

Davis, Nancy E. *The Baltimore Album Quilt Tradition.* Tokyo: Kokusai Art, 1999.

Decker, William Merrill. *Epistolary Practices: Letter Writing in America before Telecommunications.* Chapel Hill: University of North Carolina Press, 1998.

Douglas, Audrey W. "Cotton Textiles in England: The East India Company's Attempt to Exploit Developments in Fashion 1660–1721." *Journal of British Studies* 8, no. 2 (May 1969): 28-43.

Edelstein, Sidney M. *Historical Notes on the Wet-Processing Industry.* New York: Dexter Chemical Corporation, 1974.

Fischer, Roger A. *Tippecanoe and Trinkets Too: The Material Culture of American Presidential Campaigns, 1828–1984.* Chicago: University of Illinois Press, 1988.

Fox, Sandi. *For Purpose and Pleasure: Quilting Together in Nineteenth-Century America.* Nashville, Tenn.: Rutledge Hill Press, 1995.

_____. *Wrapped in Glory: Figurative Quilts & Bedcovers, 1700–1900.* New York: Thames & Hudson, 1990.

Fuller, Wayne E. *The American Mail: Enlarger of the Common Life.* Chicago: University of Chicago Press, 1972.

Goldsborough, Jennifer Faulds, and Barbara K. Weeks. *Lavish Legacies: Baltimore Album and Related Quilts in the Collection of the Maryland Historical Society.* Baltimore: Maryland Historical Society, 1994.

Harding, Deborah. *Stars and Stripes: Patriotic Motifs in American Folk Art.* New York: Rizzoli, 2002.

Harley, R. D. *Artists' Pigments c. 1600–1835.* London: Butterworths, 1970.

Hart, Avril, and Susan North. *Fashion in Detail: From the Seventeenth and Eighteenth Centuries.* New York: Rizzoli, 1998.

Hayes, Kevin J. *A Colonial Woman's Bookshelf.* Knoxville: University of Tennessee Press, 1996.

Hefford, Wendy. *The Victoria and Albert Museum's Textile Collection: Design for Printed Textiles in England from 1750 to 1850.* London: V&A Publications, 1992.

Hofenk de Graaff, Judith. *The Colourful Past: Origins, Chemistry and Identification of Natural Dyestuffs.* London: Archetype Publications, 2004.

Irwin, John, and Katharine B. Brett. *Origins of Chintz.* London: Her Majesty's Stationery Office, 1970.

Irwin, John, and P. R. Schwartz. *Studies in Indo-European Textile History.* Ahmedabad, India: Calico Museum of Textiles, 1966.

Isaacson, Philip M. *The American Eagle.* Boston: New York Graphic Society, 1975.

Keller, Patricia J. "Methodology and Meaning: Strategies for Quilt Study." *Quilt Journal* 2, no. 1 (1993): 1–4.

_____. *Of the Best Sort but Plain: Quaker Quilts from the Delaware Valley, 1760-1890.* Chadds Ford, Pa.: Brandywine River Museum, 1996.

Kerber, Linda K. *Women of the Republic: Intellect & Ideology in Revolutionary America.* Chapel Hill: University of North Carolina Press,1980.

Kiracofe, Roderick. *The American Quilt: A History of Cloth and Comfort, 1750–1950.* New York: Clarkson Potter, 1993.

Krill, John. *English Artists' Paper: Renaissance to Regency.* New Castle, Del.: Oak Knoll Press, 1992.

Lidz, Maggie. *Life at Winterthur: A Du Pont Family Album.* Winterthur, Del.: Henry Francis du Pont Winterthur Museum, 2001.

Needles, Samuel H. "The Governor's Mill and the Globe Mills, Philadelphia." *Pennsylvania Magazine* 8 (1884).

Nicoll, Jessica F. *Quilted for Friends: Delaware Valley Signature Quilts, 1840–1855.* Winterthur, Del.: Henry Francis du Pont Winterthur Museum, 1986.

Osler, Dorothy. *Traditional British Quilts.* London: B. T. Batsford Ltd., 1987.

Portugal and the East through Embroidery: 16th to 18th Century Coverlets from the Museo Nacional de Arte Antiga, Lisbon. Washington D.C.: International Exhibitions Foundation, 1981.

Powell, G. Julie. *The Fabric of Persuasion: Two Hundred Years of Political Quilts.* Chadds Ford, Pa.: Brandywine River Museum, 2000.

Riley, Noël, ed. *The Elements of Design: The Development of Design and Stylistic Elements from the Renaissance to the Postmodern Era.* London: Mitchell Beazley, 2003.

Schoeser, Mary. "The Mystery of the Printed Handkerchief." In *Disentangling Textiles: Techniques for the Study of Designed Objects,* ed. Mary Schoeser and Christine Boydell. London: Middlesex University Press, 2002.

Schwartz, Paul R. *Printing on Cotton at Ahmedabad, India in 1678.* Ahmedabad, India: Calico Museum of Textiles, 1969.

Shaw, Robert. *America's Traditional Crafts.* Southport, Conn.: Hugh Lauter Levin Associates, 1993.

Stillinger, Elizabeth. *The Antiquers.* New York: Alfred A. Knopf, 1980.

Sykas, Philip A. "Re-threading: Notes Toward a History of Sewing Thread in Britain." In *Textiles Revealed: Object Lessons in Historic Textile and Costume Research,* ed. Mary M. Brooks. London: Archetype Publications, 2000.

Synge, Lanto. *Art of Embroidery: History of Style and Technique.* London: Antique Collectors' Club, 2001.

Textiles in Daily Life: Proceedings of the Third Biennial Symposium of the Textile Society of America, Seattle, Wash.: The Textile Society of America, 1992.

Upton, Dell. "Lancasterian Schools, Republican Citizenship, and the Spatial Imagination in Early Nineteenth-Century America." *Journal of the Society of Architectural Historians* 55, no. 3 (September 1996): 238–53.

Victoria & Albert Museum. *Catalogue of an Exhibition of English Chintz: Two Centuries of Changing Taste.* London: Her Majesty's Stationery Office, 1955.

_____. *Catalogue of a Loan Exhibition of English Chintz: English Printed Furnishing Fabrics from their Origins until the Present Day.* London: Her Majesty's Stationery Office, 1960.

Withington, Ann Fairfax. "Manufacturing and Selling the American Revolution." In *Everyday Life in the Early Republic,* ed. Catherine E. Hutchins. Winterthur, Del.: Henry Francis du Pont Winterthur Museum, 1994.

Wertkin, Gerard C., and Lee Kogan. *Encyclopedia of American Folk Art.* New York: Routledge, 2004.

list of illustrations

index

Project Manager: Harriet Whelchel
Copy Editor: Julie Blattberg
Designer: Darilyn Lowe Carnes with E. Y. Lee
Production Manager: Jane Searle

Library of Congress Cataloging-in-Publication Data

Eaton, Linda.
Quilts in a material world : selections from the Winterthur Collection
/ by Linda Eaton.
    p. cm.
Includes bibliographical references and index.
ISBN–13: 978–0–8109–3012–4 (hardcover with jacket)
1. Quilting. 2. Quilts—United States—History.
3. Quiltmakers—United States—History.
4. Henry Francis du Pont Winterthur Museum.
I. Henry Francis du Pont Winterthur Museum. II.Title.

TT835.E283 2007
746.46074'7511—dc22
2006026189

Printed and bound in China

10 9 8 7 6 5 4 3 2 1

HNA
harry n. abrams, inc.
a subsidiary of La Martinière Groupe

115 West 18th Street
New York, NY 10011
www.hnabooks.com

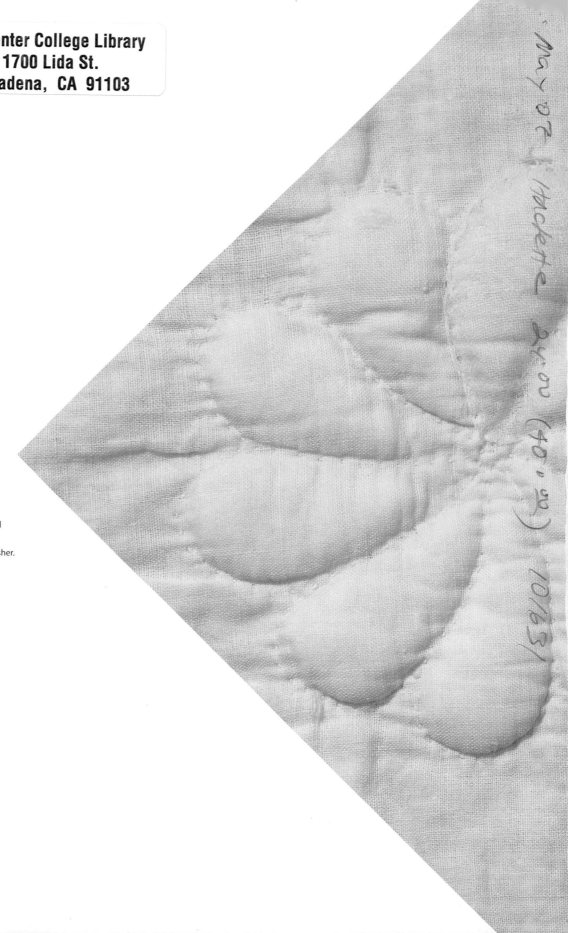